D1219060

Elizabeth Schafer was born in Britain and is a lecturer in drama and theatre studies at Royal Holloway College, the University of London. Widely travelled, she has previously lectured in Australia, and taught in Canada, France, Hungary and Brazil. *MsDirecting Shakespeare* is her third book.

Ms-Directing Shakespeare

Women Direct Shakespeare

Elizabeth Schafer

ST. MARTIN'S PRESS
NEW YORK

ISBN 0-312-22746-9

Library of Congress Cataloging-in-Publication Data is available from
the Library of Congress.

First published in Great Britain by The Women's Press Ltd, 1998.

First St. Martin's edition: April 2000.

10 9 8 7 6 5 4 3 2 1

Contents

Acknowledgements

Thanks to: CRITACS, University of Wollongong, NSW, for funding visits to theatre archives in Australia.

For help, encouragement and comments, thanks to: JS Bratton, Kirsty Dunseath, Christine Dymkowski, Penny Gay, Emma Govan, Vincent Jones, Philippa Kelly, Margaret Leask, Katherine Newey, Katie Normington, Judith Schafer and Rosemary Schafer.

Thanks especially to Joan Littlewood, Jane Howell, Yvonne Brewster, Di Trevis, Jules Wright, Helena Kaut-Howson, Deborah Paige, Jude Kelly, Gale Edwards, Judi Dench and Kim Durban, who generously found time to be interviewed for this book.

All references to Shakespeare are to *The Complete Works*, edited by Stanley Wells and Gary Taylor, Oxford University Press, 1988. However, character names are as they appeared in the productions under discussion.

List of Plates

Introduction

In *As You Like It*, Rosalind produces and presumably casts, stage-manages and directs the final masque of Hymen which ushers in her chosen, conventional happy ending of marriage.[1] As a woman theatre director Rosalind was a fantasy in Shakespeare's playhouse, where women didn't act, let alone direct, and it took a long time before Rosalind's directorial trailblazing became a real possibility for most women. However, while women theatre directors today are increasingly visible and high profile, there is still a common perception that they don't generally do Shakespeare; they do new plays, especially women's plays, fringe, and community theatre, but they don't tend to direct mainstream, mainstage professional productions of the playwright who is still the most produced, high status and high profile in British theatre, William Shakespeare. With the exception of Deborah Warner and Ariane Mnouchkine, whose Shakespeare productions have been exhaustively documented (and it is interesting to speculate why these two women *are* exceptions), women directors' productions of Shakespeare have been neglected, even ignored, by most books written on the subject of Shakespeare in performance.[2] The reality is that women have been successfully directing Shakespeare for centuries. This book seeks to acknowledge and celebrate that fact.

In order to contest the marginalisation of women directors in most traditional theatre histories of Shakespeare, this book also explores the work of eight contemporary women who have directed important and significant Shakespeare productions. As women's voices have been silenced by their exclusion from most books written on Shakespeare in performance, my aim is to give prominence to these women's own words, as they discuss their directing practice, and then their productions of specific Shakespeare plays.

For reasons of space this book can only offer a sampler of women directors' Shakespeare productions, but the notion of a sampler seems very appropriate, suggesting, as it does, a demonstration of proficiency, even excellence, as in embroidery, but also evoking a remix of different songs, different voices, different music. Both meanings are appropriate here. Proficiency and excellence are much in evidence in the productions sampled, as are differences in voice, attitude and politics. Sampling these productions and mixing them may bring out similarities and emphases perhaps never originally identified by the directors themselves, but it does also offer a clear indication that 'MsDirected Shakespeare' is something of a neglected treasure trove as far as the study of Shakespeare in performance is concerned. It also demonstrates that women directors have been at the forefront of exploring new approaches to Shakespeare, and have directed some of the most exciting theatrical productions of our day.

MsDirecting

The term 'MsDirecting' is intended initially to highlight the fact that the productions discussed here have been directed by women, not men. Studying the work of women directors in isolation from the work of their male colleagues is, of course, a contentious project, although the increasing number of published studies which *do* focus on women directors suggests there is a growing interest in this subject.[3] However, Susan Bennett (1996:167) considers focusing on 'biological sex' to be 'not at all useful and intensely problematic' for discussing directors' practice. Certainly, factors such as race, politics and class may be as important as gender in a woman director's career and artistic development: Eliza Vestris fought to get the working classes *out* of her theatre; Joan Littlewood fought to get them *into* hers. But the fact remains that traditional theatre history has unfairly neglected women directors, and contemporary theatre practice still does much to marginalise them. By asserting women's rightful place in the history of direction we can begin to overcome and compensate for the prejudices of the past.

One factor which unites all women directors of Shakespeare is that statistically they are less likely to get the work than their male colleagues.[4] Jane Lapotaire, an actress very experienced in playing Shakespeare comments: 'I've been in the business for twenty-five years and, in all that time, I have only worked with three women directors.'[5] David Scase (Goorney 1981:183) describes the 'awful shock' of being directed by Joan Littlewood, because working with a woman director 'was unknown in the profession, unbelievable, it was going against the laws of nature'. The fact that only six women have ever directed Shakespeare on the Royal Shakespeare Company (RSC) mainstage at Stratford-upon-Avon supports the notion that inequality of opportunity for male and female directors still persists in some theatres today. Indeed some would argue that those women directors who want successful, high profile careers have to adopt male identified working practices in order to enter what Lizbeth Goodman (1993:55) calls the 'traditionally paternalistic structures' of mainstream theatre, where the director used to be 'commonly known as the "Old Man"'.

The notion of 'MsDirecting Shakespeare' is complicated by the fact that many women would argue against the label 'woman director' because they feel that adding the qualification 'woman' is very loaded; male directors would never be called 'man directors'. Nancy Meckler forcibly expresses this feeling in an interview in 1984: 'I don't think of myself as a woman director. I think of myself as a director and my gender happens to be female. I want to be chosen only because I am good' (Martin, 1984:18). There is, however, one crucial factor relating to gender that has affected, and continues to affect, Nancy Meckler's Shakespeare productions. She directed several Shakespeares at the Haymarket Theatre, Leicester, a regional theatre which has a very healthy tradition of offering work to women directors; this tradition contrasts starkly with the dominant practice at the two most prestigious and best funded theatre institutions in Britain: the RSC and the Royal National Theatre. Statistically, women directors are much more likely to direct Shakespeare in the provinces than in London or at the RSC, and this has important long-term implications: not only are production resources more limited, and access to a pool of performers experienced in playing Shakespeare less attainable, but also, and crucially from the point of view of theatre historians, the archiving treatment is different. Nancy Meckler's Shakespeare productions are far more susceptible to being forgotten by Shakespeare theatre history than any production, no matter how poor, at the RSC, where so much material relating to a production – promptbooks, reviews, programmes, video records – is meticulously preserved and very conveniently located at the Shakespeare Centre, Stratford. Given that the vast majority of woman-directed Shakespeare takes place away from the RSC, it's clear that Dympna Callaghan (1991:164) is right to suggest that with Shakespeare 'the work of a woman director is likely to be excluded from the patriarchal record we accept as history'.

'MsDirecting Shakespeare' also implies that a female director will have a different perspective to a male director – that gender is an influential factor in how a play is read. It is not necessary to subscribe to essentialist notions – such as the idea that women are essentially more nurturing than men – in order to appreciate that cultural conditioning over what is 'masculine' and what is 'feminine' will have a strong impact on an individual director's working practice. In any reading of a work of art there is a tension between personal interpretation and the historical moment and circum-stances in which that work of art was originally created. Some directors, such as Dame Judi Dench, downplay the personal and take the approach that a production should replicate as closely as possible the playwright's original vision. Other directors would argue that we cannot access Shakespeare's original vision – we are too distant from him historically and politically – and, as any modern production of a Shakespeare play *has* to be a radical reworking, why not acknowledge this and use his plays as the raw material for a personal commentary on contemporary issues? Most directors believe that an element of the personal is inescapable in the interpretation of a play, and a good proportion of the women interviewed for this book felt that their gender *was* important since they brought their views and experience as women to their direction, whether or not they overtly identified themselves as feminists.

Jude Kelly is certainly clear that, because she is a woman, 'if I direct the heroines of Shakespeare it will change the way they are looked at' (Armistead, 1994:188). Kenneth Rea's survey of British directing practices also records that actors often praise women directors 'because the female roles take on more importance' (1989:51). However, for some academic writers, who now routinely treat the notion of dramatic character with intense suspicion, this is problematic. They would argue that characters must not be treated as if they were real people – they are dramatic constructions with specific narrative and political functions in the text. Tracy Davis (1989:74), for example, poses the question of whether roles written for male performers, as Shakespeare's 'female' characters were, to some extent 'always remain male'; if this is the case these characters cannot be treated as 'real women'. However, many practitioners, when they are speaking of how they work on developing a character for performance, often *will* talk about those characters as if they were real people.

This division between practitioners and academics also exists in their different uses of the word 'theory' – for academics this usually means critical theorising; for practitioners it tends to mean the theory of how to make theatre. Similarly academics are often intensely suspicious of universalism – the idea that Shakespeare's plays are fundamentally just as relevant today as they were in the early modern period, that they address a universal, essentially unchanging human condition. This ignores the important social and political differences between Shakespeare's plays and the cultures in which they are now read and performed. But for theatre directors wanting to fill their theatres, universalism, saying 'this play is about you and me, here and now', makes a lot of sense. As this book is primarily interested in what women directors have to say about their productions and their craft, I have accepted their frames of reference.

There remains the vexed question of how a contemporary woman who has experienced the benefits of women's liberation and the sexual revolution might approach Shakespeare, a non-egalitarian male writer of the early modern era. Many of the ideas and characters contained within his plays are profoundly problematic for modern women – the ending of *The Taming of the Shrew* being the most obvious example here. It is also important to acknowledge that even with a director like Jules Wright, who unequivocally identifies herself as a feminist, the impact of her politics on a production may not be at all straightforward. In directing *Macbeth*, Wright not only had to confront the gender politics of the play but also had to negotiate with individual performers, designers, management, reviewers (many of whom missed the point) and a constantly changing, politically very diverse audience. Lorraine Helms (1990) takes a particularly pessimistic line here and argues that Shakespearean characterisation, language, and even metre, will always defeat feminist direction of his plays.[6] However, given the very large amounts of money spent in Britain each year on Shakespeare productions, it is important that women directors should continue to direct Shakespeare, and to question the misogyny enshrined in his plays, rather than leaving these plays to directors who will endorse the misogyny and anti-feminism of the early modern period.

The notion of 'MsDirecting Shakespeare' is also a helpful one because dismissing a production as 'misdirected' is an effective putdown often used by (predominantly male) reviewers when they don't like the politics of the production. *The Times* reviewer Benedict Nightingale's apoplectic reaction to Gale Edwards' interventionist production of *The Taming of the Shrew* would be a case in point. This study includes several important productions that some influential critics have loathed and condemned as misguided and misdirected. However, Lizbeth Goodman (1993:235–6) stresses the role of academic and market forces in shaping the criteria of what is good, and 'the difficulty of arriving at any fair set of measure for the valuing of feminist work'. As reviewer Carole Woddis contends, most spectators and reviewers at any play will have passed 'through a male educational system' (Woddis, in Goodman, 1996:291), where many contentious issues raised by

Shakespeare's plays will have gone unchallenged, and so, on a subconscious level, what a reviewer sees as good is often simply what fulfils the expectations and criteria they have been taught to have of a play.

In the context of this book, 'misdirecting' is often a positive term, as by 'misdirecting' or 'MsDirecting' and deviating from the norm, women directors are asserting their right to bring their own, very distinctive vision to the Shakespearean canon; a vision that is not only refreshing, but also reveals much about the social and political climates in which they work.

The focus of this book is on British productions, with some reference to Australian productions. This reflects my own personal experience of Shakespeare in performance in England, the land of Shakespeare's birth and the centre of the Shakespeare industry, and Australia, a country where Shakespeare has a rather different profile, associated, as he inevitably is, with British cultural imperialism.

It would be impossible to document all female directors of Shakespeare, particularly as so many women have worked on the theatrical margins and their work has been poorly archived. But I hope that by presenting this sampler of directors, I can demonstrate that a long history of women directing Shakespeare exists. While my focus on Shakespeare will contribute further to the already extensive privileging of 'the Bard' in Anglo theatre culture, that privilege is a crucial part of the equation for women directors: the more prestige attached to a production – be it by author, institution or theatre space – the less likely women directors are to gain access to it. In addition, as audiences are often familiar with Shakespeare's plays, they will be more aware of directorial interventions in production than with new or lesser known works; this means that the directorial function itself has a higher profile.

The one really consistent theme which emerges in this study is the determination, the courage, the intelligence as well as the creativity displayed by all these MsDirectors. Claiming Rosalind as a figurehead for them all, in all their diversity, might seem something of a sweeping gesture – but then Rosalind can be so many different things: a male disguised as a female and a female disguised as a male; a male playwright's creation written for a boy to perform as well as a pioneering, active, assertive female character, a gift for the modern actress. It is precisely because Rosalind is such a paradoxical site for the blurring, collapsing and contesting of gender boundaries that s/he offers such an appropriate figurehead for women directors who follow her lead into traditionally masculine territory.

PART 1 – The MsDirectors

Theatre history can never be objective; it is constructed according to the particular interests and politics of those writing that history. Although women are now increasingly participating in the writing of history (something which has resulted in an increase in the attention paid to women's achievements), a primary resource in the writing of theatre history – production reviews – is still dominated by male voices. This is simply because the vast majority of the theatre reviewers who are writing for serious newspapers and journals are male. Partly as a response to this imbalance, I want to offer an alternative approach to theatre history here and privilege the voices of women directors discussing their craft, before moving on to focus in detail on their Shakespeare productions and on how these productions have been received.[1] These women directors' backgrounds, their training, their theatrical experiences, their approach to directing and their attitude towards Shakespeare will all impact on their productions, and hearing what they have to say on the subject of directing Shakespeare in general will help provide a context for understanding the productions they have created.

I particularly asked these women about how they became directors because theatre directing, like so many jobs in the arts, can seem like a privileged enclave for the chosen few. Kenneth Rea's *A Better Direction*, which was commissioned to examine opportunities (or lack of them) for training theatre directors in the UK, reveals much frustration on behalf of directors – both female and male – who felt they didn't know how to break into the charmed circle of practising directors. The majority of the directors interviewed here made this break after some experience as a performer.[2] Taking a route from performing to directing has the weight of tradition behind it; until very recently the vast majority of directors, both male and female, began as performers. However, Rea also identifies other strategies which have proved sensible career moves for aspiring directors: among the most popular are working in stage management (and so observing other directors in action), and forming your own theatre company. The latter option was adopted by several of the directors interviewed here; however, forming your own company often entails financial hardship (unless family background permits otherwise) and an ability to convince a group of friends or colleagues to take part in a high risk/low pay venture. As part of the job of a theatre director is to convince actors to do extraordinary things onstage, success in forming a theatre company may be a particularly significant rite of passage.

Another issue I asked the directors to discuss is that of gender stereotypes. These tend to suggest that women directors, in comparison with men, will be more nurturing, collaborative, intuitive, emotional and open; leadership style will be an issue for them; women directors will tend to work in small theatre spaces and will be ignorant of the technical side of theatre. While they were generally impatient with this kind of stereotype, most of the directors interviewed had met it at some stage – from performers or production crew or theatrical boards.[3]

I also asked the directors about female role models, predecessors or mentors. Most felt a lack here, particularly when it came to directing Shakespeare. When I asked the directors to situate their work in relation to feminism, responses varied very widely – but a particularly interesting response in relation to this issue came from Deborah Warner. Warner declined to be interviewed as she considered this study would provide a 'regressive and reductive' context for her work.[4] However, Warner's success, both in winning the approval of theatre reviewers and in being accepted relatively quickly by those writing accounts of Shakespeare theatre history, is in direct contrast with the experience of the majority of women directors, whose Shakespeare productions have generally received scant critical attention.

By being attentive to what the women directors interviewed here have to say about their craft, what they bring to that craft as women, and what they bring to Shakespeare, it is possible to begin an alternative theatre history of Shakespeare, to counterpoint the traditional theatre history which has, so far, always been dominated by the achievements of male directors. These women directors have brought vibrancy, intelligence and controversy to Shakespeare production, and what they have to say will be just as contentious for some readers, as their productions were for some reviewers.

Joan Littlewood

Joan Littlewood became a director by walking most of the way from London to Manchester and joining forces with Jimmie Miller to create agitprop theatre. Littlewood is famous for her long career directing overtly politicised theatre: theatre which was left wing, collaborative, based on popular theatre styles such as music hall, anti what Littlewood saw as bourgeois illusionistic realism, and the antithesis of the theatre promoted by her RADA training. With Theatre of Action, Theatre Union and finally Theatre Workshop (based at Stratford, in east London, from 1953), Littlewood pursued a theatre practice which stressed the physicality of the performer, using ideas from Meyerhold, Laban, Stanislavski; the intelligence of the performer; and the performer's resourcefulness. Performers were often required to improvise and to research for a show as well as to make costumes, clean the theatre and scrounge for funding. Littlewood encouraged an energised, upfront performance style which influenced generations of theatre workers, and her personal charisma and ability to inspire people held Theatre Workshop together despite years of grinding poverty.

Littlewood has enormous status in the world of theatre but she is known today for her big commercial successes such as *Oh What a Lovely War!*, and has largely been ignored in terms of Shakespeare theatre history even though she directed controversial productions of *Richard II, Macbeth* and *Henry IV Part 1*, and adaptations for schools of *Twelfth Night, As You Like It* and *A Midsummer Night's Dream*.[5]

Although she is the one woman consistently mentioned as a

source of inspiration by other women directors, Littlewood is an uncomfortable role model or mentor figure for some, partly because her focus is always resolutely on class politics:

Joan Littlewood: I've never been involved in and I don't like all of this thing that's going on about liberate women; liberate everybody!

Luckily I'm a hopeless 'woman', I've been a bum. When you're working you don't notice yourself do you? It's never been drawn to my attention, 'You're only a woman.'

In an interview with Murray Bramwell (1997:108), Littlewood commented on her early career:

Back then [women] got married at sixteen, got tied up. If you say children – I've got children all over the world but they're not from myself. I couldn't. I couldn't have managed. You'd have to leave our theatre if you'd had a baby. Maybe if you'd been subsidised you could have managed.

Consequently when she became pregnant Littlewood (1994:99) decided to 'find a backstreet Celestina' and although it 'was a brutalised, sordid business' it was 'not as bad as being trapped'.

Clare Venables (1980:5) describes Littlewood as being seen by her company as 'an all-powerful, extraordinary, loving, terrifying mother-figure'; however, Avis Bunnage, a longstanding member of Theatre Workshop, felt that women found the going particularly tough there:

Of the women, I think I survived longer than any of them because I wouldn't always give in to Joan. There was always a girl in tears somewhere because Joan was very hard on women. (Goorney, 1981:171)

In addition Theatre Workshop's house style of rough and tumble,

full-on physical contact, challenging and confronting improvisations, and energised vocal work might have been more comfortable
for those socialised as men than for women.

Littlewood's directorial practice has been much discussed and
reminisced about by many who worked with her (and by some she
claims never worked with her at all!). John Wells (1994:210–12)
describes Littlewood's standard procedure as consisting of: an
introductory talk on the play including a lot of obscenities, smoking
and references to contemporary politics; an extremely detailed
analysis of the text, breaking it into units and finding the 'active verb'
(211); improvisations; lectures by all the cast on related topics they
had researched; finally 'Very late in the rehearsal schedule, she added
"the feet"' (212). Wells stresses Littlewood's ability to teach, to release
performers from inhibitions and to create a 'chemical reaction' in
theatre (212). Littlewood also had a tendency to cast against type, so
performers had to work harder because they didn't look the part and
swapping roles in a production was common. When these (now
orthodox but then unorthodox) methods were applied to
Shakespeare, the effects could be electric: Goodwin and Milne
describe working with Littlewood as 'like watching Shakespeare in
one continuous shaft of lightning' (1964:394).

Although Littlewood's distinctive approach to theatre was evident in
many Theatre Workshop productions, the theatre was run as a co-
operative and Littlewood always saw herself as working along co-
operative lines – *with* the actors, taking what they had to offer and
working with that. In 1965 she wrote: 'I do not believe in the
supremacy of the director, designer, actor or even of the writer. It is
through collaboration that this knockabout art of theatre survives and
kicks' (Littlewood, 1965:133). In her autobiography she also states:
'The director deciding on the interpretation alone cannot compare
with the work of a composite mind' (Littlewood, 1994: 321).
Certainly the one feature of her classical productions which was most
often identified by reviewers as Littlewood's 'trademark' – sympathy
with the workers and impatience with aristocratic maunderings – was
in keeping with the Theatre Workshop ethos in general.

Littlewood's attitude to the subject of directing is still brusque:

Joan Littlewood: I don't see myself as a theatre director. Those 'geniuses' give me a pain – the directors who say 'move', 'do this', they do groupings and use stylised bloody costumes that haven't grown with the role or the actor. No I can't stand any of it, I never could.

Littlewood particularly dislikes what she sees as the excesses of directors in some subsidised theatres:

Joan Littlewood: They're all ignorant camp university types as far as I can make out.

One of my people, Vic Spinetti, he was on the floor and they'd offered him a job at Stratford-upon-Avon. He was shattered really; he wasn't used to being given an artistic costume and corsets and shoes. They said to Spinetti, 'We thought you didn't rehearse at Theatre Workshop.' He said, 'Yes, that's right. We'd spend hours to get to the point when it didn't look as if we were rehearsing.'

Littlewood's initial interest in Shakespeare started at the Old Vic Theatre run by Lilian Baylis:

Joan Littlewood: I used to go down to the Old Vic, which was walking distance from where I lived. I knew the bloody place by heart. Talk about Shakespeare! My God, how many did I see? You could get in at the Old Vic for 5 pence I think it was, with all the old tramps in the gallery. It was a bit Edwardian, really, but much better than anything that came later. I went to all the shows when the old Baylis was doing them. It was 'God and Shakespeare' for her. Old Baylis was frying sausages in the wings, and they did it all with only four costumes!

Littlewood's first pre-Stratford Shakespeare productions, however, were motivated by Shakespeare's box office pulling power:

Joan Littlewood: Shakespeare? I had to do them because we were broke and we could get a bit of money from schools. We were always broke; lucky if we could afford digs. I did so many of those Shakespeares because we had to, but I don't like his comedies compared with Ben Jonson – you know, we did all these boring *As You Like Its* and *Twelfth Nights* and stuff like that. I don't go much for the Violas and Rosalinds; they're not real women.

Despite this, Littlewood opened Stratford East with *Twelfth Night* (2 February 1953). George Cooper (Goorney, 1981:99) recalls the audience shouting and throwing toffees and pennies at the stage. *The Stage* (5 February 1953) thought that the Crazy Gang had 'invaded Illyria' and that all subtlety had been lost.

Despite the fact that so little attention has been paid to her classical productions, Littlewood is still proud of them:

Joan Littlewood: The classics were the best thing we ever did. Mostly the critics didn't come when we were doing really good work; it took a long time before anyone came.

She has fond memories of the Theatre Workshop company, especially in its early days:

Joan Littlewood: You can't imagine that company; we were *commedia dell'arte*. There were all classes working together; they could throw a box to each other in the dark and they caught it. Early on we played to places where there was no theatre and where I'd have to mind the bloody kids; they'd bring the kids and dump them and I'd have to entertain them. We played all over in ordinary working-class halls – we didn't have scenery – didn't need it really.

The name 'Theatre Workshop' – everyone said at the time, 'What a dreadful name!' Now everyone loves it. I should have patented it.

However, she also remembers the high cost to all concerned, especially to her partner Gerry Raffles:

Joan Littlewood: Our life was hard, physically hard; you didn't have any luxuries at all. Women are tougher than men; Theatre Workshop killed Gerry.

Littlewood's view of Shakespeare is also coloured by her vision of the Renaissance period, a vision which she expounds with relish:

Joan Littlewood: I lived in that period – I loved it and it was partly Elizabeth I. She was a marvellous actress and theatre director and she'd no money; she had all those ambassadors trying to marry her off to their fellas and she played them off. Elizabeth stood up and ad libbed in Latin and Italian and she had Greek and Hebrew as well. You have to see this *glorious* time – Marlowe, Ben Jonson – as to do with *that* woman. Then 'crash' – in come those puritans and put the gravestone on theatre and we have never recovered.

A similarly unapologetic appropriation of history takes place in Theatre Workshop's Manifesto which declares roundly:

> The great theatres of all times have been popular theatres which reflected the dreams and struggles of the people. The theatre of Aeschylus and Sophocles, of Shakespeare and Ben Jonson, of Commedia dell'Arte and Molière derived their inspiration, their language, their art from the people. (Goorney, 1981:41)

Historians might disagree with Littlewood's vision of Elizabeth I (which has some features in common with descriptions of Littlewood during her reign at Stratford East) but this is the vision that during the fifties and early sixties helped generate a series of Renaissance productions at Theatre Workshop which shook reviewers, sometimes outraged them, but also offered a distinctively alternative vision of the Renaissance classics from that available in the mainstream theatre of the time. Littlewood looked for and found what she wanted in classical theatre; an anti-establishment voice, and an unruly, vibrant theatre connecting with and speaking for the people.

Littlewood comes across as irrepressible, even now in her eighties, but her formidable ability to unsettle and upset has sometimes disconcerted her supporters as well as her political opponents. Pam Brighton (1984:49), an admirer of all Littlewood stands for, recalls seeing her at the LSE:

> I found her overwhelmingly eccentric, sitting there surrounded by classy Marxist students who patronized her like mad. I wished she'd been more socially acceptable. It was to be years later before I realised that to be a woman who holds on to a singular vision with passion is practically equivalent to appearing to most people to be crazy, perverse and rather frightening.

Littlewood's particular talent was for upsetting some elements of the establishment:

Joan Littlewood: I used to get turds wrapped in paper sent to me when I did *Lovely War*, from people in the army. They said I was an insult to the memory of officers.

Generally, however, Littlewood doesn't like dwelling on the past:

Joan Littlewood: My memory was better. They're not having a go at me now. I think I'm getting all these awards and things now because they think I'm dead. But I'm really not interested in the past; what about the future?

Jane Howell

Jane Howell is best known for her work in television drama, and in particular for transferring plays written for the stage to the small screen. She directed six of the BBC Shakespeares and was particularly praised for her startling and highly successful work with the first tetralogy, *Henry VI Parts 1, 2* and *3* and *Richard III*. Howell was the only woman director to work on the BBC Shakespeare at a time when, as Henry Fenwick (1981:17) comments, women directors were 'still distressingly few on the ground in television'.

Howell first gained critical acclaim in the theatre with a production of Anne Jellicoe's *The Sport of My Mad Mother*; later she became well known for her work on the plays of Edward Bond. Howell worked at the Royal Court in the late sixties and became artistic director at the Northcott Theatre, Exeter, in the seventies before moving into television work. She got the theatre bug when she was three:

Jane Howell: I saw a pantomime at the Golders Green Empire and I can still sing you the song sheet. Theatre was a magical world; it seemed to offer a lot of answers. Later on, directing at grammar school unlocked something for me. I was very shy, everything was locked in, because of being alone a lot when I was evacuated during the war and was with older people all the time. Theatre was the perfect therapy because I felt I instinctively knew what was going on underneath the play, the emotions, the shadows behind the words and I then had something to talk about.

Howell worked as a performer but gradually moved towards directing:

Jane Howell: When I left Bristol University, I set up and ran an amateur company with Dud Livingstone, at Lynton in Devon, doing weekly rep in the Town Hall. It worked out well and I wanted to go into the theatre professionally but I didn't know how to do it. My family had nothing to do with theatre; they were working class: my dad was a policeman and his dad was a farm labourer. So I supply-taught until I got a grant to go to the Bristol Old Vic drama school as a director.

Howell then went on to work as a stage manager at Coventry and while there directed *All My Sons*. After that she moved to Hornchurch where she worked for two years:

Jane Howell: I was doing one play a month in fortnightly rep, doing all sorts of plays, and this is where I really trained: farces, Shakespeare, thrillers, Noël Coward – you name it, we did it – with a few exciting modern plays like *Roots*. That's where I learned my craft.

Howell was conscious of a lack of women mentors and role models apart from Joan Littlewood, but she sees the pressures she felt as a woman director as self-generated:

Jane Howell: When I started directing there were very few women directors and one was up the sharp end of the ship and instinctively, and probably from inner need, one was challenging what the men were doing. This for me wasn't a conscious political gesture at all; it came from my own circumstances and my own life.

I think it was required at that time, in the sixties, on a wide, almost spiritual level, that women should start to challenge men or to believe that they were capable of doing the same things. It *was* uncomfortable and I did feel I needed to be better than the men but that was *my* drive, *not* anyone saying that to me.

In her directing practice, Howell uses a standard procedure:

Jane Howell: With any play I'm directing I'll section and unit it. I search the actual words used – I *love* words – and the fact that it's one word that's used and not another word becomes very important to me. There is also the finding of what I call the hook; it's defining what the play means to you. You can't always articulate it exactly but for me it's crucial finding that emotional link, that secret or inner relationship to a play.

When Howell talks about rehearsals, her concern and consideration for her performers helps explain why she, along with Max Stafford-Clark, was voted 'favourite' director to work with in a poll conducted by Sheila Hancock at the RSC (Hancock, 1987:30):

Jane Howell: Actors are wonderful, extraordinary people; they go out and do it – the director doesn't. Actors need nurturing, they need care and it's an intuitive process helping actors to develop.

Howell also sets out in rehearsals to create a safe environment:

Jane Howell: In a rehearsal room the director makes the rules; so you can have a safe, island society and you can run it how you like. You call the tune, you make the atmosphere; you don't have to talk about it, you do it by what you are and what you expect and how you treat people. There are always unspoken values in any rehearsal situation and I think mine are that together we can do more than we can do individually – and please try not to hurt each other. One *can* work from a basis of love, without being soppy.

In discussing her work, Howell is wary of the word 'feminist' but happy to talk in terms of the 'feminine':

Jane Howell: One has to acknowledge, and try to find a balance between the feminine and masculine in oneself and in one's living experience. My work isn't from a feminist point of view, but it has been feminine because I am feminine.

For Howell, this 'feminine' is crucial:

Jane Howell: For myself the feminine is where the original intuition comes from, but the masculine is the control and power. I enslaved the feminine to the masculine for a long time because I needed control and security. It's been a slow, difficult and very painful process to get back to where the feminine is in the lead and the masculine energy is subservient to it. That's the right balance for me, but it is a danger area for women today.

Howell rarely directs now:

Jane Howell: I'm working as a healer and reflexologist. I've just passed 60 and it's time for change. I teach design, I teach at film school, I teach acting courses. I'm not saying I'm not going to direct any more but I think 60 is about letting go of a lot of things.

Looking back on her long and varied career, Howell feels that one of her Shakespeare productions reflected how she felt about being the only woman director working at the male dominated Royal Court in the late sixties:

Jane Howell: When I arrived at the Court it was a time of great certainty. It felt as if we were going up a very new motorway and we were the front vehicle and everyone else was tagging on behind. We really did the author's play – everyone will claim they do that, but there was a *scrupulous* attention to what was being said to leading with the mind and allowing the emotions to follow – so you played the sense and saw what it made you feel.

The Court was a homosexual environment and the men who ran it were *very* intelligent men, very well educated, and they would play sort of parlour games with you to pass the time. I wouldn't even understand the answer, let alone the question. I didn't come from that world, I came from an instinctive, completely different environment, not Oxbridge. So the Court was a strange world, and out in the street people were wearing fancy dress and flowers in their hair.

When I did *Twelfth Night* (January, 1968) the whole of that *Twelfth Night* was based on 'What country, friends, is this?' (1.2.1) – which was my response really to the Court and London in the sixties. There was a degree of savagery in my portrayal of Orsino and Olivia as somewhat self-indulgent – just a touch – and Viola and Sebastian as rather lost souls, not quite understanding what was going on in this world. It was Carnaby Street but it was also what was in my head, wondering where I was and trying to understand the complexity of relationships and sexual puzzles between people.

Yvonne Brewster

Yvonne Brewster trained as an actor at Rose Bruford and studied at the Royal Academy of Music before embarking on a career which encompassed acting, radio announcing and producing, TV presenting and film. Brewster is the co-founder and director of Talawa Theatre Company, which was established in 1985 to provide better opportunities for black performers in Britain. The company ranges widely in its work but Brewster has now directed four Renaissance plays for the company: *Antony and Cleopatra, King Lear, 'Tis Pity She's A Whore,* and *Othello.*[6] Talawa also produces a lot of work by black playwrights, and Brewster has edited three anthologies of black plays for Methuen.

Like Littlewood and Howell, Brewster also came to directing via acting:

Yvonne Brewster: When I acted, I was always on the outside, looking – and complaining bitterly – and I realised that I had a little to offer in terms of being a third eye for people, saying to them, 'Look, I'm not believing you now.'

While training as an actor Brewster had the opportunity to observe Joan Littlewood in action:

Yvonne Brewster: When I was at Rose Bruford I used to creep through the back door entrance of the Theatre Royal to see Joan Littlewood. They never use that exit at the back of the stalls any more. The language! At eighteen I thought she was just amazing.

Brewster started directing in Jamaica:

Yvonne Brewster: I had one of the first professional theatre companies in Jamaica. Trevor Rhone was writing plays at the time so we started to do them. I am a very privileged Jamaican and my father had a garage that would take four of those old fishtail American cars. So I said to him one day, 'I want this as a theatre', and I chucked him out. It's still a theatre and it still produces four new plays a year and I run it by fax.

Brewster is very conscious of the prejudice she encounters in the UK in terms of preconceptions about what sort of work she ought to be doing:

Yvonne Brewster: I came to the UK in 1972 but I didn't really start directing here until 1984. Here, because black people have been exoticised for so long, we begin to believe it if we're not careful. Because I'm a bit off the wall, I believe I have a right to do everything, including Shakespeare, and if the English people don't like that, well, tough! There are lots of plays that Talawa could do that are really easy and we could have a good laugh, but I choose to remain on this harder road with Shakespeare or John Ford, the more 'inaccessible' plays, although it's not supposed to be my area. You know, I sing and I dance and I jig around and that's fine, it's lovely, it's charming and it's ethnic, but if I do anything that's coming from the European canon then all of a sudden it's 'Wow, what are you doing with our play?'

I'm freer when I work in Europe. If I only worked in England I would die; it's too constraining and restricting. I did Pinter in Italy last year; no one would ever ask me to do Pinter here because they would think I wouldn't understand the cups of tea darrrling. I can only take so many knives in the back, and the 'she really thinks she's someone', but I stick with just getting up their noses by doing their English classics and I think we learn quite a lot from it.

However, Brewster doesn't like to feel she is confined by a black agenda when she directs:

Yvonne Brewster: I have a great respect for writers and I don't direct a play because I want to *do* anything with it, I just want to research it, dig as deep as I can into it and find if it is saying anything to me personally. But because there are not many directors of plays here who are black, as in African or Caribbean, I find that, if I pick up a play, immediately someone asks, 'How does it speak to *you* specifically?' I really have never been put in a box until I came to England. Why am I always referred to as some sort of sub-species? Why do I specially have to want to do something with a play? Why can't I just want to do the play for the play's sake?

Having said that, whatever you bring to a play has to come from your perspective, so in fact you do something to it as a matter of course, because of being who you are. But it's an essential for me *not* to *start out* to try and prove any kind of social economic point or any other thing apart from the literary or physical or imagistic values of the play.

Brewster's decision to do classical plays is also often sparked by her desire to see a particular actor in a particular role. She directed *King Lear* because Norman Beaton wanted to play Lear and she directed *'Tis Pity* as a vehicle for a young actress, Ginny Holder. This commitment to providing opportunities for black performers also inspired Brewster to direct a black *Importance of Being Earnest.*

Yvonne Brewster: We did *The Importance of Being Earnest* because Mona Hammond [co-founder of Talawa] said to me, 'I'm tired of doing these women in the kitchen sink and watching my navel. Lord, I want to do Lady Bracknell.' I said 'You're on – and we didn't change the joke about the spade. We know that they call black people 'spade' but you could celebrate that word. I could easily have cut those lines but that's the easy way out. You have to find a way that's not going to make it racially ridiculous, but on the other hand I need to give more thought to the colour blind business; I don't see why black people should have to pretend they don't have colour. Sometimes I find it really important to go through to the racial connotations of a play and sometimes I don't.

Brewster's perception is that in England her age also tells against her:

Yvonne Brewster: People here ask me my age and they write me off immediately as if to say 'Oh God, you should get your bus pass. Forget it, you don't count any more.' I'll go on because it keeps you young and it keeps you interested.

Brewster feels her concept of feminism has to be contextualised by her Jamaican background:

Yvonne Brewster: My mother is an undertaker with a big empire, she employs God knows how many people. There have been blokes around in my family, they're all sweet, but it's the women who have always done everything and it's always very matriarchal.

Talawa has been going for ten years and I think in the whole history of the company we've had very few blokes working there – apart from actors – and it's not for any reason other than the fact that the women have been better. But when you are the victim of a lack of equal opportunities, you are very keen on at least *attempting* to be equal in terms of access. At Talawa, I would say we are female led and we have quite a female way of looking at things.

Brewster extends this idea of 'a female way of looking at things' into talking about her directing practice:

Yvonne Brewster: Because I used to act I know I rehearse differently from any of the male directors who directed me. My approach results in much more of an ensemble and much less of a star-studded vehicle, because I can't stand that at all. My process allows great freedom for the actor and I don't go in with a big heavy concept.

The rehearsal situation, if people allow themselves to be vulnerable, is so attractive and the most vulnerable person is the director. At the end of the process, normally, everybody has grown. And the Talawa casts form themselves into groups – like the 'Lear jets' – and they come and see Talawa shows together. I think that that bonding thing is helped by a female kind of rehearsal process because, as a woman, I'm accustomed to keeping things together, keeping house, bringing up baby.

Brewster's position as a black director of classics in Britain is full of paradoxes. For example, the *London Theatre Record* in listing Brewster's *Othello* in its future London schedule section announced, 'Talawa tackle the big one at last.' Yet, while *Othello*'s concern with race undoubtedly makes it a 'big one' for a black theatre company, if the play is cast according to the race of the characters, there is only one black role – Othello. This would make it one of the *last* plays a company dedicated to providing opportunities for black actors should produce. Brewster got round this by offering a heady cocktail of references to famous, ill-fated mixed race relations (Diana and Dodi, Nicole and OJ Simpson) and by making Emilia, Bianca and Cassio black. This transformed the play: Iago's racism was unforgettably underlined because not only was his wife, Emilia, black, but so was his rival, Cassio. So were most of the audience. It is indisputable that different audiences go to Talawa productions compared with most Shakespeare productions in the UK, and Brewster has tremendous support as well as critical detractors.

Di Trevis

Di Trevis worked as a performer, often for Glasgow Citizens, before moving on to direct, in which capacity she has worked for the RNT and the RSC. She has had successes with *The Taming of The Shrew* for the RSC touring company, and *The Revenger's Tragedy* on the Swan stage. Then came *Much Ado About Nothing* on the Stratford mainstage, a production which was lambasted with extraordinary, and, I would say, unwarranted ferocity by reviewers.

Trevis is very clear about why she began working as a performer before moving on to directing:

Di Trevis: In my day women didn't start as directors; they didn't yet come out of university saying they wanted to be directors. What you did was that you worked in the theatre in some other way, where it was acceptable for women to work, and you started to direct things. There were a few women directors then working in television. Sarah Pia Anderson was making her name and she'd had television training. Deborah Warner was around, but there were no women claiming the big national stages or the great historical plays. I have to say there aren't many of them still.

She is also cynical about what women directors have achieved so far:

Di Trevis: Everybody thinks that the battles are won for women, but it isn't so at all. I was one of the first women at the RSC but when you look at what I did, I actually did very little. Me and a few other women pushed open a door, but we've hardly got access to the classical stage at all, frankly. One of the things that happens is that if there is a woman in one of the companies then it's thought there are enough.

Trevis felt very strongly about her transition from performer to director, and closer to the time of that transition she commented:

I had felt disgusted by the passivity of the actor, waiting to be chosen, wanting to please, trying not to offend. This appalling situation I felt in some ways echoed my experience of being a woman in the world. By being an actress I was being a woman *twice*. (Trevis, 1984:15)

Elsewhere she commented:

I hated being an actress. I felt I was penalised for things I'd been told were 'virtues' – being well-read, holding opinions, having political commitment. (*Time Out*, 12 September 1985)

After encouragement from director Peter Gill, Trevis convinced the Glasgow Citizens to give her some directing work on the condition she would also do some acting for them:

Di Trevis: I thought I was going to be regarded as some kind of flibbertigibbet because I'd been an actress. With the Citizens I finished acting in a play on the Saturday and on the Monday I went in as a director with the same people, which is a real baptism of fire, because they're bound to say, 'Who does she think she is? One minute she's laughing in the dressing room, the next minute she's the director!' Because it *is* hierarchical and you can't get away from that.

In her directing practice, however, Trevis very deliberately tries to avoid the traditional, authoritarian model of the director who imposes a concept on a production:

Di Trevis: I prefer not actually to make up my mind about a play before I've got it into rehearsal. The play changes during rehearsal quite incredibly. I know that sounds very hippie as if I'm a deeply, wonderfully organic director, but I do feel a play can speak to you on so many levels and that is to do with the people who are in it, the experiences they bring to it and where you do it in your own biography. There is a moment in everybody's life for certain plays and if you can do the play at that moment then you can make a masterpiece out of it, if you're talented.

I also do a lot of etymology, looking up the origins of words, and I always read the plays in the original or have a literal translation. I research my work quite a lot but I don't read academics; if I read some half-cooked theory about a play, because it's in print, in a book and it's got a terribly deadening respectability, then it crushes me intellectually.

Not surprisingly Trevis is also extremely unimpressed by the traditional academic route travelled by many prominent male directors in England:

Di Trevis: One of the great failures of the English theatre is that lots and lots of people came to directing from reading English at university, usually Oxbridge, but theatre's not intellectual, it's sensuous. You *do* need to be intelligent to do theatre, you have to have intellectual rigour, but reading English isn't the only way into it and what's funny is that the women on the whole haven't gone that route.

Trevis also emphasises the significance of age in how women directors' careers are perceived:

Di Trevis: Germaine Greer talks about how women become invisible when they're post menopausal. I'm very, very interested to see how this is reflected in the theatre, where we've got this cult of the young. The older women disappear, like Joan Littlewood, or they become redoubtable matrons. It's very important that we have role models of older women, that they don't disappear and that they're not considered laughable because they're not young, and they're seen to be wise.

Earlier in her career she commented that in theatre:

There's also this incredible cult of the new: new, young talent. It's the whole capitalist ethic really – new product and built-in obsolescence, even with people. (*City Limits*, 23 August 1985)

Trevis is still fairly cynical about theatre politics:

Di Trevis: You have to examine politically the means of production and in whose hands those means of production are; they're in men's hands and it's very, very difficult for young women to do a production of a Shakespeare play. You can do them on a shoestring like Deborah [Warner] did when she went up to Edinburgh with Kick, but that is very difficult.

You've got to look at who allows women to do Shakespeare.

Shakespeare is a big commodity in America at the moment: every town wants a Shakespeare festival. You can earn a lot of money in America on the Shakespeare circuit, but now everyone is making movies of Shakespeare and there's so much more money to be made out of that, you won't see the women *there*, making the films.

This comment is in sympathy with Emily Mann's often cited suggestion that women in America started getting appointed as artistic directors in theatres because, as Julia Miles phrased it, 'all the boys have gone off to Hollywood and there's no money left' (Daniels, 1996:196), and Claire Armistead's remark (1994:191) that: 'any director with any balls is foresaking this undervalued, poorly-paid minority medium [theatre] for the glamour of opera or the influence (and money) of film and television'.

Although Trevis' political awareness is important she doesn't see it as reflecting predictably on her directing practice:

Di Trevis: You are the sum of what's made you – you cannot help but bring your gender history into your work, but *how* do you do it? It indubitably does make a difference, but in what way?

However, Trevis is clear that she does try to contest misogyny in the plays she directs:

Di Trevis: There's a lot of misogyny in the canon of classics but all you can do is just place it and show it. It's absolutely wrong to say the character's just saying this, he doesn't really mean it. You can't rewrite the play, so you place the play and you make it very, very clear that you don't condone it.

Trevis is the least optimistic of all the directors I interviewed about theatre in general nowadays:

Di Trevis: If I was a young director now I'd try to do my work in buildings other than theatres. I don't think the future of theatre lies in theatre buildings any more.

Jules Wright

Of all the directors I interviewed Jules Wright was the most comfortable in speaking of her work in terms of feminism. This is hardly surprising in a director whose career has been largely associated with the Women's Playhouse Trust, whose work has shown a commitment to new plays by women, and who contributed to the revival of theatrical interest in Aphra Behn with her production of *The Lucky Chance* (1984) at the Royal Court, a production followed up more recently by her production of *The Rover* (1995) which was filmed by the BBC. Renaissance plays she has directed include *Twelfth Night* (Victoria Theatre, Stoke, 1981), *1 Henry IV* (Phoenix Theatre, Leicester, 1982), and controversial, feminist productions of *Macbeth* (Lyceum Theatre, Edinburgh, 1986) and *The Revenger's Tragedy* (Sydney Theatre Company, 1991). Wright, who came to England from Australia in the early seventies, has often worked in theatrical environments where political commitment is taken for granted, such as Stratford East and the Royal Court, and has taken the Arts Council to court in order to contest funding cuts. She also has an academic background and trained as a clinical psychologist.

Jules Wright: I directed at school and university and it's what I always wanted to do, but because of my background, family and Adelaide having only one rep, it wasn't a transition that I felt was feasible then. I did a year's postgrad. at Bristol in the drama department and then I did my PhD in the psychology department and my clinical training in various psychiatric hospitals.

When Clare Venables had just been appointed at Stratford East, she interviewed me and offered me a three-month trial. I couldn't start straight away – I was doing a lot of work with anorexics and I couldn't just walk out on them – but a few months later I went to Stratford East. That was the journey.

Wright is fairly acerbic on the subject of British feminism and the theatre:

Jules Wright: When I came to the UK in 1974, I thought I was in the backwoods; Australia's development then, in terms of feminism, was much closer to America's. Also in Australia we did have a war with Vietnam on our doorstep, which was very politicising. Later on feminism suddenly became something that many younger women who were at university in the early eighties were distancing themselves from, and looking at some women's theatre work you have to ask, '*Is* there a feminist sensibility at work here?' and in some cases, 'Where are the lesbian politics?'

However, Wright began her directing career full of optimism:

Jules Wright: When I started at Stratford East I thought the sky was my limit, that all the problems with sexism were over and my generation would have a different experience! I think that every young woman goes through that process of thinking, 'I will break the barrier, I will alter it.'

On my first day at Stratford I thought, 'I can't believe it, I am in the theatre that Joan Littlewood started, this is Theatre Workshop.' That makes you think, 'I am in a tradition.' Joan Littlewood has this fantastic charisma/myth, even though it's very difficult for us to judge what that work was like, but while it's all very well to acknowledge Joan now she's 80, at the time she was never enabled.

Another important figure for Wright is Jane Howell:

Jules Wright: I was the first woman to direct on the mainstage at the Court after Jane – there'd only been Jane – and that's partly why the Women's Playhouse Trust was started because you think, 'There's something awfully wrong here.'

Wright is cynical about current opportunities for women directors:

Jules Wright: There was a moment in the early eighties, when the RSC and the National were thinking, 'We can cope with actresses becoming directors', but *real* directors for whom that's their job, they didn't get a look in. And where are the young women directors now? And where is *my* generation? Not in the theatre, not really. They're cut out of theatre in this country.

Wright acknowledges the significance of her politics in her directing practice:

Jules Wright: My task as a director is to uncover a text's coherence, what I think the writer's point of view is – but obviously that has to do with who *I* am, *my* perspective, which is feminist, and also how the rehearsal process happens. You make a journey through a piece of work and it has to be true for everybody in the production so they're all in the same play.

I approach a classic text exactly as I would a new piece of writing – with a close examination of the text, tracking the ideas through, tracking the twists and turns and the contradictions in the characters. With a classic text actors are often dealing with received ideas and they tend to expect a director to lay on a concept rather than say, 'We're going to start on page one and look at this text together; we're going to understand the piece that we are going to make.'

Although Wright has mostly directed new writing, she sees Renaissance plays as offering exciting opportunities for a feminist director:

Jules Wright: Renaissance plays have a huge attraction in terms of dealing with the psychology and philosophy of the period and the politics of that material, but that work has to speak in some way to an audience now and it is inevitable, because of my feminist perspective, that the things I should seek out in examining a classical text are those which give me some signs as to the ways in which people were thinking then about gender.

In theatre, people are working within a male construct and of course you're making political choices. Feminism is about saying 'What is the meaning of this moment?' If you're a socialist you *are* going to read a play differently from a right-wing Tory. A director or an actor with a feminist perspective can really get hold of those characters. Look at Harriet Walter in *1 Henry IV* playing Lady Percy for the RSC; one scene and it's astonishing the difference she made to that play![8]

Wright cites a specific academic influence, that of Marilyn French, as a major influence in her approach to Shakespeare:

Jules Wright: Marilyn's book, *Shakespeare's Division of Experience*, was really important to me. Not everyone agrees with her arguments but I find them really potent, and they stack up when you're looking at the material as a director. I don't want to impose a world view on a play, but I think there is validity in turning a classic text inside out to look at the play world in terms of the role of women within it.

Inevitably, because in these plays you're often dealing with very, very large male casts, you're also looking at male behaviour and that happens at two levels: what you discover and uncover in the text (and that's not falsifying the text but obviously you seek to take a coherent line through it); it also happens in the behaviour of the men who are then invited to play those roles.

Wright sees the need for a double perspective in confronting the misogyny of classical texts:

Jules Wright: If you're going to deal with misogyny then you want the men in the cast to take on the violence, to acknowledge the journey those characters go on. Sometimes you have to display a brutality in order to confront the audience with such behaviour. Misogyny and violence are our cultural luggage and these things are deep in people's psyche. Look at a film like *Goodfellows*; look at the male behaviour there! However, you cannot understand that male behaviour now without a political and historical perspective.

What really interests me in dealing with misogyny is to really go into it and to completely re-examine that kind of material from a political perspective.

Helena Kaut-Howson

Helena Kaut-Howson's background is Polish and Jewish. In Poland she worked as a performer and director, but when she came to live in England she concentrated on directing, partly because her accent mattered less. Kaut-Howson ran Theatr Clwyd from 1992 to 1995 and recent work includes three major Shakespeares all directed in 1997: *King Lear* with Kathryn Hunter as Lear; *All's Well That Ends Well* for the Regent's Park Open Air Theatre; and *Much Ado About Nothing* for the Manchester Royal Exchange.

Helena Kaut-Howson: I grew up in post-war Poland with a lot of ruin around me. My very first encounter with theatre was *Aida*. I was about four and I remember vividly that I was very disturbed by the fact that the princess gets immured, put in a tomb to die. I couldn't sleep and my mother said, 'Don't worry, she will be up there tomorrow.' I thought this was wonderful; not only are you a princess, and love is so incredibly colourful and musical and morbid, but you also don't die.

Kaut-Howson studied as a director in Poland and in England:

Helena Kaut-Howson: I went to study direction, on a very

sophisticated course at the Polish State Theatre School, because it seemed that to create the whole picture rather than be part of it was very exciting. Then, when I came to England, it was very lucky that at RADA there was a one-off directors' course, which was an unusual thing because they found it was too expensive to train directors as you had to give them actors to work with, and actors didn't want to work with beginners.

Kaut-Howson felt, and indeed still feels, that women directors have a harder time in England compared with Poland:

Helena Kaut-Howson: When I finished RADA, many people made me feel guilty about not looking after my child; he was 15 months old and my mother was looking after him. I came from a background where it was natural for a woman to carry on working but at that time in England there were only exceptional women like Joan Littlewood and Wendy Toye directing in the theatre. In Poland it is very common for women to direct and I think it's a job that is compatible, particularly suited to a woman's sensibility. But here there are so few women anywhere in charge of things and directing is still very much a boy's job although there are more women now.

Although Kaut-Howson does not perceive herself as a feminist, she feels a sort of feminism can be found anachronistically in Shakespeare:

Helena Kaut-Howson: Theatre can so easily embrace such things as feminism. Shakespeare certainly does –with all the hang-ups of his age and his culture he somehow, because he's an artist and a poet, sees beyond that. Artists have to see so deeply into the human predicament that the issues feminism fights for are automatically taken on board, even by artists who are themselves conservative politically.

Nevertheless, Kaut-Howson went along with her actors' wishes when they wanted to change lines they found offensive in *Much Ado About Nothing*:

Helena Kaut-Howson: In my production the derogatory references to a Jew and an Ethiop were changed; 'Jew' became 'ape' and 'Ethiop' became 'Cyclops'. So was Shakespeare a racist? Yes, he probably had several of the hang-ups that were part of his culture, but with an artist's instincts he transcended them and he could present a Jew, Shylock, a black man, Othello, and see deeply into them.

Kaut-Howson's directing practice is grounded in the idea of the ensemble:

Helena Kaut-Howson: Theatre is about a company, not individual artists and it's full of contradictions: it's both elitist and populist; it's got to have a strong vision imposed on it and it can only work if actors are core creators of it. A director shouldn't be surprised if actors want to participate, want to dream that dream together with you. Without the actors' continuing contribution, a production becomes an indulgent trip by an individual director. I think Théâtre de Complicité actors are wonderful because they have the ability to be continually creatively open to contributions.

Kaut-Howson's enthusiasm for Complicité actors, who are known for the inventiveness, the surprises and the physicality of their theatre, complements her suspicion of much mainstream theatre:

Helena Kaut-Howson: Theatre has got bogged down; it's not only that so much theatre is naturalistic, but who does it serve? A Marxist would say theatre is a sort of tool, something on top of existing social structures, serving a particular class. I imagine it serves the consumer.

Deborah Paige

Deborah Paige worked as an actress and as a news reader before becoming a director. She was artistic director at Salisbury Playhouse for four years, where she directed *The Winter's Tale, A Midsummer Night's Dream, The Tempest* and *Twelfth Night*. She has also directed the *Dream* for the Open Air Theatre in Regent's Park. Paige is currently artistic director at the Crucible Theatre, Sheffield, where she has recently directed *Merchant of Venice* and *King Lear*.

Deborah Paige: My coming into directing was largely a result of my personal life; when my husband and I split up, my two daughters stayed with him, so I had to have enough money for a lifestyle that would allow my kids to come and stay with me, and I couldn't see myself doing that as an actor. I did the directors' course at the Bristol Old Vic, which is where I trained as an actor. I imagined I would go into front of house, management, run the arts centre, something 'adminny' and not too ambitious, and the course would give me a kick start. I knew I was not going to work for no money or do profit sharing and fringe stuff, so I learnt how to bully a bit to get what I wanted out of people.

Paige believes that starting directing after a career in acting was a definite plus:

Deborah Paige: One of the reasons I'm good is because I didn't start directing until I was in my mid-thirties. You've been through various traumatic parts of life and you understand a bit more about how people behave.

She also stresses the importance of her administrative skills:

Deborah Paige: My first five years as a director was that incredible period of the late eighties when we all learnt about central funding. Instead of training directors, people were sending them

off to work at Marks and Spencer to work out how to get money. I got the job at Salisbury because I *did* know what I was talking about in terms of three-year funding, and dealing with councils.

As artistic director I gave myself all the plays I didn't know how to do and that I wanted to learn how to do. As a freelance, I would never have the opportunities that I was able to give myself then. That's the wheeze, because artistic director is a nightmare job, but I've also done my best work at theatres that I've run. When I've worked in other people's buildings I've been over accommodating and not put my foot down about what I wanted for my production in the way that I would if I were in a building that I ran.

When Paige took on the job of artistic director at Salisbury she felt that nobody had expected that a woman might be appointed:

Deborah Paige: People kept saying, 'It's really unusual to have a woman as a director', and I kept saying, 'Actually, you're making a whole load of women invisible: Clare Venables, Pat Truman, Garry Hynes in Ireland, Pip Broughton, Joan Knight up in Perth in Scotland, Jane Howell. And think of the women who moved theatre on, like Joan Littlewood and Lilian Baylis.'

Paige also mentions Sue Wilson and Glen Walford as directors who have inspired, encouraged and been mentors to her. In addition she stresses how much things have improved for aspiring women directors nowadays:

Deborah Paige: When I was at school there was no drama, no theatre studies. In the Crucible auditorium the other day some school girls who want to do lighting were asking for a plan of the rig for a school project. I didn't know *any* girls at school who wanted to do lighting. And I meet a lot of young women directors who've grown up wanting to be directors. It would not have *occurred* to me when I was 20. Not because there weren't women directors around but somehow it wasn't expected and most of all I wouldn't have expected it myself for myself.

The main problem Paige identifies in her directing practice isn't necessarily to do with gender:

Deborah Paige: I really want actors to be physically able and open to exploring things in a non-verbal way. I do come across actors who will go along with it, because I don't give them any choice, but they think it's a waste of time. I just long for actors who are as good physically as they are vocally and imaginatively. It's not just about being fit, but it's about finding out things, releasing ideas which aren't just coming through the head.

Of all the directors I interviewed Paige is the most tentative about Shakespeare.

Deborah Paige: Doing Shakespeare was scary, partly because I thought, 'I've never been to university, I don't know about Shakespeare, I don't know all the things you ought to know about.' I don't know what I thought you ought to know about it, except that with Shakespeare you've got to have a concept and that there are always loads of academics sitting around, whinging on about the language.

However, Paige, as artistic director of a major theatre like the Crucible in Sheffield, is under pressure from exam syllabuses and the associated buying power of the schools' audiences, to produce, if not direct, at least one Shakespeare production a year.

Jude Kelly

After graduating from Birmingham University, Jude Kelly had a short stint as an actress before moving completely into directing.

She was director of the Solent People's Theatre from 1976 to 1980, where she concentrated on devised theatre. From 1980 she was artistic director of the Battersea Arts Centre in London as well as working as a director and writer for the spoof epic specialists, the National Theatre of Brent. From 1989 onwards Kelly has been artistic director and chief executive of the West Yorkshire Playhouse (WYP) in Leeds where she has directed *The Revenger's Tragedy* as well as Shakespeare's *Taming of the Shrew, Merchant of Venice* and *King Lear*. Her most recent Shakespeare production is *Othello*, which she directed in 1997 in Washington, with Patrick Stewart playing the lead in an otherwise all black cast.

Jude Kelly: When I was at university it was still perceived as being odd that I wanted to be a director. I only knew of three women directors: Joan Littlewood who had retired; Buzz Goodbody who was dead; and Joan Knight in Perth. I was also very committed to the relationship between art and access, and art for everybody, and I didn't know of anyone working in that field either.

Kelly's commitment to increasing access to the arts, to convincing people of their own creativity and to combating the idea that access means a lowering of standards can be seen in daily practice at the WYP, where the large open foyer is used for a range of access activities and classes, as well as for theatre management meetings. As there's no back-stage canteen, performers, directors, designers and administration staff all eat in the cafeteria in the foyer, and anyone can come up and talk to them.

Kelly's commitment to access has also resulted in several of her classical productions – *The Merchant of Venice, King Lear* and *The Revenger's Tragedy* – using local, non-professional actors to provide a sense of the society in which the play action takes place.

Jude Kelly: I've always wanted to force the debate about art and its intrinsic value to everyone in society and how you have to change education opportunities and access opportunities within the arts profession.

For 20 years, ever since I've been in the theatre, I've always worked on the idea of personal art, and developing people to be expressive through theatre is natural. If you've got the skill it takes, why not? And when non-professionals are embarking on these journeys, I think it's really fantastic for them to be part of a professional production, to be in something which has so many areas of precision at the same time as it has the need for you to keep releasing a truth that you can't control. There's also something about real people who are not actors; they have an undeniable authenticity.

In discussing her perception of herself as a director, Kelly makes the point that she has only very rarely been witness to any other director's rehearsal practice and so comparisons are difficult to make. However, Kelly feels sure that being a woman sometimes affects the initial reaction she gets from actors:

Jude Kelly: There are always question marks hanging in the rehearsal room before any director starts work. The questions are: 'Can they direct? Will I want their ideas? Do they have the ability to translate ideas in directorial terms? Can they, through strength of character, sustain and manage the process of directing the production – including the tech. and everything?' Those question marks are there for all directors, but it's always slightly more coloured in, in felt tip pen, for a woman, because of the notion of being an exception to the rule.

If you get rid of the question marks early then there's no difference between men and women in the rehearsal room in terms of authority, and the more personal authority you feel you have in yourself then the less likely you are to try to create an atmosphere that suggests you must have power.

Kelly feels that she is likely to engage more with the energy and intelligence of the female actors:

Jude Kelly: They recognise that as a woman director I am likely to be reading a piece of material and considering how the women in that material are dealing with the world and I will judge whether the playwright has understood how women may have felt about the world.

Such engagement carries some risk as far as the male actors are concerned:

Jude Kelly: There may equally be an anxiety in the males: will their role be sensitised in a way that they don't think it should? Or will they somehow lose their masculine element if they have to fit in with some feminist scenario? This sort of paranoia has to be very, very quickly resolved.

At the end of the day, whatever your politics and rhetoric are like, you will never solve the problem of communicating if you can't actually direct. So something much deeper than politics and rhetoric must also be at work creatively; and your own disturbances, terrors, fears and aspirations are part of your work. If you try to hold on to any notion of yourself either as a kind of manager in a rehearsal room or as a holder of a particular political view, if you are very rigidly constructing your work around either of those two things, you are very likely to limit what I call this chaotic aspect of creativity which you have to have and you can't really control.

Whilst warning against the dangers of dogmatism, Kelly does, however, stress the importance of ideas in directing:

Jude Kelly: To direct a play successfully it has to be something you want to speak of. You don't put on plays to be nice. I am less concerned with how you create a beautiful production and more concerned with what ideas you want to explore.

Kelly came quite late to directing Shakespeare but now feels very attracted to the work:

Jude Kelly: I didn't direct any Shakespeare professionally until 1989 when I did *The Tempest* in New York. Before that I didn't have a need to direct Shakespeare but then I did need to after that. It's a total privilege to be able to direct Shakespeare's plays.

One of the things I feel very strongly about Shakespeare is that, though women have a particular position in his world order, he's able to give space for them to question that world order quite vigorously, both in personal relationships with lovers or would-be lovers and also quite often in terms of the larger scale.

Kelly acknowledges the importance of feminism in her directing practice but in addition stresses the politics of child rearing:

Jude Kelly: When I was in my early and middle twenties, I went to meetings of a group called Women Directors and Theatre Administrators. I don't think any of them had children and they felt that if they got off the career path on to the parenting one, they would never be able to get on to the career one again.

For me, part of women's great strength is to have this fan-like understanding and to be able to make these cross connections between ordinary tiny moments of tenderness and love, and major views about how the world order could be different.

There is also a complete myth around still, which it is useful for some to propagate, that deep creativity by women is impossible to achieve in the way of work either because it is serviced through child bearing or because it is all stopped up if you're not going to have children. But the things that are disturbed in you by having children are equal to those things that are satisfied for you, so it produces another set of understandings.

Kelly's own family life has included tragedy; she lost a baby to cot death and a sister died young. It hardly seems surprising then that Kelly often seems especially focused on ruptures within families in the Renaissance plays she has directed – obviously in *King Lear*, but also in *The Merchant of Venice* (Portia and her father, Shylock and Jessica), and *The Taming of the Shrew* (Baptista and Katherine and Bianca).

Kelly's success and position of power have brought her detractors – as she commented in a newspaper interview (The *Guardian*, 17 September 1997): 'An awful lot of short, balding, middle-aged men find powerful women frightening', and 'Ambition is still seen to be perfectly acceptable in a man, but not in a woman.' However, there are also great advantages to her position:

Jude Kelly: I'm aware that my force of personality and moving up through the ranks, if you like, has given me a greater platform from which to say things with a more demanding air. When I was at the Battersea Arts Centre I began to realise that younger women look at me and whether or not they agree with anything I've done doesn't really matter, the point is that they know that I'm here and that they could be here if they wanted to be – so that's good.

Kelly is, however, still sensitive to the obstacles young women face and has spoken elsewhere about the 'enemy within' for women artists: 'I think women find it harder to accept that they are artists. It's a word and an image which implies a certain dedication. It's harder for women to give themselves that permission.' (Armistead, 1994:189)

Gale Edwards

Gale Edwards is currently best known in the UK for her direction of large-scale productions of Andrew Lloyd Webber musicals, particularly revivals of *Aspects of Love* and *Jesus Christ Superstar*, and the British première of *Whistle Down the Wind*. Before working in England, Edwards directed a very large range of productions in Australia, mostly on mainstages, often of classical texts. Major

Shakespeare productions in Australia have included *Much Ado About Nothing*, *The Winter's Tale*, *King Lear* and *Coriolanus*. Edwards moved into English theatre with a production of Shaw's *St Joan* for Helena Kaut-Howson at Theatr Clwyd, a production which transferred successfully to the West End. This was followed up by two productions for the RSC: a controversial *Taming of the Shrew* and an acclaimed production of Webster's *White Devil*.

Edwards is a bold and interventionist director, who stamps her mark on a play. She is dynamic, focused and not afraid of upsetting the reviewers. She's also very clear on what she wants from her career.

Gale Edwards: When I was 27 I decided I wanted to become a theatre director. At 29 I started a youth theatre company, Energy Connection, in Adelaide. Now I'm doing productions with the RSC and in the West End. The success thing builds, and for me it's happening in England and in Australia now – I can walk around both playgrounds with confidence.

Both productions that Edwards directed for the RSC opened the RSC season for that year in their respective theatres. This opening slot brings extra pressure but:

Gale Edwards: It launches the season, it's seen like a talisman for how the season's going to go. If you get great reviews for the first show, you're off to a good start. It's a kind of honour when you open the season.

I have a very good relation with the RSC, but the RSC is an elaborate system and you do have to work out how it works.

Despite all her success, Edwards is ruefully aware of the personal costs involved:

Gale Edwards: Directing is a nervy, courageous, completely obsessive occupation. It requires a phenomenal energy; any

distractions have to be pushed out of the way. The other side of you is neglected. I have had no personal life for 15 years. I fly around the world, get off planes, do a show, get on planes, get off planes and do a show. I spend my spare time reading books, keeping up with my craft. I have no relationships, no family; I gave up all those things. It's a killing job, just killing. I'm 42 and I think, 'How long can I keep doing this?' It's tremendously costly to do what I have done.

In 1991 in an interview in the Adelaide *Advertiser* (23 March) Edwards spelled out what she sees as the gruelling nature of the job of directing in more detail:

> One of the important things about being a director is sheer bloody stamina. It is a tremendously difficult job. You've got to be a good communicator and leader; you've got to be a diplomat and a visionary and an interpreter of other people's work.
>
> You've got to be a psychiatrist to deal with some of the actors' problems. You've got to be a friend, a bully, a nurturer. And finally the buck stops with you. It's a tremendously stress-ridden life.
>
> I think a lot of people don't know what directors do. I think they think directors have coffee with the actors and have a bit of chit-chat, and somehow the play emerges.

Edwards acknowledges that some of her productions, such as her *Coriolanus*, have made 'a very feminist statement on the world', and she believes that the role of the personal in directing is crucial:

Gale Edwards: Any director who's good at what they do brings a unique and personalised interpretation to any script; therefore that interpretation is going to be coloured by a world view and history and background and education and all those sorts of

things. The fact that I'm a woman must be colouring my interpretation of the work. I don't interpret things from a distinctly feminist point of view in a conscious way, although I'm sure that feminism is very present in the way I see things.

Edwards is also quick to point to inequalities which still affect women directors:

Gale Edwards: Being a woman makes it double the pressure. Coming up through the ranks I felt such pressure that I'd got to be great, and you have to ask questions about the forces that operate. A hidden agenda does still exist although it may have gone underground because it's not acceptable to talk about it. For women the stakes are always higher; men are more able to weather the productions that don't work. I'm appalled at the fact that young men in this business get play after play after play to cut their teeth on until they get better (and there's no doubt you do get better with practice) and it has been a historical fact, less true now, that young women who fuck up once don't get a second chance – we can all think of examples.

In a related vein in 1990 Edwards commented caustically: 'We sometimes read about young male directors who are wunderkinds. When did you last read about a woman who was described as a wunderkind?' (*The Australian*, 4 December) However, Edwards considers that in her career she has been helped by men, not women:

Gale Edwards: I have no women mentors apart from Madame Zora Semberova in the eighties in Adelaide, at Flinders University. Since then Trevor Nunn's been a mentor; Andrew Lloyd Webber is a great champion of mine; John Gaden got me into the South Australia Theatre Company in Adelaide, and that was the leg-up that got me onto the mainstage. Otherwise I would still be doing what most women do, which is working in small spaces.

When she first worked in England, Edwards had to start again from scratch to build her reputation:

Gale Edwards: Being Australian made a difference. The English have an island mentality and they don't believe they've got a lot to learn from other cultures – otherwise there'd be more international theatre work done in England. In addition the European Economic Community, by forming very strong bonds and alliances within itself, has largely excluded Australia.

Shakespeare presents a host of challenges that Edwards relishes:

Gale Edwards: Shakespeare takes very particular skills whether it's a woman or a man who's directing. I think they're fiendishly difficult to do, very *testing* and challenging, but they're inspiring plays and you've got to go up a few steps in order to do them, and that's what's great about them.

I'm made better as a director because I direct Shakespeare. Every time it's like going into this tunnel of exploration; you have to do so much detective work, technical work, historical work and *thinking* and I love that. I could happily spend the rest of my life doing Shakespeare and never do anything else.

Edwards works primarily as a freelancer, a term which has its origins in mercenary warfare, something which appropriately reflects the fierce competitiveness needed to survive as a freelance director. One of the oddities of freelance directing is that prospective directors are often assigned productions on the basis of an interview (and here the political make-up of the appointing board becomes crucial) where candidates have to demonstrate that they are articulate, verbally skilled and adversarial – rather than whether they can direct. This interview system may well disadvantage directors who would say with Di Trevis 'theatre's not intellectual, it's sensuous' or who, like Deborah Paige, long to work with actors who are 'releasing ideas which aren't just coming through the head' – unless the directors concerned can also justify these non-verbal approaches in the verbal forum of an interview.

Freelancing does allow a director freedom from the administrative responsibilities of running a building, arts centre, or theatre company, but it also exposes a director to the demands of the market and those controlling the market. For a freelancer to be identified as politicised in any way is risky, as it might jeopardise her chances of getting work from artistic directors with different politics or in theatres with, for example, a very conservative catchment area. It's a measure of Edwards' confidence and toughness that she is not inhibited in this way.

Several of the women directors interviewed here are, or have been, artistic directors and this is a position of some power, opening up opportunities to direct Shakespeare although also bringing a pressure to direct or produce schools' set text plays. However, the artistic directorships concerned are without exception either in the provinces or out of the mainstream, positionings which have important implications in terms of funding and prestige.

It's also noticeable that all of the women interviewed have university degrees except for Littlewood, who trained at RADA and rejected everything she was taught there, and Paige, who studied as an actress and director at the Old Vic, but still feels slightly wary about doing Shakespeare, partly because she doesn't have a degree.

Because of the diversity of these directors' tastes and experiences, it was impossible, and undesirable, when discussing their Shakespeare productions, to fit them into a neat or elegantly developing argument. Not only have they all directed completely different plays, only allowing for substantial comparisons between productions in a few cases, but also, on occasion, individual directors just weren't interested in discussing a particular production. The time factor was also important here – Joan Littlewood was amused I wanted to talk about her Shakespeare productions of forty years ago; Jane Howell had only a very few memories of a 'good' *Comedy of Errors* she directed at Lincoln. So the discussion of Shakespeare's plays in production which follows has a slightly random feel. The analogy of the sampler is again useful here. In sampling these productions, it is possible to gain a feel for what these women have attempted to bring to Shakespeare and to identify common trends and difficulties which they have had to overcome. However, whether it is Joan Littlewood being reprimanded by reviewers for her class politics, Jules Wright insisting that Lady Macbeth is not a monster, or Jane Howell mourning the cost of war in the battle plays she directed for the BBC, all of these women bring a fresh, distinctive voice to the production history of Shakespeare's plays.

PART 2 – The Plays

The Taming of the Shrew

A woman directing *The Taming of the Shrew*, whoever she is, might as well get a loaded shotgun and put it against her temple, because half the critics will be disappointed and will criticise it if the view of the play is not radical and feminist because they expect that from a woman; then the other half will shoot you down in flames because you're doing a feminist, 'limited' view of a play which is meant to be about the surrender of love. So you *cannot* possibly win. You're absolutely fucked.

Gale Edwards

The Taming of the Shrew is one of Shakespeare's most controversial plays in terms of gender politics: the main plot features an unruly and obstreperous woman being tamed by marriage and confirming her newly tamed state, at the end of the play, by publicly submitting to her husband, lecturing other women on the ideal of wifely submission and abasing herself by offering to place her hand under her husband's foot. Despite this unsavoury storyline, *The Taming of the Shrew* is still very frequently revived, especially by the RSC, and because the play is a farce, full of physical and visual jokes, it often plays very well in the theatre. However, this is also true of *The Merry Wives of Windsor*, a play which doesn't get revived quite as often – possibly because that play revolves around the humiliation of male characters, Ford and Falstaff, by the active, assertive wives, and features a husband, Ford, submitting to his wife as utterly (if less loquaciously), as Katherine submits to Petruchio.

Increasing disquiet about *The Taming of the Shrew* has begun to have an impact on the play in the theatre[1] and the three productions discussed here – directed by Di Trevis, Jude Kelly and Gale Edwards – all reflected feminist critiques of *The Taming of the Shrew*, even though the productions took Katherine, the shrew, on very different journeys. In particular, these productions provided very different contexts for Katherine's story by the ways in which they recast the Christopher Sly framework.

In the received Folio text of *The Taming of the Shrew*, the play opens with two scenes in which a tinker, Christopher Sly, is subjected to a practical joke and made to believe he is a lord. In this capacity he is entertained by travelling players who perform for him the inner play of *The Taming of the Shrew*. In the Folio text that is the extent of Sly's contribution to proceedings, but in the Quarto text of *The Taming of A Shrew* several later Sly scenes exist. Despite the ongoing debate about the authenticity of these later Sly scenes, it is incontestable that when the whole framework is performed, it makes an enormous difference theatrically. *The Taming of the Shrew* becomes far more Brechtian: with Sly onstage, the audience are always at an extra remove from the Katherine and Petruchio narrative, they are aware of the theatricality of what they are witnessing and they are less likely to be sucked in by the supposedly comic ending when Katherine's submission is immediately undercut by Sly's crass responses. However, perhaps partly because the later Sly scenes are not indubitably Shakespeare's, directors have often felt free to adapt them extensively so that they make explicit political comment on Katherine's story.

For Di Trevis with her 1985 RSC production of *The Taming of the Shrew*, the potential of the Sly framework was partly what attracted her towards directing the play.

Di Trevis: I thought I wasn't interested in *The Taming of the Shrew* because I had a completely false picture of it; then I looked at the first page, the Sly scenes, and I didn't recognise any of it. I was completely taken by that; I thought, 'Why don't I *know* this part of the play?'

I felt with the structure of a play within a play, I could make all the comments I wanted about the role of the women and this became intensely interesting to me. With that very sadistic trick played on the poor man, Sly, I realised that I could draw a parallel between the powerlessness of the women in the play and the powerlessness of that beggar. And I didn't have to do that terrible thing of making Katherine send up the last speech because I had a structure whereby, after the ending of the play within the play, I could then make a theatrical comment about the position of the actress playing Katherine in the inner play – she and the beggar were finally left alone on the stage together and one saw that they were fellows. I was very, very excited about doing that.

At the end of the play Trevis underlined this bond between Sly and the actress/Katherine when Sly generously offered Katherine some of the money the Lord had just contemptuously chucked at him (Cousin, 1986:281).

Trevis also capitalised on the Sly framework to create an emphasis on class as well as gender politics. The frame was used to stress that the inner taming play was performed by impoverished, hard-working, nineteenth-century travelling players, and two of the 'actresses' in the inner play were seen to be nursing babies between their acting scenes as well as being very visibly involved in the heavy physical labour needed to get the show going.

Di Trevis: The point was that the women did all the work. I had seen a marvellous film by Ariane Mnouchkine about the life of Molière – nobody ever has original ideas; your brilliance is measured in terms of what you choose to steal. When Molière joined the theatre company that was run by Madeleine Béjàrt, there was a marvellous shot of them tugging this cart over a stream. It felt as if among these travelling players the women had to work like mad (as usual) on the least interesting jobs, the worst drudgery, for long hours. I was very taken by that image and I used it [see plate 1], but as soon as you see a woman pulling a cart it's Brecht and Mother Courage.

Several reviewers did indeed comment on the Brechtian dynamics of the production, dynamics enhanced by the use of a chalk circle on the floor to focus the acting, chalked place names to indicate locations and the pairing of the production on tour with *Happy End* by Brecht and Elisabeth Hauptmann.

Di Trevis: I also kept showing that the players were acting; just little things like when they all danced at Kate's wedding, and it was the end of the first half, all the players came out dancing but Kate came out nursing the baby as if the baby had been woken up by the music.

The whole production actually opened with the sound of a baby crying, and then the dishevelled travelling players, including two violin-playing gypsy women, appeared onstage. It was only *after* this overtly theatrical context had been established that Christopher Sly was introduced, pissing and vomiting onstage in his drunkenness.

Sly then watched and responded to the whole of the inner play; for example, his reaction 'I say we'll have no sending to prison' was so heartfelt that it threatened to disrupt the performance and he had to be calmed down and reminded that what he was watching was only a play.[2] The continuing presence onstage of Sly's 'wife' also emphasised the layers of artifice in the production as the audience had seen this 'wife' come into existence when, during scene 2 of the Induction, Bartholomew the page was made to stand on a stool and was dressed up as a woman.

In addition Sly was frequently acknowledged by the performers of the inner play and for Petruchio's crucial 'Thus have I politicly begun my reign' speech (4.1.174), which spells out what Petruchio thinks he is doing to Katherine, the actor Alfred Molina first poured out two glasses of wine, gave one to Sly, and then sipped the other himself as he delivered Petruchio's speech directly to Sly. Perhaps most memorably of all, at the end of the inner play, as Sly watched Petruchio beginning to feel uncomfortable over what he had asked of Katherine, Sly responded by beginning to act tenderly towards his 'wife'. All he got in return was mockery as his 'wife' responded to this tenderness by whipping off his wig and revealing himself to be a page-boy (Cousin, 1986:281).

At the time of the production Trevis claimed of *The Taming of the Shrew*:

> This play is about power, not gender. Power resides in economic status. The main plot is a play-within-a-play which I see as a rich man's joke. (*Time Out*, 12 September 1985).

Elsewhere she stressed:

> at the beginning there is a scene that's often cut where a woman is throwing a man out of an inn – really *manhandling* him – and when I read through the play from *that* point I thought – it isn't just about gender and teaching a girl how to behave, but is actually about class and economics. (*City Limits*, 23 August 1985)

Trevis didn't, however, let class politics steal the show:

Di Trevis: In the text it says that the inner play of *The Taming of the Shrew* is 'a kind of history' (Induction 2.136) and I used that on a banner in the production because I felt that most plays about women were a *kind* of history but not the real history.

Trevis also found the emblem of the shrew very suggestive:

Di Trevis: I found out that a shrew has a tiny stomach and it can't eat very much, it can't store food in its system. So shrews cry out all the time and make this terrible high-pitched sound because they're always hungry. I felt that this was a fantastic image for why women are shrewish; they're so *hungry* and they're vilified if they are vocal about it. Everybody would much prefer them to quietly starve than be demanding; I just loved that.

Many reviews of Trevis' *Taming of the Shrew* commented on the production's intelligence, thoughtfulness and surprising lack of farce. The range of reactions to Katherine's submission speech was extremely varied: some reviewers felt the problem had been sidestepped, others felt the direction was feminist. Certainly anyone who read their programme would be alert to feminist possibilities as it quoted Germaine Greer, JS Mill and George Bernard Shaw on feminist issues and included photographs of a women's protest march. In interviews at the time, Trevis was also quoted as saying that she had set the production in the early- to mid-nineteenth century because that was a time when:

> women were treated as chattels, when the gulf between the agricultural poor and the city rich was widening, and there was a marked political swing to the right. (*Northamptonshire Evening Telegraph*, 28 August 1985)

She also argued that *The Taming of the Shrew* and *Happy End* went well together because:

> Both of the plays have portraits of extremely passionate and strong women in combat with strong men. But the major discussion in both plays is where the power ultimately resides. The answer is it resides in economics – everything is a commodity in a world of commodities. (*Western Morning News*, 31 August 1985)

The question of where the power ultimately resides is, of course, also relevant to the institutional context of Trevis' production. As part of the RSC's touring programme, *The Taming of the Shrew* was seen by a large number of people all over the UK, but the focus of this programme is very much on outreach, targeting audiences who may not normally see much Shakespeare. Because of this, Trevis' production did not carry with it the prestige accorded to a main house Stratford production.

In contrast to Trevis' class-conscious production, Jude Kelly's 1993 *The Taming of the Shrew*, for the West Yorkshire Playhouse, was a romantic version of the play, which recast the taming as something undergone by both Katherine and Petruchio, two non-conformists in an affluent world, who were negotiating and building an alternative lifestyle to those around them. Again, however, the Christopher Sly framework was crucial in determining the tone of the production, which was comedic. The action largely took place on a cruise ship and the trick played on Sly, who was a drunk weighed down by duty free booze, was set up by the ship's captain in the tradition of the crossing the equator celebrations. When, at the end of the play, Sly was returned to his own identity, there was a sense of a light-hearted prank being over, and the fact that Sly's 'wife' was a sailor in Doc Marten boots and a pale frock also helped keep the tone broadly comic, and helped Kelly defuse some of the potential nastiness of the play.

The dominant cruise ship setting (designed by Paul Andrew) helped create an enclosed, even claustrophobic world, in which, despite the comfort and wealth, Kate could never get away from the people who laughed at her. *The Taming of the Shrew* then became a love story between two characters who had been rejected by this Noël Coward style society:

Jude Kelly: When Petruchio first meets Kate he says, 'Why does the world report that Kate doth limp?' (2.1.247) and I thought, 'What if she *does* walk with a limp?' I was then working around the idea that in Kate you have somebody who is perceived to be ugly and disabled, and 'the shrew' is a real description of a bitter person who thinks she is going to be a spinster all her life.

Katherine's limp, emphasised by the wearing of a surgical boot, generated a strong sense of her vulnerability and took away some of the traditional farce slapstick, although an onstage swimming pool allowed for one predictable joke [see plate 2]. In addition, Nichola McAuliffe's Katherine was sad and sullen, not the clichéd fiery termagant, and she was older than most Katherines. The *Yorkshire Post* (22 April 1993) thought her 'introverted, over ripe, well beyond her marriageable sell-by date'. This passionate, disparaged woman contrasted sharply with her loved, younger, prettier, able-bodied sister, Bianca, still girlishly playing on a rocking horse. Katherine's limp also offered a useful image for a twentieth-century audience who might be slow to understand that, for Shakespeare's audience, an aggressive personality in a woman could be seen as totally crippling:

Jude Kelly: Kate is full of a jagged defensiveness. She has this father who does his best, poor thing, but is very stupid in the way he deals with his two daughters, and Bianca is also insensitive to her sister's needs. I conceived of Kate as a woman who had been assumed by her father to be the sort of person who never would get married and he used her, relied on her for the household work or whatever, but now she was making him pay for it in the way that children do sometimes when they end up living with and looking after their parents.

Katherine's defences, however, were thrown by Brian Protheroe's Petruchio, an artist/traveller, with an element of the square-jawed action hero, completely out of place on the cruise ship. Petruchio treated Katherine with great charm, there was never any physical violence, and he was intriguing to her because he represented such an alternative to everything and everyone around her. Petruchio's Bohemianism allowed the audience to hope, by calling up the traditional romantic construction of the artist as sensitive soul, that underneath his bravado there might be tenderness. Also, because the taming took place at Petruchio's paint-bespattered art studio/house, the taming of Katherine by food and sleep deprivation was played against a background which evoked the romantic notion of suffering for your art.

The taming was additionally coloured by the fact that Kelly made sure that Petruchio was also seen to suffer during the process. Initially he bounded onstage full of energy; he 'wooed' Katherine in the ship's gym and he arrived for his wedding on stilts. His air of athleticism dissipated during the taming process, however, and Petruchio's increasingly haggard looks attested to the fact that he, as well as Katherine, wasn't getting any sleep:

Jude Kelly: Petruchio is another kind of outsider because he doesn't seem to sit anywhere with anybody in a very easy kind of way and, although he's very comic, he's very unconventional, quite a problematic personality, and I was looking at how Katherine and Petruchio might need each other; they might really work well for each other.

What I worked on was that he actually did fall in love with her very, very early and that his problem was that she didn't fall in love with him. He gives a long speech when he won't let her have the new clothes when he says, 'is the jay more precious than the lark?' (4.3.173), and I did that for real; he was trying to say to her, 'As far as I'm concerned you are beautiful, you don't need all those things.' It really worked and it was funny as well; it was really about Kate getting to the stage where she thought, 'I am beautiful.' So when they went back to the party at the end of the play, she was completely differently dressed in a way that said, 'I am allowing myself to be attractive.' Kate wasn't already gorgeous at the beginning of the play because that didn't make sense. There has to be a real human need to be solved; the play's not just a romp.

As a consequence of this humanising vision of *The Taming of the Shrew*, Kelly directed the submission speech as a private and moving negotiation between Katherine and Petruchio.

Jude Kelly: At the end, the play is full of people sitting around who have laughed at Kate, who have humiliated her. What I was working on was Petruchio's belief that Kate would not humiliate him in front of everybody. He was saying to her, 'Tell them how you feel about me', and there was the potential for her to say, 'Get lost', but she began to realise that there was something going on and then there was a private discussion between them, in front of other people, which ended with her saying, 'If necessary I'll put my hand under your foot.' The implication was, 'I *do* love you enough to do that, if you ever ask me, but I do *trust* you enough to know you'll never ask me.' Unconditional love is something which you must be prepared to give but at the same time you hope it won't be asked for.

Kate's speech isn't *a speech*, it's something that's happening onstage; she happens to be doing all the talking, but what's Petruchio doing? Actually what he was doing towards the end of it was not exactly crying but it was close. It was the first time really that Kate was saying, 'It's all right, I do love you and she clearly did.

Kelly actually chose to direct *The Taming of the Shrew* because of the strength of her response to the ending of the play:

Jude Kelly: I'd never seen *The Taming of the Shrew* when I read it but I'd seen Thelma Holt do Marowitz's adaptation of the *Shrew*. She did that speech in chains – Kate had just been raped, and Holt was absolutely magnificent. I was expecting when I read *The Taming of the Shrew* to find that speech full of anger. It wasn't, I didn't find anger there at all.

This absence of anger was epitomised in the closing images of Kelly's production. As Katherine and Petruchio posed like happy honeymooners on the ocean liner, an elderly and clearly very loving couple appeared, holding hands, and seeming to prefigure Katherine and Petruchio in years to come. This image of happiness and resolution got a very mixed reaction from reviewers, some of whom were won over by the sentimentality whilst others were unimpressed.

Kelly also introduced a mellower tone than usual into the taming of Katherine by making her clearly overhear Petruchio's 'Thus have I politicly begun my reign' (4.1.174) speech. This not only allowed Katherine to understand what Petruchio thought he was doing (something which is denied to Shakespeare's character) but, because Petruchio actually looked up at Katherine during the speech, and acknowledged that she had overheard him, a sense of communication was established plus, crucially, a sense that by not protesting, Katherine was partly agreeing to go along with Petruchio's ideas.

In complete contrast to this, in Gale Edwards' production of *The Taming of the Shrew* for the RSC in 1995, this same moment was one of horror: as with Kelly's production, Katherine was onstage for Petruchio's soliloquy but Josie Lawrence's Katherine appeared isolated upstage, walking slowly and painfully across the stage, heedless of Petruchio's words and enclosed by her world of suffering. Katherine remained onstage still, in shock, during Bianca's high jinks in 4.2. After this Katherine rose and delivered a soliloquy made up of the bewildered questions Katherine puts to Grumio in 4.3., when she is trying to find out what Petruchio is hoping to achieve by his oppression of her. By delaying Grumio's entrance until the end of this speech, Edwards not only created a soliloquy for Katherine but also gave her the opportunity to establish direct contact with the audience, again something which Shakespeare denies his character. Lorraine Helms (1990:198–203) identifies the paucity of soliloquies given to Shakespeare's female characters as a crucial factor in making feminist directing of Shakespeare difficult. Here Edwards partly circumvented this problem.

Edwards also palpably undercut the value of what Katherine was learning: all Katherine's submissions were painful to witness and when, after a very long and painful pause, she first submitted to Petruchio and agreed to call the sun 'the moon' (4.6.), Josie Lawrence deliberately overplayed the submission, thereby anticipating the overstated mode of her final, public submission speech. Lawrence delivered the submission speech loudly, often angrily, stressing the extreme nature of what was being said, and growling ferociously when telling the other women off. The total effect of her performance was to confront Petruchio with the question: 'Is this really what you want?' His implied 'no' was reinforced by a programme note which stated: 'Petruchio slowly realises what he has been attempting to do to Katherine in the name of love. By the end of the speech his dream has become a nightmare.'

Part of the power of this ending was made possible by the way Edwards completely appropriated the Sly scenes and made a political statement about *The Taming of the Shrew*. The whole production opened with a loud unShakespearean argument between a drunken Sly (Michael Siberry, doubling this role with Petruchio) and his wife (Josie Lawrence, doubling this role with Katherine), to the accompaniment of storm clouds on the cyclorama, thunder and lightning. After driving his wife away from him, Sly fell asleep and dreamt the main play action but immediately after the interval the opening storm was reprised, to make sure the audience had not forgotten the Sly framework. Because the Lord and his pink-jacketed hunting party who played the trick on Sly kept appearing during the production to shift furniture and help out with scenery, the framework was kept in the audience's minds and the hunting party also witnessed Katherine's final submission.

This submission speech was actually the last speech spoken in the production. Immediately it was finished the action cut back to Sly, denying the audience the comfort of 'Why, there's a wench! Come on, and kiss me, Kate' (5.2.185). As the inner play dissolved, and Katherine left, Petruchio was left onstage in shock, heedless of the money he had won from the wager and crumbling back into the role of Christopher Sly. After a few moments, Josie Lawrence reappeared as Sly's wife and, full of remorse for what he had done or dreamt, a kneeling Sly clasped his wife's waist like a small child needing comfort; Mrs Sly didn't respond but stared into the distance, leaving the state of the relationship and the amount of damage done, ambiguous. The accompanying string music certainly suggested lamentation rather than comedy. Crucially, however, as Penny Gay (1998) has pointed out, the final focus was on the woman Katherine/Mrs Sly, and the cutting meant that the last clear speech of the play, the final say, was Katherine's.

Because it was a mainstage RSC production, Edwards' *Taming of the Shrew* was reviewed in all the national papers. Several reviewers complained at having to review *The Taming of the Shrew* yet again at the RSC, and they were divided on the question of how much interference with the text was permissible. *The Times* was outraged at Edwards' interventions and misdirections and, in response to seeing the production for a second time in London, fulminated that the central couple 'become exemplars in a marriage guidance manual aimed at unreconstructed males' and:

> Edwards' handling of the play's sexual politics is not exactly liberating either. She reinvents the Christopher Sly 'induction'; she makes wholly unjustified cuts and additions at the close; she forces Siberry and Lawrence to finish the play in ways that directly contradict the Bard's wishes; and all for the sake of extracting a right-on moral for the right-thinking 1990s (11 April 1996).

Edwards was astonished by the virulence of some of the reviews:

Gale Edwards: *Taming of the Shrew* got the most vicious reviews I've ever had in my life, they were sexist, they were absolutely savage and it was like I'd pissed on sacred ground or something. The vitriol in them! All directors get bad reviews but I thought that a lot of these reviews had a *tone* to them which was just unnecessarily savage and directly aimed at me. I'd never seen a body of reviews – and in Britain 12 newspapers come out and talk about you – so clearly aimed at crucifying the director. I thought, 'Well, I've obviously pushed a nerve.'

What I find remarkable about *The Times* review is that the reviewer, Benedict Nightingale, never considered what women in the audience might have made of Edwards' production. Personally I've never seen the ending of the play performed so intelligently before.

One aspect of Edwards' production which many reviews agreed on was that the Bianca subplot was unfunny, despite attempts to conjure up broad comedy by pulling faces, 'ad libs', overstated gestures and costume gags. Edwards, however, again directed this plot line unconventionally; Bianca seemed more interested in Tranio than in her husband, but although Mark Lockyer's Tranio was dazzling with his Gary Glitter costumes and his Prince/Michael Jackson posturings, he, like Christopher Sly, ended up back in the gutter and was in attendance at the final wedding feast only to collect up the garbage.

Tranio's outlandish costumes suited the world of the film *The Adventures of Priscilla, Queen of the Desert*, which was consciously evoked in this production. *Priscilla* is a film about drag queens, that is, male embodied, exaggerated, fantasy enactments of femaleness, something which complemented Edwards' construction of *The Taming of the Shrew* as Sly's dream of remodelling his wife into a fantasy woman. The reading of the play as a dream also suited the production's anarchic mixture of Elizabethan and modern visual gags; Petruchio drove a bubble car, his wedding outfit was a chicken suit with a huge red glittery codpiece, while Grumio wore a pink ballet dress.

Penny Gay argues (1998) that this mishmash of costumes created an 'over-the-top comic carnival, an assertion of the validity of popular and working-class modes of performance' and in line with this Gay reads Michael Siberry's Petruchio as Australian, blokish, Ocker and, something implicit in these last two descriptions, working class. The Melbourne *Age* (12 September 1995) also identified 'something inescapably antipodean' about Edwards' *Taming of the Shrew*, an 'irreverence' and 'extrovert exuberance' all the more notable for being located 'in the centre of the RSC's heartland, in Stratford'. In an interview in 1996, Edwards herself commented: 'I think the critics who were outraged by [*The Taming of the Shrew*] just did not think that a woman – let alone an Australian woman – should go to work at the RSC and tamper with Shakespeare' (*Panorama* magazine, January 1996). Elsewhere in this interview she described herself as 'this girl from the sticks' and 'an impostor from Australia'. However, Edwards' position as an Australian occupying the Stratford mainstage 12,000 miles from home territory, and there producing an irreverent and Ocker *Taming of the Shrew*, also offered a memorable riposte to the British cultural imperialism which foisted overly Anglicised Shakespeare, delivered in cut-glass English accents, on generations of theatre-going Australians up until the mid seventies.[3]

Edwards initially resisted the idea of directing *The Taming of the Shrew* as her début production for the RSC:

Gale Edwards: I begged not to do it. Adrian Noble had seen *St Joan*, which I'd done on the West End, and he said it was very hard to find directors who could direct on a big landscape and would I like to come to the RSC? I was chuffed and so I said 'yes'. Then he said, 'And direct *The Taming of the Shrew*?' I said, 'Oh no, no, I don't want to direct *The Taming of the Shrew*.'

I went because I was so seduced by the idea of working in the RSC and I had the vanity to think that I could do something with it and of course it was controversial. Kate did not do the last speech subserviently because I couldn't bring myself to do it that way.

Edwards was quite consciously misdirecting the play:

Gale Edwards: My theory about *The Taming of the Shrew* is that it is about the surrender of love and it *is* about her giving up everything and saying, 'I love you and you can tread on my hand.' That is the right way to do it and I couldn't do that production. That was a *huge* artistic and moral dilemma for me.

An RSC press release for Edwards' *Taming of the Shrew* announced that this was the first production of the play to be directed by a woman 'in the Royal Shakespeare Theatre'. This got converted in the *Guardian* (24 April 1995) into presenting Edwards as 'the first woman to direct the play for the RSC', which, of course, ignored Di Trevis' earlier production. All directors are prone to invisibility once a production has opened – it's easier to remember who starred in a play rather than who directed it – but when women directors become invisible in this way there's more at stake, because women have been and still are a minority group in professional Shakespeare production.

These three productions of *The Taming of the Shrew* suggest that, as the wretched play is still good box office, it might be preferable to have women, or those with a sensitivity to gender issues, directing it. However, it is still a very dangerous play. Jude Kelly's production found humanity and romance in *The Taming of the Shrew* but hid some of the nastiness and made the play acceptable, even comfortable; Di Trevis' Brechtian production, which stressed the economic and material conditions of the characters, risked emphasising class politics at the expense of gender politics; Gale Edwards' production, with its radically reworked Christopher Sly framework, also contained a romanticism of sorts in that it implied that really, when you come down to it, men *will* always acknowledge that dreams of controlling women are shameful. It may be that treating the taming of Katherine as a foolish male fantasy makes *The Taming of the Shrew* seem more palatable – because the implication is that sensible men could never harbour such fantasies.

Much Ado About Nothing

Eight years earlier, in Adelaide in 1987, Gale Edwards had directed the Shakeseare play which reworks and softens the woman-taming motif of *The Taming of the Shrew* – *Much Ado About Nothing*. This play focuses around the so-called 'merry war' (1.1.59) of battles of wit between Beatrice, a woman who considers herself to be 'on the shelf', and Benedick, a man who considers himself a confirmed bachelor. By the end of the play, the intelligent, vocal and outspoken Beatrice is silenced; she is to marry Benedick who declares 'Peace; I will stop your mouth' (5.4.97) as he kisses her. Gender issues are perhaps raised most clearly in the play when Beatrice's cousin, Hero, is humiliatingly rejected by her bridegroom, Claudio, at the altar and Beatrice proclaims her frustration at being a woman and therefore unable to call Claudio to account for his appalling behaviour: 'O that I were a man!...O God, that I were a man! I would eat his heart in the market-place!...O that I were a man for his sake!...I cannot be a man with wishing, therefore I will die a woman with grieving' (4.1.304,307,318,323–4).

The central pairing of Beatrice and Benedick particularly attracted Edwards:

Gale Edwards: I love the central debate between Beatrice and Benedick. I love that frisson that's at the centre of the play, the untameable woman and the maverick, outcast man. She's an old maid and she's a bit weird and everyone thinks she's too loud-mouthed and too opinionated. He's equally unconventional and that they should find some way to come together and make the great fiery match – *that* **has an enormous life spirit at the centre of it. It's a play with a great life spirit beating in it;** *Much Ado About Nothing* **is blood rushing through the veins: it's a very exciting play to do.**

Edwards' production made Beatrice an intellectual, clearly equal to any man. In notes produced for school study days in association with the production, Beatrice's position was described thus: 'She refuses the commodity status and insists on the right to dispose of herself.' Meanwhile William Zappa as Benedick started off as broadly comic but charted a growth in seriousness as he moved beyond being merely a 'larrikinised aristocrat' (*Australian*, 3 March 1987) into a mature and trustworthy husband for Beatrice. The *Adelaide Review* (March 1987) commented that Zappa clearly delineated Benedick's journey:

> from wary cynic through feckless suitor to compleat (sic) lover... Benedick begins to see just how destructive all that Boys' Own Annual stuff can be. He is shaken to his spurs at Beatrice's vehemence in demanding that he revenge her by killing...Claudio. She begins sabre-rattling just when he is about to stop all that sort of thing.

This *Much Ado About Nothing* was Edwards' second co-production with John Gaden, and the first of Edwards' and Gaden's three Shakespeare collaborations. *Much Ado About Nothing* opened a season which included Gaden playing Leontes in an Edwards/Gaden *Winter's Tale*, and theatre publicity stressed the intersection between these two plays in terms of the calumnied woman, male jealousy, emotional damage and the possibility of forgiveness. The question of how Hero could forgive Claudio and, what is more, marry him at the end of the play was partly answered by this production's setting, an 1890s Messina with lots of Italian gothic in the costumes and decor. The notes for school students explained that this placed the action:

> within a recognizable social structure where women were still viewed as possessions to be disposed of between fathers and husbands, where chastity before marriage was still a major and vital social ethic, and where the behaviour of the men in the play could find some justification.

A social context which was 'both impetuously Sicilian and priggishly Victorian' (*Adelaide Review*) was evoked; huge candles and incense were brought in for Hero's marriage, an enormous tomb, complete with a St Teresa and a starburst Madonna, appeared for Claudio's penance, and the basic set consisted of an elegant colonnaded courtyard, with curtains hanging across the pillared archways, offering ample opportunities for eavesdropping, spying and 'noting'. In counterpoint to this grandness, the production also used broad, *commedia*-style clowning for Dogberry and Verges, and Dogberry's role was substantially increased as he doubled as a Harlequin/master of ceremonies, opening and closing the proceedings and blowing a half-time whistle for the interval.

Although the Edwards/Gaden *Much Ado About Nothing* was well received, the stark combination of grand drama and *commedia* clowning points to a recurring challenge posed by the play: how broadly should the comedy be played and how much should the darker elements be stressed? This challenge was particularly highlighted in the contrasting fortunes of two 1988 productions of *Much Ado About Nothing*, both of which were directed by women – Judi Dench and Di Trevis. Trevis' production got panned so vitriolically that for years afterwards she woke every morning thinking of the denunciations contained in those reviews. Trevis' experience of directing the play was also affected by the fact that during the rehearsal period her adopted son was diagnosed as having cerebral palsy. Her distress over this made directing an RSC mainstage production even more difficult.

Trevis' production was accused of several kinds of misdirection. Firstly, the set got out of hand, which she concedes is the case. Maggie Steed (1993:42), in a sensitive and intelligent discussion of the experience of playing Beatrice in this production, describes the set: 'we performed this domestic play in a vast, pillared setting (which dwarfed the actors) and wore a series of glossy costumes over-indicating wealth and an obsession with style'. Secondly, Trevis was accused of misdirecting by bringing in too much farce.[1] For example, for Beatrice's overhearing scene Steed had to hide in a small ornamental pool, emerge dripping wet and wring out her designer dress. One piece of classic farce business, a recalcitrant deck-chair routine, used in Benedick's overhearing scene, made a successful reappearance in Kenneth Branagh's film of *Much Ado About Nothing*. The third major complaint by reviewers was that Benedick was made into a obnoxious character, and the personalised attacks on Clive Merrison, who played Benedick, approached the libellous.

Maggie Steed was an older than usual Beatrice, her pairing with a short Benedick broke height taboos, and both Beatrice and Benedick were not conventionally beautiful. Beatrice was assertive and threatening to 'the status quo of a male-controlled world' (*Rugby Advertiser*, 14 April 1988). However, Steed's reflections on playing Beatrice stress a melancholic side to her character: she is caught in the 'tyranny' of always being 'the entertainer, providing the laughter in other people's lives' (1993:45); she uses a 'rhythm almost characteristic of the stand-up comic' (44) but she is 'marked' by sadness, specifically the tragic life of her mother, a 'life' which Steed (47) describes creating in rehearsal. Steed also saw Beatrice as using the 'language of men, not simply in the sexual innuendo, but also in the warmly combative, almost packaged way that Beatrice lays her cards on the table' (46).

Trevis is clear about what went wrong with her production but the reviewers reacted with venom. The *Independent* (15 April 1988) called Steed's Beatrice 'a man in drag' and 'what you might get if you sent' drag artist 'Dame Hilda Bracket on an assertiveness training course'; the then Prime Minister Margaret Thatcher was invoked by the *Mail on Sunday* (17 April 1988) and the *Daily Telegraph* (16 April 1988). The *Daily Telegraph* reviewer also confided to his readers, in case they couldn't work it out, that he had written his review 'in anger'. As John Cox (1997:78) comments:

Trevis's production offered a scathing critique of modern affluence from a materialist-feminist perspective...Most critics anatomised the production, scandalised, one suspects, at the appropriation of the play with such polemical intent.

The dominant theatrical tradition in relation to *Much Ado About Nothing* offers the play as a good-natured comedy; critical raptures have been inspired by warm-hearted, merry Beatrices such as Ellen Terry, or Beatrices with just an occasional catch of sadness in their voice, such as Judi Dench. Reviewers wanting a warm-hearted *Much Ado About Nothing* were bound to dislike Trevis' production right from the very opening moments, when the auditorium was suddenly overwhelmed by the threatening, deafening noise of a helicopter descending and bringing the men back from war, to the very end, when Trevis 'questioned with bitter scepticism whether marriage was in any sense a happy or a comic outcome' (Cox, 1997:235). Nostalgia for less confrontational visions of *Much Ado About Nothing* certainly operated in several reviews, which referred approvingly to past productions which *had* warmed their hearts: John Barton's 1976 RSC production (where racially crass 'comedy' was supplied by white actors guying Indians, serving the British Memsahibs), and Franco Zeffirelli's Old Vic production were particularly mentioned.[2] The idea that a comedy which has been seen as increasingly problematic in much academic writing, especially in terms of its gender dynamics, could be given a bleakly serious production or that Trevis may have felt 'some ambivalence about a play so implicated in patriarchal ideology' (Gay, 1994:171) was not countenanced by most reviewers, although *The Times* (15 April 1988) could see 'substance in the production's feminist angle; as where Hero...collapses in church and is immediately surrounded by a flock of sympathetic girls, while the men all retire to nurse their personal grievances'.

John Cox (1997:78) is also right to point to Trevis' confrontational class politics in this production. All the main characters were over privileged, wealthy ex-pats. The parade of fashion costumes and the overpowering set contributed to the evocation of the decadent rich, although this atmosphere adversely affected the pacing of the production, which occasionally became as drawn-out as some of the languid, drawling RP accents. A sense of privilege and languor was generated as characters sunbathed and lazed about – as Penny Gay (1994:171) suggests, the production seemed to be set 'in the 1950s, in some tropical haven of the rich, with the British Army not too far away'. In addition, the women's impractical costumes – lots of big fifties skirts – attested to their primarily decorative function in life, with nothing to do except look glamorous.

Joan Lipkin, who discusses strategies for 'Surviving the Reviews' in relation to an overtly feminist theatre piece she directed on abortion rights, comments judiciously on the impact adverse reviews have on a production: actors wilt, audiences who don't cancel sit glumly expecting the worst, telegraphing 'any ambivalence it may feel to the actors, short-circuiting the dynamic exchange that constitutes the experience of live theater and undermining the leadership of the director' (1991:317–18).

The leadership of Trevis as a director was certainly under attack in the *Much Ado About Nothing* reviews: the *Financial Times* (14 April 1988) claimed Trevis 'should never be allowed within a five-mile radius of comedy' as she 'painfully lacks a sense of humour' and for confirmation of this point reminded readers of her unfunny *School for Wives* at the RNT. The fact that the obnoxious gender politics of *School for Wives* rival those of *The Taming of the Shrew* (a comedy Trevis *had* received praise for) wasn't mentioned. Moreover the question of what constitutes comedy, and what constitutes a joke, was rarely raised in these reviews. Trevis was simply condemned for her production's 'prevailing strident humourless-ness' (*Guardian*, 15 April 1988) despite the fact that there were also complaints about the use of broad comedy; the *Daily Telegraph* (14 April 1988) particularly attacked the production's 'heavy-handed and totally irrelevant gags' and the use of visual jokes such as making Benedick 'a bald and unattractive assistant bank manager drafted into the army where he is made to wear Bombay bloomers'.

Alan Sinfield (1985:176) argues that 'A major role of theatre criticism is to police the boundaries of the permissible', and certainly the reviews of Trevis' *Much Ado About Nothing* support this impression. The boundary which was most frequently invoked by reviewers, that between the conventionally physically attractive and the unattractive, is particularly significant. Reviewers were very disturbed by the way this Beatrice and Benedick looked, and yet there is no reason why this odd couple, who both insist on their own unorthodoxy – in resisting marriage, in mocking social norms – should be cast and costumed as conventionally beautiful. The reviewers' collective condemnation of the lack of conventional beauty in the protagonists suggests a deeply conservative element in their reviews.

Trevis was the first woman to direct on the Stratford mainstage since Buzz Goodbody's production of *As You Like It* was savaged by the critics in 1973. Although she was devastated at the time, Trevis is philosophical now:

Di Trevis: You can't afford not to plough straight on when you've had a failure and I ploughed right on and had a baby because I was 41. Although I've done a lot of work, and some good work, since then, my career has never gone back to the point it was at before *Much Ado About Nothing* when I was turning down three times more work than I actually did.

One of the profound lessons that I learnt from doing *Much Ado About Nothing* is that the theatre isn't the most important thing in my life. There are other things like life itself, like there are thousands of children with cerebral palsy.

The attacks on Trevis' production contrasted starkly with the praise heaped earlier in the year on the *Much Ado About Nothing* directed by Judi Dench. Reviewers commented on how much Samantha Bond's Beatrice reminded them of Dench's own performance of the role (in John Barton's 1976 production), a performance tinged with sadness at a real betrayal by Benedick in the past, but not as pain-marked as Maggie Steed's interpretation of the role. Dench placed her production in the nineteenth century, with lots of pretty white dresses for the women and white tight-fitting trousers for the men; Dench saw the costumes as 'very Degas and Impressionist' (Cook, 1993:128). There was nothing misdirectional about this production as far as reviewers were concerned, and the inevitable comparisons with the *Much Ado About Nothing* at Stratford cast Dench as the success story and Trevis as the disaster.

The unanimity of the reviewers' praise for Dench's production is extremely pronounced. Almost all of them invoked Jane Austen, *Pride and Prejudice*, and Elizabeth Bennett, but the most overused word to describe Dench's production was 'warm'. The nearest anyone got to criticising Dench was *City Limits* (1 August 1988), which praised the production but ventured to suggest that 'the play's darker moments – Claudio's rant at Hero, for instance – are dealt with tentatively, edging into the bland'. The moral of this tale of two *Much Ado About Nothing*s is clear: if you want to please the reviewers, keep it warm, sunny and happy – and steer clear of farce mixed with pain.

Dench's production formed part of a Kenneth Branagh project to give directing opportunities to leading and experienced performers, and to avoid working with directors who were not also actors. Other productions included in this project were a Derek Jacobi directed *Hamlet* and a Geraldine McEwan directed *As You Like It*. Dench comments on the experience of directing *Much Ado About Nothing*:[3]

Judi Dench: I was reluctant to direct when Ken Branagh asked me, but Peter Hall pushed me, so I did it. The job of a director is to tell the story that the author has written. When I directed *Much Ado About Nothing*, I wanted it to be Shakespeare's *Much Ado About Nothing*, not Judi Dench's. As a director, and as an actor, I don't believe in coming to rehearsals with preconceived ideas of how the play should ultimately turn out. The input of the actors is vital, as is a sense of humour.

Given this working approach, it is hardly surprising that Dench resisted discussing what she saw as the heart of her *Much Ado About Nothing*.

Unlike the other directors considered in this study, Judi Dench has a vast experience of being directed and has encountered a very large number of different directors' methods. She is sceptical about difference in terms of gender:

Judi Dench: Shakespeare wrote from a man's and a woman's point

of view. I have been directed by a woman and found that experience no different to being directed by a man.[4] I have never really been aware of 'gender relations' and 'power relations' in rehearsals. It is important to me that a company works well together, which means it must be led from the top by the director and the leading actors.

Two women directors Dench has encountered in Shakespeare productions are Margaret Webster and Wendy Toye.[5] However, Dench names only male directors as sources of inspiration:

Judi Dench: I have been inspired by Michael Benthall, Franco Zeffirelli, Frank Hauser, Peter Hall, John Barton, Trevor Nunn and Sam Mendes.

The contrast between Dench's self-effacing stance – 'I wanted it to be Shakespeare's *Much Ado About Nothing*, not Judi Dench's' – and Trevis' more openly political positioning was very much reflected in the relative acceptability of their productions as far as the reviewers were concerned.

In 1997, having incurred the wrath of many theatre reviewers for casting a woman as Lear and then not doing what the reviewers felt she should do with this striking idea, Helena Kaut-Howson went on to direct *All's Well That Ends Well* and *Much Ado About Nothing* in quick succession:

Helena Kaut-Howson: *Much Ado About Nothing* **was sprung upon me, offered me, I didn't choose it. I was a little scared because I would have no time to discover things as I would like.**

However, with this *Much Ado About Nothing*, at the Manchester Royal Exchange, Kaut-Howson managed the considerable feat of confronting the play's more unpleasant aspects, getting a lot of laughs, pleasing some of her most ardent critics and achieving a box office sell-out.

For Kaut-Howson getting the Hero story right was crucial:

Helena Kaut-Howson: It's a very strange and rich play, a world where you follow what somebody tells you, something that was overheard, rather than trust your own feelings.

We took the dark sub-plot, Hero's story, very seriously. I was very lucky with my Hero, Niamh Daly, who completely understood Hero. Niamh is a Catholic, Irish and a modern girl. I asked Niamh, 'How does Hero forgive Claudio?', and she said, 'Because she would have done the same if she believed he betrayed her.' Because Claudio *believed* Hero betrayed him.

This reading, stressing Hero's internalisation of the rules of the society she lives in also fed into the way she responded to her father Leonato:

Helena Kaut-Howson: Leonato almost strangled Hero in the production but, again, she would have done the same: she was the best thing that he ever had and then, suddenly, she was false.

This enabled Kaut-Howson to make sense of the ending of Hero's story:

Helena Kaut-Howson: I set the play in Sicily at the time of Garibaldi, the 1860s. Like in some Arab communities now, Sicilian fathers then, if they had a daughter who was not a virgin, they could kill her.

I realised that when Leonato gives Hero again to Claudio at the end of the play and we always consider it to be this perfunctory happy ending, Leonato is not like Father Christmas just giving Claudio a gift: Claudio *must* marry her, he *must* be *seen* to marry her. It is crucial to Hero's reputation that she is married to vindicate her properly; the marriage is the recovery of her reputation.

This element was stressed in the production by making the aborted wedding a very public event, so that Hero's humiliation was in front of her whole community. For this sequence Hero was positioned centrally and alone on a raised part of the stage, exposed and vulnerable, reacting as if physically struck as the terrible accusations were hurled at her, crying out inarticulately in pain and in protest when she had no lines. Appropriately there was also a very public and elaborate mourning ritual performed in honour of Hero's supposed death. Claudio was also made so passionate, so distraught in his attacks on Hero, so close to relenting in the face of her suffering, and so clearly out of his depth in his relations with Don John, that Hero's forgiveness became more understandable.

Hero was also crucial in helping to create a strong sense of a woman's world in the production. The second half opened with 3.4., the dressing of the bride. This allowed for an elaborate staging to be set up during the interval, so that the second half could start with Hero having a bath onstage, behind lots of muslin curtains. This set created a sense of women's space; open, relaxed but also fragile, because the audience knew of the impending disaster. Using slightly different terms, the *Independent* (26 September 1997) review spoke of a 'beautifully played boudoir scene' where 'we have a real sense of the world behind the veil'.

This strong sense of a woman's world was also present in the opening scene, where women were taking a siesta in the heat of the day. *The Times* (25 September 1997) read this as a 'world of women waiting for something interesting to happen to them. In a word, men'. However, the *Independent* was able to take this a little further and praised the production for its 'definition of the women and of their side of the patriarchal medallion'. In a programme interview, Kaut-Howson herself spoke of the play's world of double standards where 'the men's world and the women's world were very different but met strongly, producing terrific tension because of the expectations and mutual mistrust.'

Kaut-Howson, however, wanted to guard against the dangers of what she felt to be an inappropriate kind of feminist approach to the world of *Much Ado About Nothing*:

Helena Kaut-Howson: It is a limitation to impose a feminist view

on an historical world which culturally could not have had those views. The thing is to embrace the past parts of the culture and to let them reach out to our perception of the world.

Using the past to reflect on the present, however, also presents problems:

Helena Kaut-Howson: How do you make *Much Ado About Nothing* modern without Beatrice wearing jeans? Beatrice and Benedick are a very modern couple – they are both very demanding of their partners – but the play as a whole is a little remote. That's why I wanted the production to be in nineteenth-century costume – so that Beatrice and Benedick could be properly modern but I could also put them in the context of their slightly remote world.

I wanted to treat Beatrice and Benedick as real human beings and also as people who were not particularly young. I thought that the reason they hadn't got married wasn't only because they believed what they said about not wanting to get married but because of a real insecurity inside, a fear that either they would fail themselves, or that others would fail them.

This sense of damage and fear was clear in the production: the *Daily Telegraph* (25 September 1997) commented that both Beatrice and Benedick seemed 'deeply insecure, and their banter is both bitter and self-protective' while the 'sense of psychological damage on both sides makes the eventual triumph of their love especially moving'. Indeed once the eavesdropping tricks had been played on this Beatrice and Benedick, both relaxed completely and behaved as besotted lovers. At the same time things never got sentimental, with comedy specialist Josie Lawrence playing Beatrice and with both Beatrice and Benedick shamelessly milking the audience. During her eavesdropping scene, for example, on hearing that Benedick loved her Beatrice fainted into the arms of a man sitting in the front row of the audience and then proceeded to steal his programme to use as 'camouflage' in order to creep closer and hear what Hero and Ursula were saying.

Kaut-Howson also developed a very strong motivation for Don John. It was not new to suggest that Don John is, as the *Daily Telegraph* described it, 'a repressed screwed-up homosexual who verges on the psychopathic'; however, the production made sense of this motivation. Don John was clearly passionately obsessed with Claudio, and his actions against Claudio's marriage fitted in with this passion, as did his cruelty during the ball scene when he physically hurt Hero, staring intensely into her eyes and holding her face too hard with his hands.

The production programme interview with Helena Kaut-Howson recorded that after *Lear*, she was looking forward to 'doing a sunny play with a happy ending' although by the time the production opened she was 'not even sure about that happy ending'. In this interview Kaut-Howson also stressed the importance of insecurity in *Much Ado About Nothing* – where someone like Claudio 'given the slightest pretext for jealousy or doubting their partner' would stick with that doubt. In his insecurity, Claudio lashed out and Hero suffered as a consequence.

The reviews of Kaut-Howson's *Much Ado About Nothing* were very enthusiastic: even Charles Spencer in the *Daily Telegraph*, who admitted that 'Over the years I've written some horrid things about Helena Kaut-Howson', praised this production very highly indeed. Kaut-Howson balanced the superb comic skills of her Beatrice and Benedick with a very serious presentation of Hero's sufferings and discovered she had a critical and box office success on her hands.

While it is important to acknowledge and celebrate the success achieved by Gale Edwards, Judi Dench and Helena Kaut-Howson in their productions of *Much Ado About Nothing*, in some ways Di Trevis' supposedly disastrous, MsDirected production is the most revealing of all, especially as the production video suggests that it is very unfairly represented by the reviews;[6] on the video the audience seem to be having a good time, they laugh at the broad comedy and they applaud loudly at the end. However, Trevis' production was also by far the most overtly political of the *Much Ado About Nothings* studied here, with its sharp class commentary and its refusal of the gender stereotypes that heroines (and heroes) should be kept young and beautiful. The question of whether it was a good or bad production becomes much more complicated when the reviews are read with the production's political stance in mind.

A Midsummer Night's Dream

Katherine in *The Shrew* and Beatrice in *Much Ado* are sisters in kind to the shrews tamed in another popular Shakespeare play, *A Midsummer Night's Dream*. Here the formerly aggressive Queen of the Amazons, Hippolyta, now defeated in battle, is about to be married to her vanquisher Theseus. Meanwhile the fairy queen Titania, a name which evokes chthonic female power, is tamed by her husband Oberon in a humiliating process which, in modern productions, usually involves Titania having sex with an ass-headed man.

A Midsummer Night's Dream is much concerned with theatre magic, as well as fairy magic, and the play's principal magic maker, Oberon, has often been seen as a playwright figure. He is also a kind of stage director, setting up environments and situations in which characters – mortals and fairies – will perform. In this respect Oberon has to be placed alongside Peter Quince, the stage director of the theatre troupe who will entertain Theseus at his wedding; a company whose all-male identity reflects the fact that *A Midsummer Night's Dream* itself would originally have been staged by an all-male cast, something which is comically stressed by Flute's reluctance to take on the role of a woman (Thisbe).

Deborah Paige directed *A Midsummer Night's Dream* for the Salisbury Playhouse in 1992 and turned the play's secondary directorial figure, Peter Quince, into a woman.[1]

Deborah Paige: I was absolutely determined to have a half female, half male company, six women and six men no matter how *Midsummer Night's Dream* got cast. So Egeus became a woman, a mother instead of a father, and the same actress also played Quince, and she became Pat Quince. It was very funny. Puck was also a woman.

Because Egeus is a rabid patriarchal figure in *A Midsummer Night's Dream*, demanding the right as a father to absolute control over his daughter Hermia's future, changing Egeus to a woman has a huge knock-on effect in terms of the gender politics of the play. Patriarchal oppression is turned into matriarchal. Nikki Slade's 'Egea' was a horsy, county type, 'a fox-huntin lady' while her 'Pat' Quince was 'a Yorkshire woman in a red wig' (Salisbury *Journal*, 1 October 1992). The female Puck, Tracy Mitchell, appeared as a naughty but gymnastic schoolgirl and she was one of three black actors in the cast.

The fairies, who owed 'more to *Twin Peaks* than to the Flower Fairies' (*Western Gazette*, 1 October 1992), created a big impact with reviewers partly because of the way the set was used. The designer was Isabella Bywater:

Deborah Paige: I like working with women designers very much and I've worked a lot with Isabella Bywater. I love being open to what a designer will come up with, and the women designers I've worked with tend to be more open whereas the male designers tend to go away and come up with something. Isabella and I were both always very busy with kids so we had to start early and then have short periods of time together with long bits of thinking in between.

We wanted to set the play in a room and for it to be very English. Isabella made the walls of the room with latex panels so you could walk through the walls. It was an inside-out room; it could become the forest and fairies could put arms through the walls and things could disappear. There was also a hole up through the floor and so Puck's first entrance was bursting up through the floorboards. The room had a dado rail which was so wide that you could come through one of these panels into a very high level of the set. The whole production looked hugely acrobatic.

This design was very popular with reviewers, who particularly enjoyed the magical effect as characters disappeared through the walls. Yvonne Bradbury in a radio review for 'Wiltshire Sound' also commented perceptively on the use of 'an apparently ordinary room

– except that a giant sunflower is growing out of the wall', which hinted 'that the wild wood is not far below the surface of the civilised palace'. Bradbury goes on:

> what seemed to be solid walls becomes a permeable membrane through which fairies appear and disappear at random, and the shapes of trees are revealed – they were there all the time but I didn't notice them. The effect of this is to suggest that the worlds exist simultaneously but on different levels of reality, and the human lovers are seen to be victims of forces of which they are unaware and over which they have no control – an unsettling perception.

Keen for her cast to keep a sense of the wood within themselves, Paige took them all off on location to remind them of how woods work – 'the wind whistling, things moving, brambles pulling at your clothes, as the text says' (Salisbury *Journal*, 24 September 1992). Reviewers were slightly less convinced by the 1920s costuming, which Paige described as setting the play 'in a slightly old fashioned world' where 'people would be shocked that a man and a woman, who are not married, spent the night together in a wood' (*Southern Evening Echo*, 22 September 1992).

Paige's main emphasis was always that she wanted to direct a visually, aurally and physically bold *Midsummer Night's Dream*:

Deborah Paige: I wanted to work with a choreographer and a composer as an integral part of the work all the way through the four weeks of rehearsals. The choreographer Caroline Salem and I set up a very physical way of working. I use a lot of physical work to release imaginations; it's not just about being fit, it's about finding things out.

Paige's commitment to a physicalised production of *A Midsummer Night's Dream* was highlighted by sketches of movement work which appeared in the programme, and the *Western Gazette* felt 'The movement would be a credit to a ballet company.'

A Midsummer Night's Dream was the first Shakespeare on the Salisbury mainstage in seven years and Paige also used a scaled down version of the play (which cut the lovers) for outreach into schools:

Deborah Paige: The company was 12 strong, and one half of the company was going to do *Doll's House* after *The Dream* and the other half of the company worked on a version of *The Dream* for seven-to-ten-year-olds, still using Shakespeare's language, and called *Hot Ice*. It was a fantastic opportunity to go on working on the text but in a totally different context, and it produced three quarters of an hour of magic.

Directing *Midsummer Night's Dream* was the most frightening thing I've ever done. Salisbury's full of people who go to the theatre (I think my worst claim to fame is that I stopped so many of them coming) but they loved *Midsummer Night's Dream*. It was magical and very beautiful, the text was incredibly clear. Curiously, because my *Dream* occurred at the same time as Robert Lepage's, it got more notice than it might have done.

Indeed the *Observer* reviewer (4 October 1992) even listed similarities between French Canadian Lepage's controversial, muddy *Midsummer Night's Dream* at the Royal National Theatre, London and Paige's production. The list included: an athletic female Puck; the use of a stark, single light suspended onstage; and the fact that Paige used 'Lepage's composer', Peter Salem, to create 'a similar atmospheric job with bells, gongs, xylophones and rattling forest noises'. As Peter Salem had actually composed for Paige when she directed *The Winter's Tale* the previous year at Salisbury he could just as easily have been described as *her* composer. However, overall, the *Observer* preferred 'La Paige' to Lepage and described Paige's *Midsummer Night's Dream* in very sexualised terms:

the fierce vexation of these sexy dreams is impelled like some gorgeous afterbirth, into the accommodating warmth of a marital celebration. The physical comedy, we are reminded, is one of insertion and withdrawal, of entrapment and consumption, of foreplay and performance, of going and coming.

Despite successfully generating such a heightened atmosphere, Paige ducked some of the most confrontational gender politics of *A Midsummer Night's Dream*, both in Salisbury and in her later production of the play in the Regent's Park Open Air Theatre in London, in 1994. Responding to the latter production, *The Times* (1 June 1994) certainly thought that the tamed state of Hippolyta was underplayed:

> David Collings is a clumsy Theseus stumbling about with silly benignity. It is hard to believe his boast that he wooed his bride with his sword and won her love doing her injuries. At best, one can only imagine he bounced up to Hippolyta (Kate Seaward) and tripped over somebody else's scabbard. He brings out little of the dark side: either the dictatorial patriarch or arrogant aristocrat when he offers Hermia the choice of death if she refuses to fit her fancies to her father's will or insults the mechanicals' entertainment.

In the Regent's Park production the taming of Titania, played by Estelle Kohler as 'a sexually ripe presence insistent on her freedom to frolic' (*What's On*, 8 June 1994), was also underplayed. What *was* noticed by reviewers was: the production was centred around a serious and moving portrayal of Bottom by Robert Lang; Puck was unusually virile, aggressive and Pan-like; the fairies were dressed like huge bluebottles with mirror spectacles, glittering leggings and silver wings; the whole production was Regency in setting, something which evoked Jane Austen for some, although one reviewer saw shades of the Shelleys, Byron, and 'drugged-out wife-swapping' (*Time Out*, 8 June 1994).

Paige was challenging conventional wisdom in directing Shakespeare on the mainstage at Salisbury and she was playing to a traditional theatre-going public. At Regent's Park Theatre she was directing in an open air space where subtleties are easily lost and the audience is often predominantly made up of tourists who want a good time. On both occasions she logically chose to direct *A Midsummer Night's Dream* emphasising the fun and the laughs, playing down the troubling gender issues raised by the play. Her success in attracting an audience for *A Midsummer Night's Dream* at Salisbury was also crucial in giving her the clout to argue for a staging the following year, 1993, of Shakespeare's other magic play, *The Tempest.*

The Tempest

For a female director interested in representations of gender, one of the main challenges presented by *The Tempest* is the paucity of female presence. As Prospero the magician collects together the men who cast him into exile 12 years previously and decides whether or not he can forgive them, the only clearly female voice is that of Miranda, Prospero's young and inexperienced daughter. The other female presence required by the play appears in the masque to celebrate Miranda's betrothal where (sexless?) spirits represent powerful classical goddesses – Juno, Venus and Ceres. Lurking in the background of the play's narrative are the disruptive, but now long dead, Sycorax, the witch who was Caliban's mother, and the women Miranda can vaguely remember from the time before she came as a very young child to the all-male environment of the island. Nineteenth-century theatre practice often increased the female presence in *The Tempest* by having Ariel played by a woman, but without such crosscasting, women performers have very limited opportunities in this play.

Jane Howell directed *The Tempest* at the Northcott Theatre, Exeter in 1973, as part of a season which included a focus on women's issues: *The Tempest* was followed by a production of Shaw's play about women, prostitution and economics, *Mrs Warren's Profession*, and a production called 'Women's Place' by the theatre's Young People's Department. However, today Howell's main interest in *The Tempest* is not gender. For her the figure of Prospero, who, like Oberon, is one of Shakespeare's director-like characters, illuminates her understanding of her own directing practice:

Jane Howell: You have to question the value of your work in this island society of theatre, in which you, as director, make the rules like

Prospero makes the rules. You have to question what the relationship is to the outer world – and basically people are still starving. Are we really affecting, are we really touching anything? Should we, like Prospero, come out of this world of theatre and go back to govern, having learnt something from theatre? Should we go back to where we began, go into politics, offer our services to the community? On a political level, should we break our staff, forego our magic?

Howell also reflects on the binary opposition represented, for her, by the characters of Ariel and Caliban:

Jane Howell: As an artist, you have to keep a balance between Ariel and Caliban. It's like keeping an area of you in slavery in some way, keeping part of you enthralled. It's very easy to ignore the dark side of yourself. Working in theatre you get to know a lot about actors, you get to know a lot about magic, a lot about technical things, a lot about how you can control the artistic – the Ariel part of yourself – but you don't properly deal with the dark side of yourself or the side of yourself which is earthed; you live up in your head, and there's a very high cost for that. When I was directing I could not give part of myself in a personal sense in whatever relationships I had.

Howell's memories of her *Tempest* are also very much coloured by the pressures she was feeling at Exeter:

Jane Howell: There was a sort or despair, an anger when I did *The Tempest*; that was what was motoring me. I was at a point of despair because we were doing what I believed to be very good work with a very good company and we were not getting people in.

However, Howell still recalls the stage environment of the production with great pleasure:

Jane Howell: I said to my designer, Hayden Griffin, 'What we need to provide is a space which is essentially theatrical but like that [snaps fingers] can become magical'. He devised a most wonderful set which had a sort of bowl of plain canvas but in segments like an orange. On each segment there was a pick-up point, and the segment could come up so that people could enter from anywhere and then as they came through it closed down again.

The magic was that you could screen projections onto it so you could have it become a mass of butterflies or a mass of flowers or trees. The segments provided the sails of the ship, and the storm, and they always looked like waves.

Reviewers who saw this set in all its glory (it was radically adapted for touring) were divided on its effect: the reviewer for the *Western Evening Herald* (16 May 1973) talked of 'the great cyclorama' but the Exeter *Express and Echo* (2 May 1973) thought the set 'a cross between half a giant pudding basin and a banana. Unpeel a section and out pops a character!'; however, the latter review also conceded that this created 'a cross between a circus ring and a psychedelic nightmare' and lifted the production 'into the mystical'. Psychedelia was also suggested by the programme illustrations.

Reviews concentrated mostly on Edward Petheridge's Prospero. The *Western Evening Herald* thought Petheridge 'personified the withdrawn philosopher', playing Prospero as 'a somewhat aloof austere schoolmaster' whose 'rather abrupt style made the spiritual magnitude of the character and its fantasy recede' and whose 'magical powers seemed pragmatic rather than wonders'. The *Western Morning News* (16 May 1973) agreed this Prospero was 'not a man of dark mystery' but also thought him 'a man thoughtful enough to have learned magic arts, weak enough to have been ousted from his Dukedom but strong enough to gain only a gentle revenge'. Howell's direction was most clearly commented on by the *Express and Echo*, which paid her the loaded compliment of saying 'the immortal playwright himself would be bemused and entranced if he could see the way in which his play has been interpreted'.

Like Jane Howell, Gale Edwards, in her début production for the

Melbourne Theatre Company in 1990, was drawn to speculating about the potential psychic meanings of Ariel and Caliban:

Gale Edwards: I believe that Ariel and Caliban are attributes of Prospero, that they are his id and his alter ego, or his intellect and his bestiality, or his fineness and his coarseness, gone berserk, and they're trapped there on the island with him.

He's trapped both of them and won't let them go, but they *are* him. At the end of the play he has to let *both* of them go and he has to break his staff and somehow reconcile something about himself and who he is; that's *my* version.

This interpretation was stressed in a set design (by Tony Tripp) which had Prospero's cell as a cave in the back/brain cavity of a sandy mound which was also a huge, ravaged human face lying on one side, half buried in the surrounding sand. The *Australian* (17 May 1990) commented:

> This design points to how Prospero pervades the play; how his magic and quest for revenge shape the realities experienced by everyone on the island.

The revolve on which the giant head was placed also allowed for flamboyant discoveries and spectacular apparitions such as the masque to be staged relatively easily.

The production programme pointed the audience in the direction of dreams and Jung. The *Sunday Herald* (20 May 1990) approved and spoke of the production's 'rapid pace' which helped 'sustain the effect of a dream play, as nearly all its characters fall in and out of sleep, confusing the real and the imagined'. In addition the programme printed a clear directorial statement by Edwards:

> The conflict between order and chaos raised in the play and the struggle that we as human beings are all involved in to harmonise the two within ourselves are contemporary issues.

Prospero, struggling to reconcile the extremities of his own nature, which he has at first neglected and later enslaved, becomes, in this context, a very modern and familiar figure.

Gender was not much discussed by reviewers except for Helen Thomson (*Sunday Herald*), who praised Sancia Robinson as Miranda and went on:

Miranda's is not an easy role to play. The only woman in the play, she is in one sense merely a commodity exchanged between men, formally handed over from father to husband, but in her sexual awakening she also represents the fresh start Prospero proposes for a new world.

However Edwards did excite comment for casting one of Australia's leading actresses, Helen Morse, as Ariel:

Gale Edwards: I loved the notion that a woman should play the ethereal, sensitive, thinking part of Prospero, representing the flight of fancy, the intellect, the spirit. Helen was sensational as Ariel; sometimes she rode upon Prospero's shoulders, she sat on his back, he walked with her, sometimes she wrapped herself around his body. So Ariel was played as some kind of little, bald creature, with blue feathers, and Caliban was the dark monster representing all that is coarse and vulgar.

Morse's Ariel created an ambiguous, suggestive relationship with Prospero: the *Sunday Age* (20 May 1990) commented:

There is a great tenderness between Ariel and Prospero, and, even though this 'trixie spirit' is presented as a kind of androgynous creature, the feminine side shines through, and there is just a hint of eroticism between them.

Similarly the relationship between John Gaden's Prospero – who was described in the *Australian* as 'a complex, confused and erratic man, who upon acknowledging his darker side, makes peace with his enemies and himself' – and Frank Gallacher's Caliban was appreciated for its complexity. The *Sunday Age* explained:

> By finally acknowledging, and thus redeeming [Caliban], Prospero is admitting to having a dark side, which, it is said, is a necessary step on the path towards enlightenment...
>
> Frank Gallacher is fairly forceful, as usual, as Caliban, in the way that suits him. But he also shows another, vulnerable side, which is very moving, exemplified by the embrace of reconciliation between him and Prospero in their final scene.

The darker elements of life were also evoked as: 'Magical effects were engineered by thoroughly substantial satyrs, rather than by spirits, hinting at the bestiality which continually threatens Prospero's ideal world of moral order' (*Sunday Herald*).

Edwards' memories of the production are extremely positive:

Gale Edwards: I loved doing the production. I had the best time in rehearsal, I adored the cast and I adored the mystical nature of the piece which is also a puzzle, a mystery and cerebral.

Reviews praised the production both for its clarity and its entertainment value. The one dissenter (*Financial Review*, 25 May 1990) complained obliquely, and rather ponderously, that Edwards had failed to reference *The Tempest's* treatment of white colonisation, and invoked Jonathan Miller's production for the Old Vic, which had a black Caliban and Ariel. The reviewer disliked Miller's production but commented:

> It did have a clear interpretation – ironically one just right for Australia. I won't say what it was, but a clue lies in the way Caliban is treated.

The painful topic of the white invasion of Australia and the appalling treatment meted out to the Aboriginal population, was also ducked in two other mainstream productions of *The Tempest* in Australia in the same year.[1]

By contrast, when Deborah Paige directed *The Tempest* at the Salisbury Playhouse in 1993, she provided an additional commentary on the colonial politics of the play by casting Ferdinand as black; his sister Claribel's recent marriage in Tunis then became a return to her mother's home.

Paige initially considered subverting the dominance of male characters in the play:

Deborah Paige: From the point of view of feminism, *The Tempest* was interesting. I thought, 'How can I be doing this play when there's only one woman in it?' I flirted with the idea of a female Prospero but then I thought, 'It's all absolutely about Prospero being male. It's so important that he's male and that Miranda *is* the only woman and she's coping with a totally, totally male world.

Paige's production team, however, was all female:

Deborah Paige: One actor had a problem because the director, designer and choreographer were all female. He used to call me 'sir' and then say 'joke, joke'. Not a very good joke and he was difficult, and blocked himself from being as wonderful as he could have been.

Paige also had reservations about the play itself:

Deborah Paige: *The Tempest* was quite hard following the success of *The Dream* (in 1992) because as a play there's much less charm, less narrative. I wanted to go on pursuing that spirit world idea that really gives you a lot of scope. At the same time there's reams of academic stuff about *The Tempest*, and I don't know how you ever get to the bottom of that play. I got to the end of the production

and thought, 'I want to start again now', because I didn't, and I am still not sure that I do, really understand Caliban and Ariel.

Paige's production presented an Ariel whose relation with Prospero was imbalanced; Ariel was Prospero's closest and most beloved friend, who had enabled Prospero to explore new areas – magical, spiritual, psychological – but Ariel himself was emotionally detached from Prospero, and was simply a spirit in pain, yearning to be set free. Ariel was onstage all through the action, watching when not participating, but also suffering, imprisoned, unable to leave the space. His antithesis, Caliban, was earthed, constantly touching and enjoying the feel of the sand [plate 3]. The Salisbury *Journal* (23 September 1993) added another layer of interpretation:

> Prospero's familiars, all dressed in white, are his two natures – good and bad, female and male. Andrew Price's Ariel is deadpan – and brilliant. He sings falsetto, his long hair is plaited, Prospero addresses him like a lover.
>
> The dark side of his nature, Caliban, is played as a Salisbury traveller by Christopher McHallem...[in] unkempt, tattered clothes turned grey. And, sorry to be repetitive, brilliant.

The cultural loading here is weighted by the proximity of Salisbury to Stonehenge, a site popular with travellers.

The setting of Paige's *Tempest*, however, was not Salisbury plain but always very clearly an island. Onstage, three large screens, each painted with an image of a stormy sea, defined the playing space:

Deborah Paige: It was a very challenging set, just six inches of damp sand. It was visually extraordinary. We'd made a very early decision to use no props; the feast wouldn't be a real feast.

So the feast was created very simply by the actors playing spirits: Ariel lay down and defined the table space by drawing in the sand with his fingers. Meanwhile four spirits sat around him 'cross-legged' and proceeded to 'feed' each other 'with imaginary delicacies with two-foot long sticks, one in each hand, using graceful balletic arm movements' (Carter, 1994:26).

Looking at these three *Tempests* side by side, it is striking how focused all three of the directors were on Ariel and Caliban and their relationship with Prospero. Given that Prospero is a theatre director figure within the play, although an extremely dictatorial and patriarchal one, it is tempting to see all three of these productions reflecting on how Jane Howell, Gale Edwards and Deborah Paige see their craft and their relationships with their own personal Ariels and Calibans.

The Winter's Tale

In contrast to *The Tempest*, another late Shakespeare play, *The Winter's Tale*, has a very powerful sense of female presence. Women, Hermione and Paulina, bond together to work against the destructive behaviour of a man, Hermione's husband Leontes. Hermione is particularly impressive in her resoluteness when she stands trial unjustly accused of adultery by Leontes, and endures a very public humiliation with dignity, within days of giving birth. Paulina is less dignified and speaks out in her anger, evoking the misogynist stereotype of the shrew. As the audience find out at the end of the play, these two women work together, in secret, keeping up the pretence that Hermione has died, in the hope that Hermione's lost daughter Perdita will return – reunion with Perdita is their primary goal, *not* Leontes' repentance.

The play is also infused with the feminine and is full of images of pregnancy, birth and women bringing regeneration and grace. The feminine breaks through even in a moment of rampant masculinity when Antigonus is in the midst of protesting at Leontes' outrageous behaviour, he suddenly digresses into a discussion of his three daughters (2.1.146–52). This is totally unnecessary in terms of furthering the plot and the digression's main dramatic purpose seems to be to continue to build an image of the play world as one imbued by the feminine, even if that feminine is often in danger.

The Winter's Tale has particularly powerful resonance for Jane Howell, and she had already directed the play several times previously when she was asked to direct it for the BBC Shakespeare.[1] However, Howell's memories of the initial contact over the BBC production are very pragmatic:

Jane Howell: *The Winter's Tale* was just offered me; that's how telly works. It was just a straight offer and I thought, 'Do you want to do it or don't you? Where's your life going? Is this right for now or not? Do I need the money? *Yes!*'

Howell's interpretative 'hook' on *The Winter's Tale* was second chances:

Jane Howell: I have always believed very deeply in reincarnation. I believed in it as a child and I couldn't see any other sensible explanation of spring following winter. When the statue of Hermione comes to life it is stupid and ludicrous but it always works, and it always makes me cry however bad or good the production because one longs…

I believe that at any moment of the day, you can have that regeneration; all you have to do is ask for it and let go of the damage we all do to ourselves, let go of what is unnecessary. I think we all cry at *The Winter's Tale* because none of us can quite believe it, that we are worthy of a second chance. We are guilty, fear gets in the way, so do questions, but mostly it's a lack of self-worth, a deep feeling of being set apart from whatever the higher power is, being set apart from and not worthy of grace.

Howell sees the operation of 'grace' in *The Winter's Tale* as being very much in the province of the feminine:

Jane Howell: In some strange way the women are the same person: Hermione is the wife, Perdita the virgin and the crone is Paulina, who has gone beyond worrying about what she says, which is a wonderful stage of life to be in. So you've got the three aspects of the feminine there moving through to bring healing, and it's the quality of the girl, Perdita, that makes the healing really count. Then, for Leontes, the decline of his winter can move through to spring. The movement of *Winter's Tale* is towards that act of regeneration of the spirit, towards the reconciliation of the masculine and feminine and towards the

feminine finding its own way back, through Perdita, after it has been abandoned.

Despite Howell's deep concern for the regeneration of Leontes, aspects of her production appeared threatening to some critics. Kenneth Rothwell (1981:401) complained 'everything about Leontes in the first act confirms the darkest feminist visions of male aggression leading to the "battered-wives" syndrome'. Howell certainly wanted to create some sense of menace here; during the first half of the play Leontes wears 'more and more fur and by the trial scene he looks more debased and animal-like' (Howell, cited in Fenwick, 1981:23) and it is important to remember the extent of the destruction Leontes causes. The body count includes his son, Mamillius, his courtier Antigonus and an entire ship full of working-class men. He also appears to cause the deaths of his wife and daughter. In fact, emphasising the damage done by Leontes has a positive effect in that the more the audience registers his *de*generation, the more they can also register the miraculous quality of his subsequent *re*generation.

Leontes' abrupt shift from loving husband to jealous tyrant is notoriously difficult to play realistically and, given that audiences watching plays on television tend to expect a high level of realism, playing that transition was almost bound to be problematic. Howell chose to follow Jeremy Kemp as Leontes in close-up, with him whispering intently to the camera: sometimes only part of Leontes' face was in shot while Hermione and Polixenes were visible together in the background. This close-up work was untheatrical and so was in tension with the performance of Robert Stephens, as Polixenes, an actor known for his deliberate theatricality. For Howell, gauging the appropriate level of theatricality at any given moment was one of the most difficult challenges in this production:

Jane Howell: It is hard to find the right level for yourself *and* for your individual actors when you are doing a theatre piece on telly. You do need energy for that stuff; you can't bring it down to just everyday conversation. It *was* theatrical, but I hope it was never overburdening.

One actor who got the balance right was Rikki Fulton. As Autolycus, Fulton often played close-up to the camera, taking the audience into his confidence, but he was also able to be knowingly theatrical at the same time, laughing at the absurdity of it all. Howell still feels slightly uncomfortable, however, with the production's overall level of theatricality:

Jane Howell: We were trying to get towards something which I thought resolved itself more in the *Henries*, there we were deliberately theatrical at the beginning and then tried to take it down as we went through. *The Winter's Tale* I think was stylistically too harsh. It was a very harsh set.

Appropriately, however, the harshness of *The Winter's Tale*'s set was much more noticeable in the first half of the play where, despite the patterned floor suggesting an interior, the action was played alongside a wintry, stricken and dying tree. This tree began to bud as regeneration began in the second half of the play and the dominant colours changed from the stark, icy whites of Sicily to the golden warmth of Bohemia. The costumes enhanced this seasonal change as the heavy, quasi-Tudor hats and robes of freezing Sicily were left behind for the spring world of Perdita, who was dressed as the Botticelli Primavera.

When Gale Edwards directed *The Winter's Tale* in Adelaide in 1987, it was her second Shakespeare co-directed with John Gaden. The notion of co-directing clearly unsettled some reviewers, one of whom had responded to Edwards' and Gaden's previous co-production, *Much Ado About Nothing*, by attempting to identify 'his' and 'hers' sections. Edwards and Gaden explained how they saw their co-directing at the time in a jointly signed programme note:

It is not easy to examine the subtleties of how any artistic partnership works, but one thing is certain: we do it *together*. From the very first discussions about the play, through the development of the concept and design, to opening night, we share each step of the working process.

Stressing that the resulting production was 'mutually owned' and that flexibility was crucial, they commented on their choice to co-direct:

> We are both convinced that, in this particular partnership, two minds are better than one and the loneliness traditionally associated with the role of director is alleviated by having a trusted sounding board for ideas. Having another perspective, another eye and ear in the rehearsal room is an enormous asset and security in the rehearsal process, especially for the actors.

> We believe that, by working together, the creative process is enriched. And finally we enjoy it.

Co-direction is a relatively rare phenomenon, the classic model still being that of director and assistant, rather than a co-operation between equals.

Gale Edwards: Co-directing's a funny term. We had a lot of talks together about the play and with Mary Moore our designer, but inevitably when we started rehearsals, because John was playing Leontes he had to move into actor mode, so he was on the floor and I was sitting out the front.

The resulting production of *The Winter's Tale* was particularly rigorous in its engagement with the experience of Hermione at the end of the play.

Gale Edwards: When Hermione comes back to life, from being dead, from being a statue, as if she's been frozen for 16 years, and when she's rejoined her husband Leontes, he wants to skate off, to reel off to celebrate. I had him saying the last line of the text 'Hastily lead away' then everyone left the stage except Leontes and Hermione, and he stared at her and she wouldn't move. She just looked at him, she wouldn't go off to celebrate. Then he slowly

walked towards her – there were just the two of them onstage – and he fell down on his knees at her feet. So the curtain went out on the image of him holding onto her, half childlike, begging forgiveness for what he'd done.

That's to do with my interpretation of the world. I can't just go, 'Oh, the woman's been tortured, humiliated and denied for 16 years but hey, let's go off and have fun!' I can't do that. Hermione doesn't speak to Leontes in that scene but I think she's not very happy. I don't think I'd be very happy if I'd had to pretend to be a statue.

The *Adelaide Review* (August 1987) commented on this representation of Leontes and Hermione's reunion, 'Their reconciliation remains a provisional and ceremonial one – it is only with the brave new world of Perdita and Florizel that Sicilia will be redeemed.'

This interpretation of the final scene was very much enhanced by designer Mary Moore's representation of Paulina's art gallery as including images of the *Mona Lisa*, the *Venus de Milo*, Raphael's *Madonna and Child* and Warhol's *Marilyn Monroe* [see plate 4]. All of these artworks, as the *Adelaide Review* commented, showed 'women idolised and immobilised' and 'destroyed by the pedestals they are placed upon'. In addition the statue of Hermione was a huge caryatid with Hermione half encased, half entombed within it.

Moore's set was generally much acclaimed. The action took place on a large raked disk which changed colour according to seasons and emotions. The move to spring, regeneration and fun in a very 'Bohemian' Bohemia was signalled visually as the black and white of Sicily were disturbed by the entry of the Old Shepherd wielding a bright yellow umbrella, heralding a move to a world of vibrant colours and hippie beach costumes. Four curved perspex tubes hung in the air, creating a jolly rainbow and promising peace and reconciliation.[2] Moore (1994:230) comments of the set:

In monochrome Sicilia, the 'masculine world' was represented by a series of symmetrically placed phallic poles cut diagonally through the circular mass of the horizontal plane. Behind the poles, caryatids (drawn from classical Greek architecture) symbolised women acting as the supporting structures of their own oppression. In colourful Bohemia, the 'feminine world', the vertical bars were curved in the shape of a rainbow to harmonise with the circular floor.

Elsewhere Moore spoke of how 'great' it was 'to work with two directors who haven't said "we think all that political stuff is crap"' (*Adelaide Advertiser*, 11 July 1987), and Gaden and Edwards' programme note clearly complemented Moore's thinking on the play:

> We saw it as important to make a clear distinction between the two kingdoms of Sicily and Bohemia. We saw Sicily as being formal, courtly, hierarchical and structured. A society that works so long as the man at the top remains humane, rational and balanced. When he loses these qualities, the world is blown apart resulting in injustice, misery and death. A Winter world.
>
> Bohemia, on the other hand, is a pastoral world, of simple shepherds, feasts, innocence and young love. There are rogues (Autolycus), savage animals, duplicity and heavy fathers, but the spirit is gentle, open, even 'Bohemian', in our modern sense of the word. It is above all a world of hope imbued with the optimism of young love. A Summer world.

Edwards and Gaden's *Winter's Tale* was also much praised for the comic inventiveness of Geoffrey Rush's spiv Autolycus and the clever solution to the problem of staging *Exit pursued by a bear* (3.3.57). The bear, evoked amidst deafening thunder and threatening darkness, was actually Antigonus' own shadow 'devouring' him up.

In 1991 Deborah Paige directed *The Winter's Tale* at Salisbury. Her main memories of this production are to do not with interpretation but with finances:

Deborah Paige: I did *Winter's Tale*, when I first went to Salisbury, in the Studio. And of course, it bloody sold out and that was an early lesson. I'd never run a theatre; I didn't know that we could be sold out for three weeks doing *Winter's Tale* and lose money. With nine people in the Studio, you lose money after two performances because the Studio just doesn't seat enough.

Paige paired *The Winter's Tale* with the play she was directing in the main house, Pinero's *The Second Mrs Tanqueray*, another play which focuses on a family disrupted by the question of a wife's chastity – although in the Pinero play the strong and intelligent wife really does die.

Deborah Paige: A lot of people who saw *Winter's Tale* loved it. It was very much a chamber piece, and it was glorious doing *Mrs Tanqueray* and *Winter's Tale* close together with such reverberations between them. They're both totally strong on the subject of family.

In a programme note Paige described the production as 'exploring the domestic worlds' of the play.

As with most productions taking place outside London and Stratford, Paige's *Winter's Tale* got little press coverage, but it was highly praised by the Salisbury *Journal* (25 April 1991) for its paciness and narrative drive. The same review commended the effectiveness of the move from Sicilia to Bohemia: 'sepia panels slide back to let in the sea air and Antigonus' famous exit (pursued by a wonderful story-book bear) gives way to some doleful sounding sheep'. In this modern dress production, Bohemia had 'a far more foppish feel' than Sicilia; Autolycus was a 'disco rapping wide-boy'; and the climax of the play was 'magical'. The review also commented on the strenuous doubling, whereby a nine-strong company occasionally aided by 'the unobtrusive use of voice-overs', peopled the stage 'with more than 20 characters'. Helen Schlesinger was kept busy playing Hermione, Mopsa and Time while Polly March doubled as Paulina and the Clown.

At the end of *The Winter's Tale*, the audience find out that Paulina has been acting for 16 years, lying to the remorseful Leontes and only pretending that Hermione is dead. We also see Paulina stage-manage and, in a sense, direct a piece of theatre magic, when what appears to be a statue of Hermione transforms and turns out to be the real thing. The three directors considered here made very different decisions about what that moment meant for Hermione: Jane Howell focused on regeneration; Gale Edwards still saw the pain unforgivably inflicted on Hermione; Deborah Paige found magic. All of these readings are plausible, because Shakespeare chose to leave open the question of what Hermione thinks of her ending. The only lines he gave her are entirely focused on her daughter, not on herself, nor on her husband.

All's Well That Ends Well

The Winter's Tale is often linked to *All's Well That Ends Well* because both plays include women characters who prevail without donning doublet and hose, who band together with other women to outmanoeuvre men behaving badly and whose visible pregnancy, a condition comparatively rarely represented in Shakespeare's plays, is central to the narrative. However, the heroine of *All's Well That Ends Well*, Helena, is a long way from the largely passive Hermione, waiting, withdrawn for 16 years.

First Helena sets off on her own to travel to the court of France and cure the King of his illness. When the King rewards her by giving her the choice of any man at court as husband, Helena chooses the man she loves, Bertram, and is publicly rejected by him. The King enforces the marriage, Bertram runs off to war and Helena sets off on her own again, this time travelling to the war zone, where she finds her husband and tricks him into fulfilling the seemingly impossible conditions Bertram set for cohabiting with her: that she should gain possession of a ring of his and also conceive his child. Helena manipulates Bertram's urgent desire to have sex with another woman, Diana, substitutes herself for Diana in bed (thus utterly deceiving Bertram at the moment of sexual intimacy) and conceives his child. Helena *acts* to get what she wants and uses her ingenuity to the full. Because she is focused and an achiever, Helena has been punished by generations of critics who have expressed dislike for her relentless determination and drive. Helena has also made critics uncomfortable because, early in the play, she frankly discusses with Bertram's untrustworthy hanger-on, Parolles, the problem of how she should lose her virginity to her own liking.

Helena is also that dangerous thing in the Renaissance period – a woman healer. She has inherited her knowledge of healing from her father, which somewhat legitimises her as far as the patriarchy is concerned, but her success where so many men have failed, in healing the King of France, is potentially very threatening.

Harriet Walter, who played Helena in Trevor Nunn's well-received *All's Well That Ends Well* for the RSC in 1981, has spoken persuasively about how much Helena has been pilloried for achieving 'in a male way' and getting 'her hands dirty and enter[ing] the male world' (Rutter, 1988:75). Walter tried to contest the image of the 'devouring tiger-female' (Rutter, 1988:74) and stressed that Helena is 'desperately tentative' as well as heroic. However, it is revealing that her director, Trevor Nunn, wanting a sympathetic Helena, gave Walter 'two character points' which would chip away at Helena's air of success:

> The first was that she should be self-critical and apologetic, not triumphant or smugly self-vindicating. The second was that where she had signs of a sense of humour, of self-irony, we should bring that out. He believed these traits would stand her in good stead when she does things in the play that the audience don't approve of. (Rutter, 1988:81)

Helena Kaut-Howson has directed *All's Well That Ends Well* on three occasions:

Helena Kaut-Howson: I did *All's Well That Ends Well* in Leicester, where Kathryn Hunter played the Countess for me, in Clwyd and then in Regent's Park. I was always fascinated by the play because it was such a dark, cynical comedy. Shakespeare takes a conventional, fashionable plot and he mixes it with real life, and then the story itself doesn't really work, but I am interested in how these people, the characters, cope with the fairy tale test, and the way Helena has to do these strange things in order to achieve her aims.

Kaut-Howson's 1987 production at the Leicester Haymarket had a cast of seven, presented the play as a 'soap opera' and gave the war 'an Arab setting' (*Leicester Mercury*, 20 February 1987). The programme included a photograph of the family of arms dealer Adnan Khashoggi, in order to evoke both the life of the fabulously rich and the insidious influence of 'power-brokers, arms dealers, or image-makers' (programme note) in our lives. Computers and TV sets featured in the set, suggesting a hi-tech world where it was impossible to escape exposure by the media.

Kaut-Howson's 1993 Theatr Clwyd production of *All's Well That Ends Well* explored some of these ideas further and completely divided reviewers because of its snazzy updating of the action, characterised by the *Evening Leader* (20 January 1993) as 'Shockspeare'. Parolles was high camp, Bertram 'an excoriating portrayal of the pampered public school playboy' and Helena, in Doc Martens and a New Age dress, seemed in her 'man-grabbing' to be exhibiting 'direct, open, honest assertiveness' (*Guardian*, 26 January 1993).[1] The opening image – eight television screens, two newscasters and the Stock Exchange latest – set the tone, and the sequence where Helena chooses herself a husband involved a roving cameraman accompanying Helena into the audience in search of suitable candidates and relaying images of audience members on to the TV screens. The social context was 'a hi-tech society where the moneyed class manipulate the media' a society awash with 'fawning video footage of the royal soap opera' (*Guardian*). The Middle Eastern setting for the war suddenly became alarmingly topical, as the *Guardian* noted, as tensions again rose in that part of the world.

Kaut-Howson still sees one of the major problems faced by the high-ranking characters in *All's Well That Ends Well* as the strain, on the famous, of living a life in public view.

Helena Kaut-Howson: In *A Midsummer Night's Dream* there are those fairies who manipulate people's lives; today it's the paparazzi and the media. Suddenly we become enchanted; our lives become magical because they're captured for a moment in the dream of the glossy photograph, the flash of the camera.

Given this high-flying milieu, outsiders stand out:

Helena Kaut-Howson: The play has important things to say about society, about a closed world, an inner circle, versus outsiders like Parolles or Helena. Society is ruled by its own rules, and whatever you think of the values of that day, like honour and virtue, some characters are able to follow paths which allow them to stay walking that thin line, staying true to their own integrity.

Of course, there are double standards, different standards for women and for men, but I am also interested in these odd human beings who are against those standards and remain outside society. The play asks, 'How do you cope with double standards?'

Kaut-Howson's 1997 *All's Well That Ends Well* in the Regent's Park Open Air Theatre, London, again cast Helena as a palpable outsider in a filthy rich society. In the production programme, James Shaw suggested that Helena 'can be viewed as a proto-feminist, drawing on her own resources to ascend beyond the limitations dictated by society', and this idea of an alternative ethos was evoked by presenting Helena as a very young, frail-looking, neo-hippie. New Age music played when Helena cured the King, which she did by simply laying her hands on his head. Helena thus contrasted starkly with the conspicuous materialism on display all around her.

The Regent's Park Theatre, which has a healthy history of employing women to direct its Shakespeare productions, only operates during the summer season, and the beauty of the theatre's location is tempered by the fact that productions are subject to interruption not only by rain but also by jets flying overhead. As the theatre space demands big, not subtle effects, Kaut-Howson gave several characters theme tunes – Helena was accompanied by mystical pan pipes, in striking contrast to the cheerful, cockney Diana, in platform trainers and boob tube, who bounced around to Spice Girls music. Other large-scale theatrical gestures included the noise of bomber planes, a camouflaged Citroën driven onstage and soldiers hurtling around the auditorium, practising manoeuvres.

The death of Princess Diana during the run of this production made Kaut-Howson's use of paparazzi characters particularly provocative. Whenever the King of France appeared, even though the courtiers clearly thought him a bit of a bore, the paparazzi buzzed around him, flashing cameras at the ready. Multiple photo opportunities were staged during the production and there was an overpowering sense of the phoniness of such images.

Kaut-Howson's ongoing interest in *All's Well That Ends Well* is partly inspired by its problematic ending. Helena gets what she wants – Bertram – but by now he has been exposed as a liar, an adulterer (in intention), and a very unattractive character. He has agreed to live with Helena as her husband, but has only half-heartedly suggested he might love her:

Helena Kaut-Howson: What has always attracted me to *All's Well That Ends Well* was the question of how can you make a very dark vision of human morals, of human learning and the process of learning, still seductive and entertaining? I believe that what Helena learns about herself and about Bertram is unspeakable really. You know that they won't be happy, that they'll break up after a year; but the seduction of the theatrical moment of the 'happy end' is such that you believe, for a little while, they are in love.

Kaut-Howson was also attracted to *All's Well That Ends Well* because of the close and loving relationship between Helena and Bertram's mother, the Countess of Roussillon:

Helena Kaut-Howson: One reason I originally did *All's Well That Ends Well* was that after directing Shakespeare's heroic, male-driven history plays I wanted to direct a *woman's* Shakespeare. I was looking through the collected works and I came upon the conversation between Helena and the Countess and I thought of an agony aunt. I also thought it was like women talking in the bedroom, and that was very appealing.

However, with the Regent's Park production, many reviewers found Frances Cuka as the Countess insufficiently dignified. *The Times*

(14 June 1997) described Cuka's Countess as 'a genial but coarse-grained old bat who dresses in fake zebra or gaudy red' but didn't suggest that this flashiness might be an intentional contrast to Helena's other-worldliness. Frances Cuka doubled the Countess with Diana's mother, the widow Capilet, playing the latter role as 'a modern day Mother Courage selling drink to the soldiers from the side of her Citroën van' (*Time Out*, 18 June 1997)

Reviewers found lots of references to 'Girl Power' but Kaut-Howson was also exploring the presentation of masculinity in the play – something which is subject to scrutiny because of the callowness of Bertram and the sense that the play traces his growing up, his initiation into manhood. Homoeroticism was hinted at in the relationship between Parolles and Bertram as well as in that between Parolles and Lafew. The torture of Parolles, who was stripped to his underpants, included the threat of homosexual rape, and Nigel Planer as Parolles played this moment as completely traumatic. Other alternative versions of masculinity appeared in the production: a man in drag, conspicuous in high platform shoes, stood among the Florentine crowd; when Helena was given the chance to choose her husband, the prospective candidates had to twirl and strut their stuff as if they were models on a cat walk; and the clown Lavatch, whose comic set turns were much commented on by reviewers, included a Madame Butterfly in his repertoire. Several of these ideas were developed from Kaut-Howson's earlier *All's Well That Ends Well* productions – in 1987 Jon Strickland played Lavatch for Kaut-Howson as 'a kinky fool' (*Leicester Mercury*, 20 February); John Baxter's Parolles in 1993 was a 'cross between Adam Ant and Gary Glitter with a liberal dash of fishnet and chiffon' (*Evening Leader*, 20 January). This suggests that the idea of competing notions of masculinity is central to Kaut-Howson's vision of *All's Well That Ends Well*, and it is something she stages in a visually arresting and memorable way.

Kaut-Howson's Regent's Park production was busy and noisy, and several reviewers for 'quality' papers complained about this as well as about interpolated funny business. The *Daily Telegraph* (June 1997) commented:

Helena Kaut-Howson is a personally delightful Polish woman whose work often gives the impression that she has a grudge against the English classics. No trick too meretricious for this director, no gimmick too brazen.

However, despite declaring this *All's Well That Ends Well* to be laden with Kaut-Howson's 'usual panoply of wizard wheezes', the reviewer had to confess that not only did he enjoy the production but he found it 'fresh, funny and genuinely disturbing' especially the 'harrowingly' cruel torture of Parolles. Kaut-Howson's stress on Helena and Parolles' shared positioning as outsiders in relation to the world of the play clearly communicated to the reviewer in the *Independent* (16 June 1997) who commented:

You realise how far these two talkie, cerebral characters are divorced from the society around them; the play sees Helena learning to marry thought to action, while Parolles' failure to act leads to his humiliation.

Kaut-Howson's three productions of *All's Well That Ends Well* reveal a sustained interest in several key aspects of the play: the problematic ending, the public lives of the ruling classes, the role of the outsider, double standards, and challenges to the conventions of feminine and masculine behaviour (Helena's assertiveness, camp masculinity). While most productions of *All's Well That Ends Well* confront the problem of the not very happy ending – Bertram doesn't seem worth Helena's trouble and few would bet on this marriage being a successful one – very few have addressed notions of differing masculinities in the play with as much verve and enthusiastic theatricality as Kaut-Howson. The emphasis on the super rich is also very distinctive to Kaut-Howson's vision of the play although the idea raises as many problems as it solves – the notion of putting on a good show for the cameras is useful at the end of the play, but if Helena really is an alternative voice, why does she want to join the ranks of the filthy rich? Perhaps by the end Helena is guilty of double standards, compromise and selling out as she joins the ranks of the social elite, while the other outsider, Parolles, has been rejected, publicly humiliated and very definitely placed as belonging to the servant class.

In *All's Well That Ends Well* a lower-class woman pursues and obtains an upper-class husband. In *The Merchant of Venice* the opposite happens: an impoverished man, Bassanio, pursues and obtains the wealthy Portia. However, in some ways Portia has to display as much, if not more, assertion, determination and tenacity as Helena, before she can take real possession of her husband.

The Merchant of Venice

The major question in dealing with *The Merchant of Venice* is whether the play discusses racism, colludes with it, or challenges it. Post-Holocaust productions of the play can never be comfortable with its articulation of anti-Semitism, or with the total defeat and humiliation of the Jew Shylock after his attempt to implement his bond and exact a pound of flesh from the merchant Antonio's body. However, when actors play Shylock sympathetically, the so-called 'comedy' of *The Merchant of Venice* teeters closer and closer to tragedy.

The play is also a particularly problematic text for directors interested in contesting passive feminine stereotypes: Portia is initially stuck in a bizarre patriarchal fairy tale, bound to marry the man who guesses the meaning of her dead father's riddles and chooses a lead, rather than gold or silver, casket. Portia may dress as a man, travel to the court of Venice and win a legal battle, but she also voluntarily submits to Bassanio ('You see me, Lord Bassanio, where I stand...' (3.2.149) in terms even more extreme than Katherine's submission speech in *The Taming of the Shrew*. Another problematic area is the play's depiction of Antonio's love for Bassanio; productions which highlight and expand on the homosexual potential in the play cannot present this dimension positively because Antonio and his friends are the most virulently anti-Semitic characters of all.

In her production of *The Merchant of Venice* for the West Yorkshire Playhouse in 1994, Jude Kelly sought to emphasise the problematic nature of this comedy by stressing the tragedy of Portia, as well as the more obvious tragedy of Shylock. The issue of racism, however, was still to the fore and, although Kelly's production was extremely well received critically, Francine Cohen, a local writer who also writes for the *Jewish Chronicle*, attacked Kelly for staging an anti-Semitic play. Kelly took part in an open, public debate with

Francine Cohen on this question and she remains convinced that debate is what is needed:

Jude Kelly: I wanted to direct *The Merchant of Venice* because I wanted to raise all sorts of issues to do with racism and complicity in racism.

One way in which Kelly scrutinised the racism on display in *The Merchant of Venice* was by extending the focus beyond anti-Semitism: references to slaves in the trial scene were more loaded because black slaves were present; Portia's relief that the black Prince of Morocco [see plate 5] didn't win her via the casket test was emphasised. However, Kelly also built up a sense of a godly Jewish community at risk, by setting the play in the early twentieth century, not long before Hitler came to power. This sense of a community presence was mostly created by the use of a very large group of local, non-professional women performers, who appeared to be praying constantly, especially during the trial scene. The fact that this Jewish community lived in a ghetto was also stressed, and the ghetto had ominously noisy, clanging gates. Portia's victory in the court room was very quickly placed in a wider social context as she walked by the entrance to the ghetto, only to have gravel thrown at her. Portia's triumph was not only a defeat for Shylock but foreshadowed the fate of the godly Jews in Venice.

There was also a strong *Death in Venice* ambience to the production, an ambience which again evoked impending Nazism. Antonio was an Aschenbach figure, wearing steel-rimmed glasses, loitering in an art gallery at the opening; elegant and decadent and slightly gone to seed. When preparing for Shylock's knife in the trial scene, Antonio's attempts to preserve an appearance of youth became cruelly exposed when he was forced to remove his wig.

Gary Waldhorn, who is Jewish and whose family escaped from Austria in 1938, played a sympathetic Shylock who, when stripped of his property, dignity and religion at the end of the trial scene, took the process one logical step further and began to strip off his clothes to signal the totality of his defeat. As is often the case with

Kelly's productions, the disruption of the familial bond was stressed and the break in the relationship between Shylock and Jessica was seen to be tragic and a continuing source of pain. The last scene was punctuated by Jessica's remorseful prayers and chants, and the final image of the production was of Jessica, in tears, standing by a menorah, while traditional Jewish music played. Kelly wanted to suggest that Lorenzo was trying to respect Jessica's Jewishness and that the mixed marriage might work, but many saw the ending as pessimistic.

Kelly's approach to Portia was to emphasise the love triangle she unwittingly enters into when she marries Bassanio:

Jude Kelly: I read the opening, the 'In sooth I know not why I am so sad' (1.1.1), and I thought that was so upsetting and awful. It seemed to be so vividly obvious that Antonio was in love with Bassanio and suffering in the way that you do when you aren't able to go directly towards something, and whatever turn you make will involve distortion of your personality and a compromise of some kind.

Then you have Bassanio, with his opportunism, feeding on Antonio's love. And Portia, who has to deal with the burden of her father's legacy, the properties in the country, the fortune, the fortune hunters, which is a huge burden to carry – she seemed really to want Bassanio. But he had already told the audience how much he actually needed her money. Her need for him was blinding her to certain things.

Kelly saw a contest going on between Portia and Antonio for possession of Bassanio:

Jude Kelly: When that contract with Shylock is made out of apparent good humour it is actually quite an aggressive act on Antonio's behalf. And if Portia hadn't gone to court to show off to her lover, rightly or wrongly, Shylock would not have been destroyed. I find it very interesting that she says 'The quality of mercy is not strained' (4.1.181), but when Shylock won't give in she is totally ruthless and she hasn't got any choice. She's now got to go down that road and destroy him utterly, and yet she's got his daughter Jessica in her house!

In the court scene, Portia has also seen, there in front of her eyes, that her lover is actually in love with another man. The ring she has given to Bassanio he gives away and she realises that everything she's done has all been for fool's gold.

As a consequence of this Kelly gave unusual weight to the lines at the beginning of Act 5 telling us that Portia is absent visiting 'holy crosses, where she kneels and prays/For happy wedlock hours' (5.1.31–2). In Kelly's view Portia was desperately praying that she might salvage something from the wreckage of her marriage.

Jude Kelly: The fifth act is all about the tragedy of Portia revealing to Bassanio what she knows. In the end it's 'We'll discuss it', but can they move forward or not? Because they have destroyed *so much*. The issues here are about responsibility and about only seeing, only holding on to your half truth because you need that half truth, and what happens when that all comes back to bear down on you. *Merchant of Venice* is the most fantastic play but *only* if you play the fifth act as part of the same story. You can't suddenly turn it back to comedy – 'let's destroy this' and then 'let's dance'.

Nichola McAuliffe as Portia particularly suggested her bitterness in the trial scene when she clearly relished her rival Antonio's undignified panic in the face of his impending death. The *Financial Times* (26 March 1994) also described how, at the end of the trial scene, Antonio and Bassanio 'rush upon' the disguised Portia/ Balthazar 'with instant talk of love – as if to initiate her into their gay mafia'[1] and when Bassanio hands over the ring Portia gave him 'she is aghast – and teeters right back into full despair'. Logically following on from this, Portia's welcome to Antonio in the final scene was cold and she semaphored the fact that she was taking possession of Bassanio, physically separating him from Antonio and wrapping Bassanio's arms around herself. Her subsequent confrontation with Bassanio over the ring was full of 'real rage and heartbreak at his perfidy' (*Financial Times*).

The production's period setting also helped create a complex Portia, poised between her father's Victorianism and women's suffrage campaigns:

Jude Kelly: *Merchant of Venice* **was turn of the century but it wasn't slavishly concerned with absolute accuracy of detail. I don't like Shakespeare done in Shakespearean dress. Shakespeare's performers wore what was for them modern costume – with maybe a toga on top. Choices of clothing reflect the way people think about themselves, but I don't know how to read a Shakespearean dress. In my productions I'm looking for costumes to provide clarity of personality, psychological motivation, class and wealth. Corsets** *mean* **something to us, so why not draw on them to make new points?**

The corsetting helped Nichola McAuliffe create a Portia with overtones of Hedda Gabler, an angry prisoner to her father's will who practised pistol shooting in her home, put bullets into a portrait of her father and played Russian Roulette with a pistol placed inside her mouth. The portrait of Portia's father depicted him as a stern judge and McAuliffe frequently played speeches and actions to this portrait, holding up the marriage contract to him but also swigging wine, smoking marijuana, and gesturing defiantly. The *Financial Times* saw shades of Dorothy Parker; McAuliffe saw Portia as more of a Christina Onassis figure 'in some ways…incredibly gauche and naive and in others incredibly astute. She was her father's daughter, like Portia' (Sheffield *Telegraph*, 11 March 1994). Kelly, however, also stressed the potential subversive in Portia:

Jude Kelly: I felt that there's a huge amount of Portia's character

that speaks of a world that she may have to inhabit in terms of a tradition but which she doesn't necessarily agree with.

The *Financial Times* commented that Kelly's production retold 'the tale of Portia' and had nothing but praise for this retelling:

> Jude Kelly's staging keeps taking you by surprise, pushing hard against preconceptions, sending you back to re-examine the text...

> Though I have known this play for over 25 years, I followed all of this... as if I never knew what would happen next.

The *Sunday Times* (20 March 1994) agreed: 'This is a magnificent production, clear, perceptive, mature, hard as iron and deeply forgiving.' Given this production's excellence, it seems a pity that only *two* national reviewers managed to travel to Leeds to see it.

Although its engagement with anti-Semiticism makes the play controversial, *The Merchant of Venice* still regularly turns up as a set text, and it was the pressure of the play being on the schools' examination syllabus, and the captive audience that that implies, which resulted in Deborah Paige directing the play in 1996 at the Crucible Theatre, Sheffield. What she actually wanted to do was to build on the success of a programme she had done for the BBC, an extract from *Julius Caesar* in the *Shakespeare Shorts* season, and direct a full-scale *Julius Caesar* set in the Caribbean:

Deborah Paige: When I came to Sheffield, I didn't want to get stuck into the routine of 'Right, now which Shakespeare am I doing this year?' – as if I always do a Shakespeare – but I did want to do *Julius Caesar*. Then I discovered it was not on the syllabus. It was a SATS play, it's recommended reading, but the only play that hadn't been done in this theatre in the recent past but that was dominant in both GCSEs and A-Levels was *Merchant of Venice*, and it's the only play that made me feel dreary.

Paige fought a long campaign against *The Merchant of Venice*, and converted her board only to be told at the eleventh hour that *The Merchant of Venice* was back:

Deborah Paige: I went into a complete strop and said, 'Well, I'm not bloody directing it; it's a politically unacceptable play.' Various people said, 'Don't make those decisions while you're angry. Stop and think about it.' I'm now tussling with it, which is rather good. I'm having to fight with the play, which I'm enjoying. I don't know where I'm starting from yet, but at least there's one compensation with *Merchant of Venice* – it's a very female play; there are lots of stronger women's roles.

Despite Paige's initial reservations, her production was praised by the *Sunday Times* (17 September 1996) as 'deeply intelligent' if 'sombre': Niamh Linehan's Portia was 'worldly, self-possessed, almost smug' but gave a 'bitter sense of a woman being imprisoned and blighted and made wary'. Portia

> longs fiercely and recklessly for Bassanio's love, but even as she gains it she cannot forget, and needs to remind both him and herself, that this love is tainted by calculation. In one sense they are both buyers in a sellers' market.

Polly Pritchett's Jessica was 'wracked by guilt and doubt' and left in a relationship with Lorenzo which was 'shadowed by race and disloyalty' which she knew he was 'going to use...against her', while David de Keyser (who is Jewish) was praised for his 'ageing, burdened' Shylock who 'has clearly spent decades teaching himself psychological self-defence' (*Sunday Times*).

De Keyser himself saw Shylock's love for Jessica as the key to his character:

> It's not just that [Jessica] runs away, which is bad enough for any parent, but for an Orthodox Jew marrying out of the faith is horrendous. That is what breaks him. I'm using that as the

trigger that drives him to cruel viciousness (*Yorkshire Post*, 15 November 1996).

The fact that Lorenzo, Jessica's husband, was black also gave 'an added dimension to Shylock's outraged hatred of him' (*Yorkshire Post*, 14 November 1996).

The Venice created for this production by designer Lucy Hall was very much a city influenced by trade links with the east. Many reviewers commented on how much they liked the sixteenth-century costumes and characterised the production as ungimmicky, with no frills, because of its period setting. However, all the costumes had a strong eastern feel and this atmosphere of mingling cultures, something complemented by the multiracial cast of the production, helped generate a sense of the sheer stupidity as well as the offensiveness of racism.

Despite her success in tackling *The Merchant of Venice's* treatment of race, the fact that Paige, the artistic director of the Crucible, did not initially want to direct this play and had to give way to the power of the school syllabus, suggests that she, like Portia in the casket test, is very much constrained by forces beyond her control:

Deborah Paige: We have to go with the set texts because things are so diabolical financially. The issue is, you can predict more accurately what the box office figures are likely to be. I still think it's a very dubious basis on which to be doing Shakespeare but I'm not Chief Executive and I haven't been here long enough to be able to get my way.

Such constraints, however, may go beyond the decision as to which plays will be put on. If a theatre board wants to play primarily to the education market the risk is that, as with the early productions in the BBC Shakespeare, safe, conservative and traditional approaches to the texts will be favoured over artistic boldness and risk taking.

In *The Merchant of Venice* the father/daughter relationship is intensely problematic: Portia is imprisoned by her dead father's will; Jessica has to flee from her father Shylock so that she can marry the Christian man she loves. However, the father/daughter relationship reaches its nadir in Shakespeare in *King Lear*.

King Lear

King Lear is a, possibly the, great patriarchal tragedy. Lear divides his kingdom between his daughters on the basis of their public declarations of love for their father. Because Lear's youngest daughter Cordelia refuses to go along with this idea, she is rejected and gets nothing. Lear then quickly learns how foolish he was to trust the declarations of love made by his elder daughters, Goneril and Regan, who reject him and eventually plot his death. The central conflict between the patriarch and his unruly daughters reverberates suggestively when women directors take on *King Lear*. Not only are they assuming a position traditionally associated with men (director), but they will usually be directing a senior male actor as the tragic lead. Like Goneril, Regan and Cordelia, women directors will choose whether to diminish Lear or to permit him grandeur and royalty; they will choose whether to dethrone Lear or re-enthrone him as hero; they will choose whether to destroy or nurture his tragic status.

Women directors also have to confront the fact that *King Lear* contains much vividly expressed and poetically effective misogyny, much of it voiced by Lear himself. For example, in one of the most moving moments in the play when the suffering Lear meets the blinded Earl of Gloucester (4.5), Lear suddenly launches into a tirade about the grossness of women's sexuality which has nothing to do with the immediate dramatic context. Negotiating this moment without endorsing the now sympathetically positioned Lear's deep-seated loathing of women's sexuality presents a serious challenge.

King Lear is also very frequently performed; in discussing the play in performance from 1980 to 1990, Susan Bennett was able to examine seventeen *King Lear*s and *King Lear* manifestations. However, only two of these productions were directed by women – Deborah Warner and Cicely Berry, the RSC voice director. In discussing Berry's 1989 RSC *King Lear* at The Other Place, Bennett (1996:43) makes a crucial point:

> this production does not take place on the Royal Shakespeare Company's main stage. Instead it was produced in their studio space, and it is more than a little ironic that when *King Lear* is given over to a voice specialist to really let the text speak for itself, it is despatched to a stage which is generally a venue for alternative or new plays/productions.

The Other Place was also the venue for the only other *King Lear* directed by a woman at the RSC; Buzz Goodbody's production in 1974. Bennett's comment on *King Lear* and power: 'Producing *King Lear* might well be said to be, in the end, all about access and control: *King Lear* is (about) power' (1996:48) could well be extended and applied to the situation of women directors and in particular their access to and control of the theatrical production of this most produced and most studied of tragedies.[1]

Gale Edwards' *King Lear*, in Adelaide in 1988, was the first Shakespeare production in her artistic partnership with John Gaden where Edwards was identified as sole director.

Gale Edwards: I did *King Lear* because John wanted to play Lear and I was seduced by the idea of tackling such a difficult and monumental play. I thought, 'My God, in Australia I may never get this chance again.'

In the *Age* (11 May 1989) Edwards was asked to explain her 'women's-eye view' of the play and she responded:

> It certainly wasn't just a matter of siding with the daughters, more a matter of overcoming the fact that romance, sexuality and women's outlook on stage is all generally coloured by men...to the point that women in the audience don't see it as wrong any more.

What she stressed in the production programme was the 'damn good story' element and the link with the theatre of the absurd.

> As members of an ensemble working on the play we found ourselves frequently laughing during rehearsals, when the absurdity and familiarity of these very human situations suddenly came into focus. We felt, at times, that we were in the landscape of Beckett and that Vladimir and Estragon might at any moment wander onto the stage waiting for Godot.

However, reviewers were disconcerted by the absurd comedy; they complained about the fool having a joke umbrella which stopped the rain whenever it was put up, and they complained when the audience laughed as the sensationally gory balls representing Gloucester's eyes were flung into the wings after his blinding. Edwards followed Peter Brook (whom she quoted in the programme) in cutting the servants who help the blinded Gloucester from the stage and in taking the interval at this point, leaving the audience to dwell on what they had just laughed at.

Reviewers also complained about the lack of royalty in Gaden's angina-stricken king, who moved swiftly from a fiery tempered, slightly hammy public figure in the opening scene towards pathetic senility, frequently seeking comfort from Geoffrey Rush's elderly, dressing-gown-wearing fool [see plate 6]. Lear became very vulnerable, constantly forgetful, cradling his head as if to ward off madness.

Edwards spelt out her reading of Lear's journey in the programme: 'Lear's self-delusions at the beginning of the play are mighty – he even believes, in the storm, that he can command nature herself!' During the storm Lear, like Cordelia, Kent, the Fool and Edgar, becomes an outsider and 'viewed from this new perspective the world appears to be cruelly unjust and grotesquely absurd'. Lear learns at first hand that the dispossessed 'suffer while those in power, ultimately uncaring, continue to profit and expand':

Gale Edwards: The central concept of *King Lear* is the idea of someone believing their own press, and Lear's press is that he's

invincible and he's a great king, and a lot of the play is spent stripping that away.

The setting of this *King Lear* was a world of 'sound sculptures', great rumbling waves of sound. A bleak stage design by Mary Moore presented a black circular platform floor which split, at Goneril's 'We must do something, and i' th' heat' (1.1.306), into three jagged pieces, reflecting Lear's proposed division of his kingdom. Moore also created a wild rocky space for the storm scenes. The fragmented floor pieces could rise and descend to create different levels, and Lear appeared for the storm at the back of the stage on a platform three metres high, jutting out precariously into space. Lear was surrounded by swirling smoke, stranded in a terrifying no man's land.

Moore saw the landscape into which characters were cast out 'as a major character within the play' and she tried 'to create scenic elements that endowed this silent protagonist with life' (Designer's Note, programme). Elsewhere Moore (1994:230–31) commented:

> The circle echoed the symbolic link between nature and femininity that permeates the text; the cracks in the circle split open, creating a birth image revealing Edmund invoking nature as his goddess. The parts of the circle distorted and twisted, violently paralleling the movement of the tragedy; with the death of Cordelia and the resolution of the play, the circle was reformed but the crack was always already present.

Moore also linked the set to contemporary politics: 'when you are working on a play about dividing up the land and Howard [then leader of the Opposition, later Prime Minister of Australia] is saying that he doesn't think that the Aboriginals should carry on with this treaty – somehow these things waft into the same category' (*Adelaide Review*, July 1988).

Edwards' production also had a strong line on Goneril, Regan and Cordelia although several reviewers were unhappy with this, and complained that the sisters were unappealing.

Gale Edwards: As I worked on the play over the year, the thing that appealed to me was the character of Cordelia and the fact she can't lie, she *has* to tell the truth. I also believe Goneril and Regan are Lear's creatures; *he* has created them.

Goneril and Regan 'have inherited from [Lear] a love of power, possession and ambition' (Edwards, programme note). The production also built up an age difference between Goneril, Regan and Cordelia:

Gale Edwards: We had a theory that Goneril and Regan had been born a long time before Cordelia and that Lear had been a pretty lousy father, that he'd been busy being a king and building a career and perhaps being a soldier, and that he probably didn't shower much love on Regan or Goneril or even *know* them very well, and he expected them to be like little boys. With Cordelia being a late life child, Lear had been able to dote on her and hug her in a way that he hadn't for the first two. That was our turn on the play and that's why there was so little love between Goneril and Regan and Cordelia; they seemed to be a generation apart.

Edwards was very proud of her *King Lear.*

Gale Edwards: I thought it was a very good go at it. Trevor Nunn says you have to do *King Lear* three times in your life before you get it right, and I suspect that's true, but in Australia you don't get to do a Shakespeare three times; you're lucky if you get to do a Shakespeare once because we don't have enough population and theatres to do the classics frequently.

This makes Edwards' achievement in directing *King Lear* on a high-profile professional mainstage whilst still in her early thirties all the more remarkable.

Yvonne Brewster's 1994 *King Lear* for Talawa introduced a race dynamic to the play; indeed the main reason Brewster wanted to direct the play was to give a black actor the chance of playing Lear:

Yvonne Brewster: I did *King Lear* because Norman Beaton wanted to play King Lear but he never got to do it. He got sick and he died, and it was one of the most awful things. I still went on with the play because I was committed to all the other people, and they were wonderful, but it had to be something completely different. We had a 40 year old man (Ben Thomas) as King Lear and we didn't try and make Ben into some ancient of 90 or 100 with a long grey beard.

Instead Thomas played Lear as an energetic man, facing death because of coronary ill health. For Lear's first entrance, Thomas bounced onstage and spoke in a loud and healthy voice. Early in the play he was capable of large physical movements: enthusiastic hugs which were rejected disdainfully by Goneril; childish tantrums in front of Regan, who offered him a handkerchief as if her father were a misbehaving child. However, Lear was constantly attended by a retainer who carried pills around for him and at every crisis, as Lear clutched at his heart, the pills were administered. As Lear descended into madness, and the kingly gestures began to seem like parodies of the earlier Lear, the audience could plot the draining away of his energy. After the storm, when Cordelia's supporters placed Lear back on the white throne, which now looked more like an electric chair, the formerly rumbustious king looked truly shattered.

Brewster's production was controversial because of its racial mix. Claire Armistead in the *Guardian* was the major complainant here; she condemned the production on several levels, some of which depended on prescriptive images of cultural identity:

One of the production's least endearing characteristics is its flirtation with Afro-Caribbean culture, which – in the absence of any consistency – becomes a dabbling in the exotic, even the primitive...David Harewood's charismatic Edmund... becomes a Rambo figure, whose final battle is played out as a tribal dance against hooded figures beating Brixton-style riot shields. It's a dramatically effective image, but think of its implications. That Edmund, the double-crossing bastard, is an icon of black manhood, or of repressed black youth in Britain today?[2]

Brewster was angry with this response:

Yvonne Brewster: *King Lear* became a very socially important bit of theatre for black people and in a strange way for white people. When white people said, 'How can you cast Edmund as a black man? What a terrible role model it is for those black guys from Brixton!', I said, 'So with one of the best Shakespearean parts, who shall I cast? A kind of amoeba?' But black people who came to see the play – and they came in their thousands I'm glad to say – enjoyed it. When Edmund said, 'To both these sisters have I sworn my love' (5.1.56), one woman – she was sitting in the audience all dressed up for a Saturday night – she shouted out at the top of her voice; 'Typical black man!'

Brewster's culturally and racially mixed *King Lear* actually had Anglo-Celtic, Afro-Caribbean and Asian actors side by side in the same 'families'.

Yvonne Brewster: The casting wasn't colour blind (colour blind is not to see the colour of the person) but non-racially constrained. But obviously it is the job of this company to give black people work to do, so I couldn't have cast 75 per cent white because then they would say to me, 'Hello darling, goodbye. The RSC can do this far better than you can.'

Gloucester was white, David Fielder; afterwards I saw David Harewood, who is black, and I knew he could do Edmund, and Edgar was Dhirendra, who is Asian. So we ended up with a family which had a white father, a really beautiful young black man, Edmund (who was physically so wonderful we couldn't stop those two women going for him) as his son, and then his other son was this wimpish spider thing, who actually had more intelligence, and happened to be played by an Asian actor. I didn't set out to do any race games, or a racial map or anything, but once it blew open, I just went with the flow.

Dhirendra's Edgar was particularly striking and journeyed from an initially sophisticated, laughing Edgar, mockingly imitating Edmund's affected, melancholic pose of leaning on his elbow, to a Poor Tom, who was almost naked, and had mottled skin, blackened eyes and Japanese Sumo bunches in his hair. He got easy laughs with his Poor Tom rap and with his crude pelvic thrusts, seemingly performed to try and distract Lear from going mad:

Yvonne Brewster: I liked Dhirendra's work because that young man was very brave; a lot of people didn't like it and thought it was a bit odd. Edgar is not playing at being very poetically mad with his nice white shirt with the collar off. The text says Edgar's almost naked and he's actually playing a kind of sexually aggressive person in Poor Tom, and that's what we were trying to do.

The predominant sense was of a caring Edgar hidden beneath a series of fantastic role plays, which included a cringing, British caricature of a stereotyped 'Indian' when up against Oswald. This Edgar tried to comfort the traumatised fool (Mona Hammond), only to find that the fool was already dead in his arms [see plate 7], and at Dover Cliffs, it was a very tender Edgar who carried Gloucester on his back like a child. Even in his deception of Gloucester here – as Gloucester threw up a stick in the air, to test the height of the cliffs, Edgar caught it so there was no sound of it falling – the sense of Edgar having the best of intentions was strong.

Brewster feels that she read *King Lear* differently from many British directors because of her cultural background:

Yvonne Brewster: I didn't think the racial connotations would affect *King Lear* because Lear is some mythical king. However, from an African or a Caribbean perspective, old people are the

people you revere and you want them to stay alive as long as possible because you do really believe they have some wisdom, even if you may laugh at them sometimes. That was really one of my cultural lessons in England, realising that old people don't have status. In *King Lear* we had to talk about this: how could they do this to this old man just for the sake of a few shekels which they're going to get anyway? There's something really bizarre about that.

The setting for Brewster's *King Lear* also complicated easy notions about cultural location. The environment was presented as cold, and characters' bodies, and importantly their skins, were largely covered by clothes. Japanese hairstyles mixed with Middle Eastern beaded head-dresses, English Victorian ladies' riding habits and full-length leather coats. Lear had stylish grey streaks in his hair and his face was made up like a Noh mask, with heavy, beetling eyebrows. Kent's disguise included dreadlocks and speaking in patois. The fool's face was half bronze coloured and half white, with black slanting lines drawn around the eye on the white side, and the actress playing the fool, Mona Hammond, was padded out to conceal her bust and make her an androgynous figure.

Reviewers mostly characterised the production as erratic and there were many complaints about the stylisation of the storm which was represented by the white canopy (which initially hung above Lear's throne) descending and engulfing him. Red ropes hanging from the ceiling, which characters clung to during the storm, created a sense of movement and energy – they were also used pragmatically elsewhere to tie up Kent in the stocks and to secure Gloucester in readiness for his blinding. The production was a box office success and attracted predominantly black audiences.

Jude Kelly's 1995 *King Lear* also irked many reviewers, primarily because they felt the king was insufficiently regal and 'great'. Two reviews (*Guardian*, 16 November 1995; *Time Out*, 22 November 1995) also identified Kelly's production as 'feminist'. However, one of the most commented-on aspects of the production was the fact that 69-year-old Warren Mitchell, playing Lear, stripped naked in the storm scene and was joined in his nakedness by the fool and Kent. This incident was rendered particularly crassly in one (positive) review (*Today*, 17 November 1995), which opened by reporting 'on a glimpse of Alf Garnett's willy' – thus bathetically and sensationally linking Warren Mitchell's Lear with his long-running television role as the racist, ineffectual patriarch Alf Garnett in *Till Death Us Do Part*.

Although the London venue for Kelly's *King Lear*, the Hackney Empire, is some way from the West End theatre centre, it was significant that this was the first production of a Renaissance play that Kelly had brought down to London from Leeds, particularly given the fact that Kelly, at the time, was being touted as a possible incumbent for the job of artistic director at the Royal National Theatre – the most prestigious and best funded centre for theatre in the UK. Implicit in some reviews (for example, the *Daily Telegraph*, 2 October 1995) was the idea that Kelly was not 'man' enough for the National job.

Kelly's production not only had an unkingly Lear but also a love-starved Goneril, a sexually abused Regan, who bizarrely stored the body of her husband Cornwall under her bed, an unforceful Cordelia, a neurotic and uncharismatic Edmund, an obnoxious and thuggish Albany who was terrified of fighting Edmund, a Nazi Kent and a very threatening Black Panther King of France. In almost every characterisation, Kelly was breaking with tradition but she is philosophical about the reactions she provoked:

Jude Kelly: There is a big problem with people who have a notion of what the play already is. People say things like, 'Well, why did you take that angle?', and you'll say, 'It wasn't an angle, it was what *I* thought the play was.'

With *King Lear* my criticism of myself would be that I wasn't defiantly, publicly, totally brave about what I was doing, but that's because I didn't realise how radical it was. I remember people saying in the rehearsal room, 'That's really dangerous and amazing' and me thinking, 'Is it?' When I read the reviews I thought, 'That's

very stupid and conservative of them,' but it hadn't dawned on me that the production would seem so extraordinary.

By and large, *King Lear* got really good audiences in Leeds and London. You're not doing a play as part of a historical treatise on how you do *King Lear*, and we got people who obviously loved it and I don't think they were thinking, 'Oh God, this is a feminist version, it's preposterous.' For most people it was just the play and, as far as they were concerned, it seemed to stack up.

Kelly's production confronted the realm of the personal as well as the political in *King Lear*.

Jude Kelly: I was looking at dysfunctionality in the family and asking what has the king done wrong? It can't just be that he split up his kingdom. You can't really talk about *one* act; we must be talking about a lifetime of aberration. The two girls constantly refer to that, and I was trying to find a way of saying, 'This is a man who thinks of himself as the centre of the universe and that means that everything he does is important, but what he's done to the people around him in his own family is terrible.' He destroys Cordelia but he's *already* destroyed Goneril and Regan.

Of course I forgave him but, at the end of the play, he's got three dead children on the stage and those deaths are all products of his work as a father. So I was looking at the fact that not only is he a father to his children, and does that very, very badly, but also, as a parallel fact, he's a father to his kingdom and he does that badly too. Unless you are examining both things at the same time I think you're not looking at the whole play.

It was interesting to work on an idea of a character like Lear where you have to say, 'You are completely wrong about everything; *everything* you've done is wrong.'

Kelly also refused to see Goneril, Regan and Cordelia in terms of extremes of vice and virtue. Thus Regan was a deeply troubled woman, often in a state approaching breakdown, abusively fondled by Lear in public; during the gouging out of Gloucester's eyes by using her hair slide, Regan lost her way in her attempt to play the heavy villainess and began vomiting in horror. By contrast with the sexually abused Regan, Goneril was starved of sex and love; certainly Lear kept Goneril physically at a great distance, brutally rejecting any display of affection by her. Goneril's marriage to a repressed, prayer-book-wielding Albany appeared loveless and possibly unconsummated. Goneril seemed to sublimate her cravings for love by spending time in church obsessively arranging flowers, and the relationship with Edmund represented a real coming to life for her:

Jude Kelly: It's impossible for me to think that Goneril and Regan go round just being vile because they feel like it. I thought Shakespeare had set up the most extraordinarily, wonderfully problematic situation where two women are told *in public* that they are not loved, and this obviously can't be news; they say later on, 'He's always loved her best.' We know that if you are a child who is publicly less loved that can destroy your life; it is difficult to be a balanced human being in that context. I was looking at the natural consequence of starting from the position of three children, Edmund, Goneril and Regan, all of whom knew, for different reasons, that they weren't loved, and so they begin the play as damaged people.

It was definitely Regan and Edmund who interested me most, along with issues to do with redemption. People get damaged and it's interesting looking at how that gets described: for example, Edmund's speech about being a bastard – that is such a painful thing to talk about. However Edmund talks about it, it still masks or exposes hatred, and anyone who's self-loathing is going to be a destructive person.

As a consequence of this thinking, Kelly's Edmund was not the usual wicked but sexy seducer of Goneril, Regan and the audience.

Instead, Damien Goodwin played Edmund as a rather sad specimen, who, in his first scene alone, cried a lot, hugged a soft toy and tried to kill himself with a plastic bag. He was an unloved, lonely and very disturbed student in a depressing bedsit, who was finally successful in committing suicide at the end of the play. After winning the duel against Edgar, Edmund very deliberately *chose* to embrace his brother and his knife together.

Edmund's lack of charisma had the consequence of making Goneril and Regan's rivalry over him seem all the more desperate; all the more an over-reaction by love-starved women to a sudden access to passion. In contrast to Edmund, Edgar was a cool charmer until he entered the world of Poor Tom, surrounded by hordes of beggars. Played by local non-professional actors, the presence of these beggars vividly made the point that while the ruling classes played dysfunctional family games, the poor continued to starve – except for when good scavenging opportunities arose, such as the aftermath of battles.

Although Kelly's focus wasn't on Lear, the big name of the production was Warren Mitchell, playing the title role for the second time in his career.[3] The production programme included an interview with Mitchell, conducted after three weeks of rehearsal, in which Mitchell stressed Lear's vigour, claiming Lear can't have fathered Cordelia very long ago, and how recognisable the family tensions in the play are. Mitchell's Lear was often endearing and visually evoked Father Christmas, even when his henchmen wrecked Goneril's precious, flower-bedecked church. Determinedly playful at the opening of the play, making his first, unregal, entrance wearing open-toe sandals and playing a childish game, Mitchell's Lear laughed at Cordelia's first 'nothing' (1.1.87), thinking she was just playing another game:

Jude Kelly: What for me has never stacked up in *King Lear* is this sort of roaming elderly saint who's quite bad-tempered to begin with but then is absolutely the centre of sympathy and surrounded by these cats, Goneril and Regan. That's misogyny in the directing, not misogyny in writing. However, it's very difficult for

actors not to want to be loved, and it was difficult for Warren to accept the idea that Lear needed not to be centre stage, being adorable.

Choosing the play and then casting is the inspirational part of the work, but when you come to do the rest of the work, you can't make an actor do what isn't in their own soul. You can light a fire in them, you can make them turn and look this way rather than that way, but you can't force any other creative person to see the world as you would see it. So you are always in a sort of negotiating position where you're saying, 'Well, this is how I feel it and how I think it' and, if it flows, then you have total harmony, but the flow will always come from a very personal base because actors are artists.

However, Mitchell was totally in accord with Kelly's concept of an unregal king. In the programme interview he stated, 'I said at the outset that I couldn't play a regal king. I could play a warrior, a tribal chieftain – but not a gracious royal.'

Kelly also used race provocatively in her *King Lear*. The black King of France suddenly appeared menacingly at the end of the play, ready to take over the kingdom. Another break with tradition occurred as Oswald, who was black, was racially harassed by Kent, who was white. In disguise as a vicious, tattooed, Nazi thug, Kent made monkey noises at Oswald and bashed him, providing a stark contrast to the conventionally noble and loyal Kent.

When Helena Kaut-Howson directed Kathryn Hunter as Lear in 1997 at the Leicester Haymarket, the combination of woman director and woman protagonist made the production a much discussed theatre event. Kaut-Howson insists that Hunter's acting skills were the determining factor in casting her as Lear, and not her sex:

Helena Kaut-Howson: With *King Lear* people tried very much to harness it into feminism and regendering the Shakespearean role,

and both Kathryn Hunter and myself were adamant about it being *nothing* to do with feminism at all. If I hadn't known an actress like Kathryn Hunter and if it hadn't been for a particular personal reason why I wanted to do *King Lear* at that time, I would never have thought of casting a woman in that part.

The knee-jerk assumption that Kaut-Howson *must* have been making a feminist statement – because she was a woman director casting a woman as Lear – needs to be modified when some theatre history is taken into account. Not only have women played Lear before but there was also a flourishing tradition in the nineteenth century of women playing many of Shakespeare's male leads – Hamlet, Romeo, Wolsey, Macbeth and Falstaff as well as, more predictably, the fairy roles of Oberon, Puck and Ariel.[4] These productions were not automatically discussed in terms of feminism, although, as Jill Edmonds (1992:60) points out, it was significant that 'many of the nineteenth-century actresses' who played such roles 'were actor-managers in their own right, able to choose what they wished to play rather than waiting to be cast by male directors'. The practice of professional actresses playing Shakespeare's male roles reached new heights during the First World War, when there was a shortage of male actors. Indeed an actress was sacked from the Old Vic for refusing a male role. Lilian Baylis, who managed the Old Vic, commented 'after all, there should be no sex in acting – you ought to be able to understand men as well as women' (Findlater, 1975:132). Kaut-Howson's irritation over the tendency to read her production solely in terms of feminism is also understandable given that the casting was equally radical in terms of age – Hunter was in her late thirties and played Lear, extremely realistically, as very, very old [see plate 8]. This achievement tended to vanish in the excitement over gender issues.

Kaut-Howson explains the personal reason that she wanted to direct *King Lear* in moving and eloquent terms:

Helena Kaut-Howson: I never do a play because I think it's a beautiful play but because it somehow reflects what life feels like

to me now, and I would not have been ready for *King Lear* had it not been for the death of my mother. I would have felt it was a mountain too high to climb because it *is* a mountain both for a director and an actor, because it philosophically demands an enormous amount from everyone involved. Its outlook is so complex; it destroys all values and doesn't suggest anything in their place. That's why Jan Kott or Peter Brook could relate it so easily to the Beckettian world, the Post-Holocaust world of existentialism where there are no values other than what we human beings create.

My mother's death alerted me to many of the issues that are central to *King Lear*, like this difficult existential problem of ageing and changing, the shift of generations, the transfer of power from one generation to another which can never happen without a trauma. I've always been interested in that transfer of power and the shock that it causes both in those that take the power and those that relinquish it, and in all those around them – and I mean power in a family as well as in politics.

Because my mother was a single parent and to me a father and a mother, an incredibly important, powerful force in my life, I never thought of her in terms of gender, especially when she grew old. She was exceptional in many ways because she was a witness to the century and went through all the major revolutions with very open eyes and the very progressive, proactive view of somebody who *owned* the century and what was happening to it. She came from that generation of socialists that had not only to witness but participate. I thought that her death was the collapse of everything; her old age, her decline was a collapsing, and I identified it with the collapse of communism and the collapse of all the values that she stood for.

My mother survived the Holocaust and believed in socialism and all that it entailed, which means equality – of sexes and people – as an answer to humanity's problems, and she didn't quite recognise socialism's collapse. She was always an optimist, always believed that, even if there are reversals, there is continual progress. She was 87 when she died, but in the last year and a half her memory went and she seemed to refuse to acknowledge all that was happening around her. I saw her very much as a Lear figure.

Kaut-Howson's intensely personal reading of *King Lear* also had an impact on her reading of Lear as king:

Helena Kaut-Howson: Shakespeare can look at the distress and the deprivation the withdrawal of love can cause at the same time as looking at the terrible injustices to humanity that are caused by – well, what is the cause? Lear asks what is it that makes people have such hard hearts? I was suddenly aware of the commonality between those two things – the loss of love and the injustices of the world.

This for me bridged the gap between Lear as a father – an obnoxious, terrible, despotic, petty parent, expecting love as a given – and Lear as a ruler, who so often quickly switches from talking about humanity and the 'kind', humankind, and society, to talking about his daughters.

Reviewers, however, took Kaut-Howson severely to task for presuming to personalise and add a framework to *King Lear*.

Helena Kaut-Howson: Critics were *so* rude about it. I had a prologue in a geriatric ward and all the national reviewers hated that bit. So I got rid of it for the London revival. The production was still set in a geriatric ward but it was abstract.

My mother, who died in a geriatric ward of a hospital, never, never came to terms with being there, and looked at from her point of view it must have been – I'm guessing – a kind of Dantesque circle of hell with bodies being carted out. When I set *King Lear* there originally, it worked very well for the Leicester audiences; it was a very good way of making the play accessible.

This is borne out by the reviews: the London reviewers – who see a lot of *King Lear*s – moaned, but the local reviewers were intrigued. The *Harborough Mail* (6 March 1997), whose reviewer declared this 'was the first time I had ever seen the play', praised the '*ER/Casualty* prologue and epilogue' and called the production a 'brilliant introduction' to the play. There was also positive feedback from schools' audiences in post-performance discussions:

Helena Kaut-Howson: The young audiences responded very well; they completely understood how you can move from dream to reality – from reality to fantasy.

The sense of the fantastic was partly generated as the opening geriatric ward environment was maintained throughout the play and hospital paraphernalia supplied props and setting; an old bath turned into the hovel on the heath:

Helena Kaut-Howson: I very, very much wanted to flesh out the world, the society and cultural world in which the characters lived. Some people go for the bare stage, minimal approach, but I, as an artist, like to place the action in a real world – not Naturalistic theatre, but I like to have the signs and the texture of a real world onstage.

In the case of *King Lear* I especially wanted that because I placed it in the world of my mother – not just the hospital but also the wars and the hiding places. My mother, being Jewish and Polish, spent the war being hunted and continually running from place to place, hiding, and working in the fields, and then being recognised again. So that theme of hunting and being hunted in *King Lear* was very strongly fleshed out in our production. When Edgar ran away, the first thing that happened was that he hid in a hole like a rabbit. He suddenly understood that he'd lost everything – he says 'Edgar I nothing am' (2.2.184) – and he suddenly realised that they didn't even have to kill him because he'd lost his identity. So in our production he was naked and he *was* quite like an animal, hunted.

Kaut-Howson also evoked contemporary Eastern European conflicts in her production:

Helena Kaut-Howson: *King Lear* **is Beckettian, modern and primitive. Life can so easily become Stone Age when wars break out and brothers suddenly attack brothers. In our version people certainly perceived the setting as central European and maybe Bosnian.**

A personal dimension in relation to *King Lear* was also crucial for Kathryn Hunter; she had wanted to play the part of Lear 'ever since she was at school, where the play was read to her by "a very fervent, big-bosomed lady" called Miss McDonald' (*New Statesman*, 7 March 1997).

Helena Kaut-Howson: Kathryn was inspired by a school teacher and, because her teens were very traumatic, she completely identified with the storm scenes in *King Lear* **and the desire to destroy the world because it's unjust.**

Kathryn has that unique ability to transcend gender, to transform, but the reason I wanted her to play the role was because intellectually and emotionally she was capable of embracing the leaps of imagination towards old age and towards death.

Reviewers were generally impressed by Hunter's performance. There was a great sense of vulnerability, partly associated with the frailty of her frame – Hunter is only five foot tall – and two reviewers read in images of Deng Xiaoping; one even saw shades of Haile Selassie and 'an embalmed Lenin' (*Sunday Times*, 9 March 1997). Hunter's voice was quiet, gravelly and rasping, and as she couldn't command obedience by physical intimidation, she compelled attention by a sense of iron will and forcefulness. The *Independent* (2 March 1997) commented, 'Her tyrannical authority only exists in so far as it is accepted by others. Take away that fear of her and this spidery, frail autocrat is impotent.' In a break with stage tradition 'Blow, winds…'

(3.2.1) was whispered and gradually summoned the storm rather than competing with it. The *Leicester Mercury* (1 March 1997) particularly applauded Hunter's skill in creating 'an almost genderless person wrestling with the confusion of being old':

Helena Kaut-Howson: Some critics gradually came round to the idea that it's not at all about gender, and with the London production a number of them started talking about gender being irrelevant and that it was more amazing that Kathryn acted so compellingly in terms of the issues of age.

Although the production programme contained an essay or 'version of the story of King Lear' resiting the play's narrative in the mind of an old woman 'sitting alone in a nursing home', Kaut-Howson's reading of *King Lear* via the death of her mother was never made explicit. However, when one is aware of Kaut-Howson's personal investment in this production, some of the reviews are painful to read. The *Guardian* pronounced: 'It is an original concept but one that goes right against the Shakespearean grain' and then proceeded to offer a brief lecture on 'Shakespeare's genius', citing Harold Bloom on Shakespeare's 'disinterestedness', and calling for a *King Lear* 'staged with absolute moral neutrality', with Goneril and Regan seen 'objectively', and invoking the master text of Peter Brook's production. One thing which Kaut-Howson's prologue made abundantly clear was that she had chosen to direct a very individual, personal *King Lear*, but rather than saying, 'I don't like the production', the *Guardian* review was telling Kaut-Howson she was wrong, out of order, to interpret *King Lear* so subjectively. Indeed in places the review began to assume a somewhat Lear-like tone, as if Helena Kaut-Howson, like Cordelia, must be rejected for failing to love and reproduce *King Lear* correctly.

Given the number of women who have directed *King Lear* professionally, it's tempting to speculate that there is a particular attraction for these women in taking on the great patriarch.[5] Gale Edwards is unimpressed by this notion:

Gale Edwards: There's a handful of great plays, maybe ten, that crop up on almost every director's wish list, male and female, and (in the west) they are usually *The Seagull, King Lear, The Crucible. King Lear* is the great mountain. It's the great, mysterious piece for a director; it's supposed to be unsolvable, uncrackable. It's monumental; it's got the reputation for testing you – so there's a tremendous lure for the director, be they a woman or a man, to take it on.

It's also true to say that many male directors in the late twentieth century have been accused, like all of the women directors considered here, of dethroning the king and failing to stress his greatness. However, these women directors offered particularly distinctive, often very personal readings of the patriarchal tragedy. Gale Edwards played dangerously with the broadly comic side of Absurd theatre, which is so often invoked only in its most solemn form in relation to *King Lear*; Yvonne Brewster repositioned *King Lear* culturally and won the support of a black audience; Jude Kelly focused on the domestic side of the tragedy, and directed most of the characters unconventionally; Helena Kaut-Howson radically reshaped the play, cast a young woman as Lear, and invested the production heavily with her own response to the death of her mother. Accusations of MsDirection abounded, but all of these productions shed new light on a familiar play.

Macbeth

In *Macbeth* the hero turns away from 'legitimate' killing (as a career soldier) to illegitimate killing and the murder of the elderly King Duncan, Macbeth's friend Banquo, and the vulnerable Lady Macduff and her children. Lady Macbeth is often blamed for egging Macbeth on to kill King Duncan; the witches are also blamed for prophesying that Macbeth will be king. All three of the directors whose productions of *Macbeth* are considered here – Joan Littlewood, Jules Wright and Helena Kaut-Howson – decided that, despite his poetry and his imagination, the character of Macbeth needed to be seen as fully accountable for his actions, and the result was three very different, but noticeably untraditional and unromantic readings of the play.[1]

Joan Littlewood's interest in *Macbeth* started early. In *Joan's Book* (1994:51) Littlewood records that while still at convent school she saw John Gielgud ('too decorative') in the title role and decided that *Macbeth* would be an ideal school play. Littlewood herself played Macbeth and the Old Man; there were props but not much set – for the banqueting scene the schoolgirl actors 'poised on thin air, pretending to be sitting' (Littlewood, 1994:53) and the murder of Banquo, aided by a roll of drums and a lot of cochineal, was so effective that the visiting Mother Superior fainted. This appropriately prefigures the apoplectic reactions of most reviewers in response to Littlewood's 1957 Theatre Workshop production of *Macbeth*.

Littlewood put *Macbeth* into modern dress – khaki soldiers' uniforms, dress suits, and elegant gowns for the women. As so often with her productions, it was Littlewood's class politics that particularly rankled with reviewers. Accusations of misdirection abounded: reviewers were worried about satire on the army and royalty (Milne, 1965:81) and Norman Marshall (1962:299) scolded that Littlewood's:

> determinedly anti-poetic treatment of the play reduced Macbeth himself to no more than a craven killer. The attempt to portray him as a ruthlessly ambitious dictator was altogether too much at variance with the lines.

This unheroic Macbeth was executed by firing squad at the opening of the play and the rest of the action was presented as a flashback. The *Observer* (8 September 1957) felt that the presentation of the play as 'the dying fantasy of a military tyrant' didn't come off; the *New Statesman* (14 September 1957) saw Littlewood's vision of Macbeth as being 'a modern tyrant, a sort of poor man's Hitler, whom the good will eventually shoot down like a mad dog' and the *Daily Express* (4 September 1957) commented on similar lines, 'The last scene, as enemy troops close in, invokes a picture of Hitler's last hours in his Berlin rat hole'; the *Spectator* (13 September 1957) detected the influence of Brecht and Marx and could only find 'arid doctrinaire asceticism' in the production. Reviewers particularly disliked the lack of dignity in the Macbeths; *The Times* (4 September 1957) complained especially about the moment when in 3.2. 'Macbeth gave his wife a playful slap on the bottom, to which she responded by rubbing the affected place and biting her underlip as if on the verge of tears.' Littlewood's determination to see Macbeth as a product of class, as a soldier and as a thug does not seem so remarkable nowadays; however, in 1957, this line of thought completely shocked the reviewers.

Macbeth played in Zurich, Moscow, Stratford East and Oxford. The programme for Stratford East contained a note signed by Littlewood, unapologetically declaring her stance on the play:

> If Shakespeare has any significance for today, a production of his work must not be regarded as an historical reconstruction but as an instrument still sharp enough to provoke thought, to extend man's [sic] awareness of his problems and to strengthen his belief in his kind.

Above: Sian Thomas as Katherine in *The Taming of the Shrew*, directed by Di Trevis, RSC tour, 1985–6. Photo by Donald Cooper.

Below: Nichola McAuliffe as Katherine and Brian Protheroe as Petruchio in *The Taming of the Shrew*, directed by Jude Kelly, West Yorkshire Playhouse, 1993. Photo by Gerry Murray.

Above: Christopher McHallem as Caliban and Andrew Price as Ariel in *The Tempest*, directed by Deborah Paige, Salisbury Playhouse, 1993. Photo by Peter Brown.

Below: Larrington Walker as the Prince of Morocco and Nichola McAuliffe as Portia in *The Merchant of Venice*, directed by Jude Kelly, West Yorkshire Playhouse, 1994. Photo by Phil Cutts.

Above: Jane Menelaus as Hermione and Barbara West as Paulina in *The Winter's Tale*, directed by Gale Edwards, State Theatre of South Australia, 1987. Photo by David Wilson.

Below: Geoffrey Rush as the Fool and John Gaden as Lear in *King Lear*, directed by Gale Edwards, State Theatre of South Australia, 1988. Photo by David Wilson.

Opposite: Dhirendra as Edgar and Mona Hammond as the Fool in *King Lear*, directed by Yvonne Brewster, Talawa Theatre Company, 1994. Photo by Richard H Smith.

Above: Kathryn Hunter as Lear and Marcello Magni as the Fool in *King Lear*, directed by Helena Kaut-Howson, Leicester Haymarket, 1997. Photo by Tristram Kenton.

Below: Julie Covington as Lady Macbeth and Jonathan Hyde as Macbeth in *Macbeth*, directed by Jules Wright, Edingburgh Lyceum, 1986. Photo by David Liddle.

Above: Howard Goorney as the Gardener in *Richard II*, directed by Joan Littlewood, Theatre Workshop, 1954 and 1955. Photo from Howard Goorney's private collection.

Below: Michael Redgrave as Orlando and Edith Evans as Rosalind in *As You Like It*, directed by Esme Church, Old Vic, 1936 & 1937. Photo from V&A Museum Picture Library.

Above: Final scene of *Twelfth Night*, directed by Irene Hentschel,
Memorial Theatre, Stratford, 1939. Photo from the Shakespeare Centre Library.

Below: Eileen Atkins as Rosalind, Maureen Lipman as Celia and David Suchet as Orlando in
As You Like It, directed by Buzz Goodbody, RSC, 1973. Photo from the Shakespeare Centre Library.

Overleaf: Patrick Stewart as John in *King John*,
directed by Buzz Goodbody, RSC, 1970. Photo by Joe Cocks, from the Shakespeare Centre Library.

This reflects Littlewood's view of the classics as a resource to be used in an overtly political way, rather than as a collection of sacred texts whose integrity had to be respected. In the same note, however, Littlewood claimed to be rejecting traditional interpretations and conventional stage business, with the implication that Theatre Workshop productions actually got closer to the 'real' play:

We try to wipe away the dust of three hundred years, to strip off the 'poetical' interpretations which the nineteenth century sentimentalists put upon these plays and which are still current today.

Joan's Book also stresses the act of stripping away:

I…set about stripping the play of the usual trimmings – no Highland mist, no bagpipes, no dry ice for the weird sisters, mine were three old biddies with a penchant for fortune-telling, such as you might meet at any time on a road to the isles (Littlewood, 1994:480).

Littlewood didn't always just strip away; the addition of a highland lament sung over the bodies of Lady Macduff and her son (Trewin, 1956:230) demonstrated that. However, that Littlewood did cut back severely on the supernatural is very clear: the *New Statesman* thought 'the weird sisters (on the one occasion on which they appear)' were '*Mother Courage*, 1620 circa)'; the *Daily Express* (4 September 1957) described the witches as 'battlefield molls, sneak-thieving from soldiers' corpses'. Littlewood herself recalls that 4.1, Macbeth's second encounter with the witches, was 'played as a nightmare, Macbeth tossing and turning on his bed, imagining the old women in the room with him and seeing pageants of kings only in his mind's eye. This way it made sense; as usually played it is an illogical pantomime' (Littlewood, 1994:480). Macbeth also halluci-nated the Third Murderer, and a production photograph in *Plays and Players* (October 1957) confirms that Banquo's ghost was also a figment of Macbeth's imagination: a group of smartly dressed diners, the women in long white dresses and elbow-length gloves, the men in dress uniforms, gaze in perplexity at the empty stool where Macbeth can see Banquo's ghost. The accompanying review by Caryl Brahms was very negative and particularly complained about 'the buzz and whine of Bombers' in the production. However, Brahms did have to confess 'I was…far more terrified of [Littlewood's] invisible Banquo at the Feast' than the more sensational 'green Lime' stagings of the ghosts she had witnessed previously.

Brahms' review is fascinating as a record of the prejudices that Littlewood was up against. The review dismissed Littlewood's ideas as old hat and yet complained bitterly about the innovation of not playing the National Anthem routinely after performances (Brahms defiantly murmured the words of the anthem under her breath in personal protest). Brahms was displeased that the Porter was unfunny, Macbeth lacking in grandeur, Lady Macbeth 'a Deb's Mum', and she finished the review by stating her personal dislike per se for any Shakespeare production in modern dress.

Some of the modern energies so disliked by Brahms were summoned up in improvisations: 'the actors improvised the scene which Shakespeare never wrote, when Macbeth actually meets the murderers for the first time – in a pub; the murderers, two ex-RAF types; Macbeth saying, "How would you boys like to do a job for me?"' (Goodwin and Milne, 1964:392-3). Games of 'cowboys and indians' were also used (Milne, 1965:82).

Although *Joan's Book* (1994:479–81) records that *Macbeth* was something of a stop-gap production, Littlewood seized on it when she wanted to direct a play 'about the evil assumption of power' (479) which would seem relevant in contemporary Moscow. She was pleased that her mainly young, student audiences 'seemed to grasp the parallel with their own political leadership' (Littlewood, 1994:488).

Littlewood's first choice for the role of Macbeth was Jimmie Miller (who renamed himself Ewan MacColl), her former husband and her partner from her early days of agitprop theatre. Miller's response was unequivocal: 'He flew into a rage. All his early dislike of the classics surfaced. He mounted his agitprop horse and called me a bourgoise'

(Littlewood, 1994:479). Thus Littlewood's love of the classics and her determination to mount modern and meaningful productions of these plays were not only in conflict with the traditionalist reviewers but also, sometimes, in conflict with the agendas of some in Theatre Workshop. Glynn Edwards, who actually played Macbeth, had, Littlewood felt (1994:480), a 'gentle nature' which 'shone through, whatever he did' and although the reviewers were busy complaining that Littlewood had transformed Macbeth into a thug, for her Edwards seems to have been too gentle.

Although Littlewood was so severely taken to task by her reviewers, she offered a kind of riposte ten years later when she directed Barbara Garson's *Macbird*, a parody of *Macbeth* and even less respectful of the traditionalist, dignified view of Shakespeare's tragedy.

Jules Wright also ran into trouble for her politics when she directed *Macbeth* at the Royal Lyceum Theatre, Edinburgh (1986). Wright's explicitly feminist approach, particularly in relation to Lady Macbeth, was much influenced by Marilyn French's *Shakespeare's Division of Experience*, a work which sees masculine and feminine principles at war in the play and points to gender trouble spots: the bearded witches; the macho warrior culture; Lady Macbeth trying to unsex herself; the final victory by the man not 'of woman born' (5.10.13), Macduff, who was born by Caesarean section.

Jules Wright: One has to be entirely quizzical and questioning and questing. In the end, what you are doing as a director is making sense of the world you are presenting to an audience. *You* have to make sense of the play; you can't take someone's idea and say, 'I'm going to examine this play in terms of *this*.' But Marilyn's work made sense to me. In *Macbeth* there is a complete denial of the feminine principle; all the women are wiped out.

Wright was particularly interested in challenging the traditional view of Lady Macbeth as driving Macbeth forward so that 'basically it's her fault and not his'. This approach got Wright into trouble with reviewers who mostly wanted a starkly defined villainess. They complained Lady Macbeth was 'listless' (*Observer*, 16 November 1986) and 'an embarrassing non-event' (*Guardian*, 10 November 1986).[2] Two reviewers took the argument a stage further: the *Glasgow Herald* (8 November 1986) commented that Julie Covington's understated Lady Macbeth 'adds to our understanding that her husband is the true villain of the piece' and the *Scotsman* (10 November 1986) revealingly suggested:

> Julie Covington's portrayal of Lady Macbeth often contradicted the text. She seems to have set out to exonerate the woman, making her appear to be almost a victim of Macbeth's ruthlessness rather than the fiend who gloats over 'the fatal entrance of Duncan under MY battlements'.
>
> Ms Covington's performance is too subdued and lacking in force for a character who takes pride in the valour of her tongue.

Julie Covington herself, in an interview at the time, confirms something of the *Scotsman*'s suspicion that she had 'set out to exonerate' Lady Macbeth:

> She believes their plan involves only Duncan's murder, then the rewards. Instead, Macbeth commits murders she never envisages, and after Banquo's death she becomes frightened of him. He seldom consults her and finally excludes her altogether...What drives her is sexual passion and hunger for power. She wants to belong to the male ruling class. She wants equality of power (*Scotsman*, 3 November 1986).

Wright was extremely pleased with Covington's performance:

Jules Wright: I have never seen Lady Macbeth played before with that kind of intelligence and depth and making sense of her place in the world. Julie Covington is not only a brilliant actor but also a highly educated woman who has incredible perception and who can not only *have* an intellectual idea but find a way of *playing* it. If you track your way through *Macbeth*, there's a very, very clear

and interesting journey for Lady Macbeth, and it's about denying all that is female for one reason, which is to ensure that he gets what *he* wants.

Before the murder she says, 'Look what I've done for you.' She confronts him with 'I've given up all that is female within me, I've made myself a man, I've made myself stronger than you', but she's essentially saying, 'I have denied myself for you; will you pull back now? I will dash my child upon the ground; will you waver now, when I have done that?' You can play that scene as an urging scene or you can play it in a very confrontational way: '*This* is what I have done.' You have to look at the play as the journey of two people utterly engaged with each other, but she *is* the one who ultimately denies herself.

Wright was particularly intrigued by the fact that Shakespeare does not map out every stage of the journey undertaken by Lady Macbeth during the play:

Jules Wright: Characters often make choices in extremely contradictory ways. With classic texts people often look to make the character *whole* in some kind of Stanislavskian, Freudian sense, but a Freudian view of a kind of wholeness, completeness, order and unity is inappropriate. Human beings are not like that; human beings are much closer to a Brechtian model, a model in which people are different in terms of the person they think they might be interacting with at that particular moment. That makes for diversity but also for the complexity of human personality. So if an actor says, 'This character didn't act in this way in the last scene', I say 'No, they didn't, and that's what makes them extraordinary.' But then with *Macbeth* you have to explain why you have a banquet scene and then Lady Macbeth disappears from the play and the next time you see her you see a woman who's in breakdown, deep psychosis. So you have to ask what *is* it that has happened in her four or five scenes up to that point, which allows her to disappear? Shakespeare is too complex, too knowing a writer, too able to understand human behaviour to lose track of a character. So you have to understand Lady Macbeth's journey to that point so that you can make sense of the void that follows.

A major strand in this production's interpretation of Lady Macbeth's journey was the degree of passionate commitment the Macbeths initially felt for each other [see plate 9]. *The Times* (11 November 1986) commented that initially the Macbeths were 'almost one body, in love, excited by one another and quickened by the thrill of danger'. Wright was very clear about how she saw the breakdown in this relationship coming about:

Jules Wright: The scene in which Duncan's death is discovered is the beginning of the separation. Macbeth knows then that he's got the taste of blood, he knows the journey he will take, and Lady Macbeth knows that he knows this. She realises that that means separation. Then in the scene in which Banquo's ghost appears there is an astonishing exchange between Lady Macbeth and Macbeth where he completely cuts her. At the end of that scene that relationship is over and she knows that she has given *utterly, everything*, and then she is rejected by him.

One consequence of Wright's reading of Lady Macbeth was that Macbeth became more culpable than is often the case; the *Observer* described Jonathan Hyde's Macbeth as 'a silky patrician schemer' and 'a damned, villainous hero with a profile struck from a Renaissance coin'. Wright sees Macbeth as an intensely difficult role to play:

Jules Wright: An actor in that role is having to deal with half a dozen major speeches that everybody knows. There's a great rawness in the actor; he's got to go out and speak while everyone's sitting there and thinking, 'I've seen X do that before.' How *do* you bring that from inside yourself, with a depth of understanding that makes your grip on the role, at *this* moment in your life, at *this* time, secure, that makes the role *yours*?

However, Wright makes no bones about Macbeth's guilt:

Jules Wright: Macbeth makes a choice before he gets to see Lady Macbeth or even write the letter; he's standing there in 1.4., looking at Duncan, and he has that aside towards the end of the scene which in effect says, 'I know the choice I must make.'

It's a very interesting scene when Macbeth first returns to Lady Macbeth (1.5.). You can play it as Lady Macbeth saying, 'You *are* going to do it', or you can play it as her saying, '*Are* you going to do it?', and he's saying, 'What do you think?' If you can leave a kind of mutuality in that scene, then you stop the actor playing Macbeth withdrawing from the responsibilities of his actions. So often there's a 'she made me do it' element, but that's not in the text. We were challenging the conventional tracking of those two roles.

The production's emphasis on Macbeth's culpability was also enhanced by a downplaying of the supernatural elements: *The Times* considered 'the vice that grips and unites the Macbeths in this production feels unnatural, but not supernatural', and the visions of the potentially spectacular witch scene of 4.1. were reduced to tricks done by old women using mirrors.

Jules Wright: The witches needed a four-week rehearsal period by themselves to come to understand their journey. We treated them as old women, who weren't really dealing in magic. We were looking at power and so we sought to understand the real text, the real engagement between Macbeth and them and how he chose to hear and construct that which was said to him. You have to take a social context on board if you're doing the piece in the way that I did, but the witches certainly fit into *Macbeth* once you start to take it apart in terms of male and female principles.

The witches were almost upstaged by a 'giant curtain of spattering rain' which 'looked tremendous' but drowned out their voices (*Times Educational Supplement*, 14 November 1986). This curtain of pouring rain was also present during the scene in which Banquo's ghost appears, and the noise of rain made the bloody sergeant's speech in 1.2., extolling the heroism of Macbeth and Banquo in battle, almost inaudible. However, with the exception of the very end of the play, when Barrie Rutter's Macduff was savage in his excessive, frenzied stabbing of Macbeth, this production was not interested in showcasing violence, and the upstaging of the bloody sergeant seems in keeping with this. In addition to the rain there was also a soundtrack created by Ilona Sekacz and Mary Phillips of 'fluttering bells, pipes, wails and tolling piano wire' (*Observer*) and 'half-human noises and heartbeats' (*Guardian*), although the *Scotsman* was put in mind of 'a battery of video games being played backstage'.

The Times felt that the set was a forceful presence as well: 'Huge slabs of grey wall encase the stage: a Scottish castle unmistakably, but also a walled-in tomb, a dark barren cell in which Macbeth and those around him are cabined, cribbed, confined.' The approach of the English army into this domain was signalled as harshly back-lit, still, but menacing figures suddenly appeared upstage in seven giant doorways which swung open one by one.

The context most frequently invoked by reviewers of Wright's *Macbeth* was the opening of another production of the play by the RSC at Stratford. The *Guardian* brought in nationalist politics and complained of an 'English transplant' to Scotland. Although several reviewers commented on the fact that Wright was a guest director at the Lyceum and mentioned her work with the Women's Playhouse Trust, there was little attempt to take on board her feminist politics. Many reviewers complained that Covington's Lady Macbeth was not what they were used to – the traditional, ferocious, easy to blame Lady Macbeth – but they were not willing to accept this as a conscious interpretative decision; they constructed it as a weak performance and not a deliberate challenge to tradition.

Helena Kaut-Howson's last production at Theatr Clwyd in 1994 was a *Macbeth*, co-directed with Kathryn Hunter. Reviews of this production were extraordinarily polarised, loving or loathing it with a passion; however, whether they approved or disapproved, what most reviewers commented on was the unconventional playing of Macbeth. Sixty-year-old Timothy West looked old enough to be Lady Macbeth's father, and he played Macbeth as a businesslike, unpoetic, vastly experienced soldier, who by the final duel with Macduff was wearily resigned to his fate. The *Daily Telegraph* (23 September 1994) described West's Macbeth as distinguished by 'gritty, shirt-sleeves-rolled-up-realism'. The *Independent on Sunday* (18 September 1994) commented:

> Nothing…could be less unearthly than Timothy West's Macbeth; first seen wearing full pack and gaiters, and taking every supernatural development in his professional stride. Murdering Duncan is all in the day's work. Planning Banquo's assassination simply requires a military briefing. When he does fall apart, the effect is tremendous: not least in the sight of the phlegmatic recluse calmly philosophising over his wife's death, erupting into skin-saving panic at the news that the forest is on the move.

However, in counterpoint to this pragmatic Macbeth, the production played up the supernatural element, both in the set design and in the striking presentation of the witches.

Pamela Howard's set consisted of a steeply raked, slatted stage through which smoke and light poured and which suggested 'the nearness of a spirit world through the earth's fragile crust' (*Independent on Sunday*). This set split open for the cauldron scene, which was described in detail by the *Daily Telegraph*:

> The hags roll about athletically in jumble-sale clothes and have a brilliant device for conjuring up visions in a circular mirror suspended above the stage. In its reflection we see a foetus ('untimely ripped' from its mother's womb) and the parade of eight kings, while Hecate, wearing a goat's-head skull, presides over the famous cauldron recipe. It is like a scene from *The Devil Rides Out*, the best bit of bewitching I've seen.

The witches were young women who wailed, moaned, chanted and writhed: the *Sunday Express* (18 September 1994) saw them as 'the unfortunates of some dire Victorian lunatic asylum' and the *Wrexham Leader* (23 September 1994) agreed: the witches looked like 'poor, pathetic escapees from a lunatic asylum, one wearing striped bloomers and another an outsize bra'.

Half the reviewers accused Kaut-Howson of misdirection – 'The main mystery has to be why Macbeth's eager assassins didn't strike a fatal blow to the director before the opening night. The director must bear the brunt for the most fundamental mistakes…The director may as well have put the actors in strait jackets' (*North Wales Pioneer*, 22 September 1994). The other half were enthusiastic – the production bore the 'hallmarks' of Kaut-Howson and Hunter, 'two remarkably gifted and creative minds', who together have 'succeeded in revealing the many layers of this incomparable text' in a production which boasts a 'formidable' cast, a 'strikingly convincing' Macbeth and a Lady Macbeth who is 'a complex synthesis of the primitive and sophisticated' (*Western Mail*, 15 September 1994). However, additional commentary was provided by the *Guardian* (23 September 1994):

> The context here is that Helena Kaut-Howson's contract is not to be renewed and the choice of play was imposed on her. This is not the way to treat one of the most creative theatre directors in Europe.

Although these three *Macbeths* were extremely different in terms of politics and aesthetics, one feature is common to them all: the downplaying of the traditional, tragically heroic Macbeth. Littlewood was particularly chastised for her Macbeth's lack of tragic grandeur and his (and the production's) lack of poetry; Wright exonerated Lady Macbeth and so cast Macbeth as the villain of the piece, thus creating what many reviewers saw as an imbalance; Kaut-Howson directed an ageing Macbeth as a bluff soldier who ended his career without poetry or bravery but with a great sense of weariness. For this she garnered a set of reviews which, even allowing for political and aesthetic differences among the reviewers, diametrically opposed each other, on almost every facet of the production to a bewildering extent. With *Macbeth*, as with *King Lear*, presenting the tragic hero as insecurely grand or heroic renders directors particularly open to accusations of misdirection from reviewers who assume that the 'correct' way to present Shakespeare's tragic heroes is to endorse their heroism, not question it.

English History Plays

Shakespeare's English history plays are not 'good' history. Shakespeare took action packed stories from his chronicle sources, appropriated them and usually gave them a contemporary political slant. However, when Joan Littlewood tried her hand at something similar – appropriating Shakespeare's history plays and giving them a contemporary political slant – there was critical uproar. Shakespeare was allowed to interrogate history and rework it to suit his purpose but Joan Littlewood was not allowed the same leeway by her reviewers.

The English history plays are a very heterogeneous group: *Richard II* is a lyrical piece; *Richard III* mixes morality play with melodrama; *Henry IV Parts 1* and *2* are best known for the rumbustious character of Falstaff; *Henry V* is poised and theatrically self-conscious; *Henry VI* can seem like a ramshackle soap opera. However, there are important similarities between all of the English history plays: they are dominated by male characters jostling for positions of power, leading armies into the field and committing acts of violence, often onstage, accompanied by flourishes of drums and trumpets. With the important exceptions of Joan of Arc and Margaret of Anjou in the *Henry VI* plays, women characters are marginalised in the plays' narratives of macho brouhaha. Women directors who take on these plays are not only dealing with very male dominated material but they also have to confront the culturally conditioned expectation that women and violence don't go together, that a woman director is a less obvious choice for warrior culture plays. Di Trevis certainly encountered this expectation at the RSC:

Di Trevis: I wanted desperately to do *Macbeth* and I didn't want to do 'a woman's play', not because they didn't interest me but

because I felt that everybody expected it. I can't describe to you how there were underlying assumptions in those days and everybody would expect you to do an *As You Like It* or a *Twelfth Night*. When I was interviewed to be Terry Hands' assistant at the RSC, I said that the play that interested me was *Henry V* and they just went 'Oh!!!' and they absolutely didn't want me to do *Macbeth*.

Trevis' first play for RSC was actually the *Taming of the Shrew*.

Several women directors have managed to make quite an impact on Shakespeare's histories;[1] however, none has been as controversial as Joan Littlewood, whose productions of *Richard II* and *Henry IV* created critical uproar. I also want to look at Jane Howell's BBC productions of the *Henry VI* plays and *Richard III* because, as they are available on video, and as the BBC Shakespeares were very much targeted at the education market, they have had, and will continue to have, an impact far greater than most theatrical productions of the same plays.

Because it represents the deposition of a king, Richard II, and the usurpation of his throne by Henry Bolingbroke/Henry IV, *Richard II* was controversial at the time of its original performances. It is thus in some ways appropriate that Joan Littlewood's production of *Richard II*, one of the first of her classical productions to have a large critical impact, created such intense debate. Littlewood encouraged the controversy, indeed she very deliberately used *Richard II* to pull off a publicity coup. *Richard II* originally opened on 19 January 1954 and was, as usual with Theatre Workshop productions at that time, ignored by most reviewers. However, in January 1955 Littlewood revived the production specifically in order to compete with and comment on a traditional style *Richard II* which had then just opened at the Old Vic, directed by Michael Benthall.

The *Spectator* (28 January 1955) was unimpressed by Theatre Workshop's 'publicity hand-out' which explained that they were going to do *Richard II* 'better' than the Old Vic; however, Littlewood got the free publicity Theatre Workshop needed when many reviewers joined in the game of comparisons. *Plays and Players* (March 1955) did a double-page picture spread to illustrate the differences in approach.[2] Although the accompanying review definitely preferred verse-speaking in the Old Vic style, and commented magisterially that the Theatre Workshop 'players did not all show the proper Shakespearian manner', it did praise Littlewood's production for the 'sheer excitement of the first act. Here everything was alive and powerful, plunging us straight away into the unprincipled struggle for power.' Later on Littlewood herself commented (*Observer*, 15 March 1959): 'When we play "Richard the Second", the critics can't stand it because we're playing in what they call a vulgar fashion – we're playing it for action and dynamic rather than for decoration.'

The reviewers also objected, as usual, to Littlewood's class politics. The *Evening Standard* (19 January 1955) described the production as Marxist in opposition to the Old Vic's 'royalist' production; the *Spectator* sneered at the 'Marxian analyses produced by some of the audience ("Of course it's the barons taking advantage of the revolutionary feeling of the masses...")'; Norman Marshall (1962:299) saw Bolingbroke as 'the leading part, the typical Marxist hero, the revolutionary who overthrows a regime'.

Certainly working-class characters were given their due; for example, Howard Goorney gave full weight to the brief role of the politically acute, working-class gardener [see plate 10]. However, some reviewers took their dislike of the politics of the production further and responded to Harry Corbett's playing of King Richard with homophobia: Richard was 'a cringing, ranting, arrogant, capricious homosexual...an ugly, loathsome creature' (*Evening Standard*); a 'weak, treacherous, decadent pervert' (Marshall, 1962:300) who was deprived by Littlewood of 'his poetry and his pathos' with the consequence that the drama became one of 'blood sports' as 'the rebel faction hunted down their whimpering prey'; the *Truth* (28 January 1955) complained that Richard and his flatterers had 'one and all' been directed as homosexuals with very little justification; *Plays and Players* judged that Corbett's performance as a 'queenly pervert rather than a sickly, weak-minded king' was 'misdirected'.

In 1995, in suggesting Richard might be homosexual,

Littlewood's production was taking real risks and it is unsurprising that there were so many pointed attacks on the playing of this role.[3] Indeed the *Sunday Times* suggested Corbett had been directed to play Richard as quite mad:

> His high, treacherous, sing-song voice, his glazed eyes, his up-tilted chin, his fancifully managed hands, his swift, light, stopping little runs and leaps are all marks of a man who has only a distorted grasp of reality, and is living in an interior world of his own that touches objective existence only with disastrous consequences.

The review pays tribute to the powerful impact generated but adds the important rider 'it would have surprised Shakespeare considerably'. Similarly *The Times* (18 January 1955) couldn't recognise 'the play that Shakespeare wrote', and asked 'if this can possibly be Shakespeare's play at all'; under Littlewood's direction *The Times* thought John of Gaunt became 'a nightmare Old Testament prophet', the Bishop of Carlisle a 'twisted zealot almost as crazy as his king', Bolingbroke a 'swart and bloody minded adventurer' while Richard himself was a 'dangerous lunatic'. Littlewood (1994:451), on the other hand, remembers Corbett's performance with pride, especially the poignancy of his final prison scene, where, dressed in sackcloth, Corbett's Richard was 'tethered by his right ankle to a stake centre stage', and 'could only circle slowly round as he spoke his thoughts'. Today she simply comments: 'Harry Corbett did the *best* Richard II.'

Howard Goorney (1981:101) importantly stresses the issue of resources in relation to Littlewood's *Richard II*: while the Old Vic were able to go for pomp and circumstance and a cast of 45, the underfunded Theatre Workshop style was all shoestring, starkness, speed and energy, with a cast of 14. Anger and urgency underscored the Theatre Workshop production: Mowbray and Bolingbroke really spat at each other in the opening scene of the play and John of Gaunt's lines of angry prophecy were delivered as if he really was dying (Littlewood, 1994:453).

For Littlewood the stress was always on the physicality of the action. Howard Goorney (1981:167) vividly remembers 'Richard striking Gaunt with his glove as a climax to their confrontation; how the gardener handled his plants; the feel of the texture of materials' as well as several improvisations used to emphasise the violence that easily goes missing in lyrical productions of *Richard II*:

> Joan would say, 'You're in a market place and it's full of people. You're getting your shopping and a fight breaks out!' We would fight each other, go berserk, jump on each other. Then she would say; 'Now you're stabbed in the back…You're on horseback, you're knocked off, you're dragged along, you shout and scream and sweat.' (Goorney, 1981:167)

On another occasion in rehearsal for *Richard II* Littlewood told her actors: 'Pretend that stretching out before you is your future, your sons and their sons in a great long line. Behind you is a man with a dagger, about to plunge it into your back' (Goorney, 1981:171). Meanwhile, in contrast to all this violence, Littlewood herself played the role of the distressed, ineffectual, childless Duchess of Gloucester with 'genuine pathos' (*Plays and Players*).

By positioning her *Richard II* against the Old Vic's, Littlewood exploited Shakespeare in order to grab media attention for Theatre Workshop and to define their position as purveyors of an alternative, oppositional version of classical drama. With its perhaps inflated reputation for lyricism, *Richard II* was an ideal vehicle for Littlewood to make the point about her energised, iconoclastic Shakespeare, the antithesis of what was showing at the Old Vic and elsewhere. Although it is in some ways the least violent of Shakespeare's histories – featuring more aborted violence than onstage drums and trumpets – Littlewood gave the play a violent urgency which was highly charged, and highly offensive to some reviewers.

When Littlewood directed her next history, *Henry IV* at the Edinburgh Festival in 1963, she provoked even more virulent critical attacks:[4]

Joan Littlewood: The critics tore us apart. I had such fun, and that big assembly hall was packed. Usually at Edinburgh we played some place sharing between the dog shows and the parrots. We did some bloody good work there but they'd say, 'Oh yes, this is great theatre but dreadful politics', or something like that. The communists were bad on our politics too but *Henry IV* **was brilliant, I must admit it. All the critics hated** *Henry IV* **and the audiences loved it.**

At this stage in her career Littlewood had considerable standing in English theatre and, although some were suspicious of her politics, her style of theatre had many admirers. What is particularly interesting in relation to *Henry IV*, however, is that Littlewood completely confounded even her greatest admirers' expectations of what she would do with the play: she was expected to play down the troubled relationship between Henry IV and his son Hal and play up Hal's relationship with Falstaff, emphasising the love of good living, good drink and roguery that Falstaff epitomises. Instead Falstaff was a class oppressor, 'an unsentimental picture of a public-bar soldier', young, without 'the traditional whiskers and ruddiness' (Brown, 1965:154) or the customary paunch belly. The *Spectator* (28 August 1964), which had expected Littlewood 'to dote' on Falstaff's 'sack-swilling' and 'cut-pursing', was astonished. The *Scotsman* (18 August 1964) chastised George Cooper, who played Falstaff, for insufficient 'distinction in his rascality' as:

> it is this which Falstaff needs above all things to endear us to him and excuse his evil features – his bribe-taking and his cruel comments on the troops he is ashamed of being seen with.

The problem was that Littlewood had clearly decided *not* to 'excuse' Falstaff, although she also surprised critics because, despite the fact that the production was a conflation of parts 1 and 2 of *Henry IV*, there was no hint at the end of the action that Hal, or Henry V as he has now become, would now reject Falstaff.

Class sympathies also worked, more predictably, against the king and his court, who were 'cold politicians, uniform in dress and clipped and unemotional in speech'. The son of the Earl of Northumberland, Hotspur's 'grandiloquence was *meant* to sound empty' (Brown, 1965:153). Meanwhile the minor, working-class characters were strong and John Russell Brown particularly praised the presentation of Francis the serving man, who is often read as nothing more than an opportunity for a few easy laughs; here Francis was full of 'honesty, loyalty, ambition, ignorance – a small, conventional and intense imagination' (1965:154).

The class politics of the production help contextualise JC Trewin's indignation (*Illustrated London News*, 5 September 1964): the production was 'preposterous', full of 'wayward shoddiness', and 'Nobody will say that Miss Littlewood is not sincere in her defiant beliefs; but Shakespeare's Quatercentenary year and an important Festival stage are hardly the time and place for their presentation.'[5]

Howard Goorney vividly remembers the reviewers' response to *Henry IV.* They:

> objected to the way it was cut, the lack of poetry, most of the acting, and the mixture of modern and period in the costumes – Poins, for example, wore Italian slacks, a bowler hat and a leather jerkin (Goorney, 1981:130).

The most vociferous complaints, however, were directed at the theatre configuration: Littlewood 'stretched from side to side a kind of dyke, a high oblong stage that divided the audience into two halves' and 'upon this her company had to manoeuvre, with much restlessness and showing of backs, so that each half of the auditorium could get a share of what was going on' (Sprague and Trewin, 1970:113–14).[6]

Another attack, made on the actors' accents, drew an angry response from Littlewood: 'I find the accents of Leeds, East London and Manchester as acceptable as those of St John's Wood, Eton, Oxford or hangovers from Edwardian dressing rooms' (Goorney, 1981:130).

Joan Littlewood: If someone spoke with a Geordie accent it didn't matter: Geordie's better than that muck they speak at Stratford-upon-Avon.

The class dynamic, which is inevitably implicated in any discussion over accents in Britain, was again in evidence in Littlewood's statement to the press that Shakespeare's company was 'made up of leary misfits, anarchists, out of work soldiers and wits who worked at their ideas in pubs and performed them as throwaways to an uninhibited pre-Puritan audience' (Goorney, 1981:130). Whatever the historical accuracy of this vision, it helped create an attack on established Shakespeare which had reviewers in a spin.

Littlewood's *Henry IV* upset every single reviewer and it is clear that some aspects of the production – such as the acoustics – were faulty. However, the unsettling quality of Littlewood's politicised use of Shakespeare clearly went beyond class warfare. *The Times* (18 August 1964) in a revealing reference declared that this production was 'an act of theatrical pillage which in its combination of muddled purpose and bungled execution rivals the expedition to the Bay of Pigs'. Meanwhile the *Daily Telegraph* (19 August 1964) complained that with *Henry IV* Littlewood 'manufactured a sort of glum Elizabethan paraphrase of her own "Oh, What a Lovely War!"' That Littlewood's anti-war message in *Oh, What a Lovely War!* was intentionally carried across into *Henry IV*, was most clearly suggested in her use of actors playing refugees, trudging across the full length of that intensely disliked traverse stage after the battle scenes.[7]

While Joan Littlewood was able to be irreverent towards Shakespeare within the context of Theatre Workshop, when Jane Howell directed Shakespeare's first tetralogy of history plays for the BBC Shakespeare, there were strict limits on how much she could interfere with the text. The sprawling narratives of these plays – *Henry VI Parts 1, 2* and *3* and *Richard III* – with their saga of the disastrous Wars of the Roses and the reign of Henry VI – are often cut radically in production. However, the BBC series was geared to an educational market and the expectation was that as much of the received text as possible would be performed in a relatively conventional way. Howell's productions were some of the most critically acclaimed of the entire series, although Howell's initial involvement came about by chance:

Jane Howell: I had a son to bring up and I was broke, so I took what was offered as long as I didn't disagree with the plays. My attitude to the telly was, if I thought I could do it, do it well. Money was the basic driving necessity over that time, and I got the *Henries* because I was sitting in a corridor at the right time. Jonathan Miller came by; he was looking for a director for the *Henries*. I'd just done *Winter's Tale* in the series; he obviously thought it was reasonable, and he said to me, 'This would be very good for your bank balance. Do you want to do it?'

Initially Howell was unenthusiastic about the project:

Jane Howell: I read the first *Henry* and I thought, 'This is absolute rubbish', and then I started reading *Parts 2* and *3* and I became interested. Then I got an idea about it and I really wanted to do them. That's how those two years started. I loved it; it was a great privilege to do those plays and to be with all those actors for so long.

One of the important 'hooks' that Howell used with the tetralogy was the sense of a journey through all four plays; both in terms of theatrical method and in terms of the immorality of violence:

Jane Howell: The *Henries* seemed like a really interesting puzzle to me. You can see a development from very primitive, almost pageant wagon stuff up to the forerunners of the great tragedies. The verse changes; in the second play you feel as though Shakespeare's got in touch with Greek tragedy suddenly and is starting to understand those sorts of mechanisms.

It was also a puzzle because all the editors and the critics, non-theatrical people, dismissed that first play as worthless, but when you look at it, it is based on theatrical gags and it almost uses a pantomime form. Then later it changes into something very serious. The plays go on getting darker and darker and I loved that. I thought I'd perceived a pattern in it which I thought could be made to work.

As a consequence of this vision, the violence depicted in the plays was initially portrayed in a slightly cartoon-like style with little sense of real physical damage being done to flesh and blood human beings. As the tetralogy progressed, the violence became more real, more disturbing and more confrontational, even for television audiences accustomed to the horrifying bloodshed of news programmes. Howell was trying consciously to challenge the traditionally masculine battle ethic of the *Henries*.[8]

Jane Howell: I tried always to say, with all that macho battle stuff, 'But count the cost, count the cost', and I tried to undermine it all the time. That's what the very last image of the tetralogy (which was the first image that came into my head) was about. It was purely instinctive but apparently it's a classic image for revenge, a reverse pieta, with Margaret surrounded by corpses, cradling the dead Richard in her arms.

This extremely powerful final image irritated Michael Manheim (1994:138): 'Howell is more engaged with old Margaret's cacklings as she sits on her mountains of corpses during the credits – fine pacifism, but not really the point of *this* play.' Manheim's certainty that he had got the point of the play and that Howell hadn't was absolute. More appreciatively, Robert Potter (1988:118) saw the pile of corpses as evocative of Dachau, Treblinka, Flodden Field, My Lai or the Somme as much as Bosworth, and at the top of the pile 'sat a mad vindicated Margaret amid the carnage of a famous victory, cradling the body of dead King Richard like some demonic anti-Pieta, her golden curls shaking exultantly, gorgon-like'.

Crucially, in giving the final image of the tetralogy to Margaret, Howell also stressed the terrible journey taken by Margaret across the plays – from young, inexperienced woman to hag, seer and avenging fury. In *1 Henry VI*, Howell first introduced the young Margaret by means of a fade from Joan La Pucelle (Joan of Arc). There was a real sense of disorientation in the last scenes of Brenda Blethyn's Joan, a character who had grown used to having power, joining in the men's war games with 'jolly hockey sticks' enthusiasm, and beating the men at their own game effectively, and often comically. Now suddenly Joan was back in a state of gender and class disempowerment; however, the fade linking Joan to Julia Foster's Margaret, promised Joan's political legacy – as a battle-hungry, insubordinate, turbulent French woman – would live on.

Married to the feminised and unmacho Henry VI, who cannot control his competitive, aggressive barons, Margaret of Anjou begins to adopt the same masculine codes of violence as Joan. Appropriately, in Howell's production, as Margaret became more and more experienced in battle, her clothes, like her behaviour, became more and more indistinguishable from those of the men around her. Howell's careful charting of Margaret's education in violence, was made especially clear at the moment of one of Margaret's most repellent acts (*3 Henry VI* 1.4.). After taunting her enemy, Richard of York, Margaret stuck her knife into him with relish; however, Julia Foster's look of shock defined this act as Margaret's first real blooding and contrasted strongly with the casual attitude of the men around her. Later in the play, the now war-weary Margaret was able to fight dirty, brawling with Clarence in a completely undignified manner, trying to force him to kill her in her despair after the death of her son.

Howell's careful attention to Margaret made her *Richard III* unusual; one of the commonest and easiest cuts in this long play is to remove Margaret completely. The cut can be justified because Margaret never actually drives the action of the play – she prophesies, she comments, she curses but she doesn't instigate dramatic action. However, Margaret is also the only character in the play who can consistently upstage Richard, and by forcefully placing Margaret at the centre of the final image of *Richard III*, Howell added to this upstaging effect.

Richard III is traditionally one of the most spell-binding of Shakespeare's characters, one of the actor manager's dream parts. Under Howell's direction, however, much of the traditional, arch, theatrical high jinks, and the melodramatic, even comic, relish for evil often associated with Richard disappeared. This was partly a result of the increased sombreness in the presentation of the violence at this stage of the tetralogy, but it was also a natural consequence of Howell's interest in Margaret. Because Howell carefully tracked her through the whole tetralogy, the audience understood Margaret's growing monstrosity as a response to the violent world around her. In the battle culture of the *Henries*, where power mostly accrued to those who could fight and wield huge, heavy swords effectively, Margaret was a survivor (the only character still alive from *1 Henry VI*), and although Howell stressed the huge emotional cost to Margaret, as she sat nursing the dead Richard in a gloating, perverted maternalism, she was clearly identified as a victor, and a survivor.

The Times (30 January 1983) commented of Howell's *Richard III*: 'It was the women who came out of the production best.' However, Howell sees things in a more complex way and feels she brought feminine energy to the whole group of plays:

Jane Howell: With the *Henries*, for the first four weeks I was working off the feminine and dragging everything through me to see if it felt right. I worked with the major actors for three weeks upstairs in a small room, and because the fighting stuff was so dangerous, and I didn't have much time, the second company, who came in for the fights, had a week's rehearsal on their own. Then in the last week I just pulled back and said, 'What have we got? Let's make it work', and I put everything together, a bit like a musical – so that last week was spent doing a lot of shouting.

One of the strengths of Howell's production practice could also be seen in terms of traditional notions of the 'feminine': Howell's careful consideration for her cast and crew. Fenwick (1983b: 26) particularly comments on the 'strong sense of family' which Howell created in the *Henries* ensemble:[9]

Jane Howell: Because I knew with the *Henries* that we had to get married really, all of us, for the seven or eight months we were going to be together, it was essential that we were going to get on. I knew I wasn't going to have the time to deal with any nonsense. So I was very careful about the selection of the actors, and I was thinking of the experience of working over that period of time and being together every day.

Howell also felt a major strength of the production was the set, a circular space which was a cross between a reconstructed Globe theatre and a children's adventure playground.

Jane Howell: That set allowed me a lot of freedom because I could be inside or outside; I could be where I wanted, within reason. If I found out my thinking was wrong when I came to do a scene, if I was setting up a scene in a church, I could suddenly turn it round and say 'Oh no, it's outside', and that was easy.

The set further enhanced the Brechtian, non-realistic style of the productions which contrasted so vividly with the leaden realism characteristic of some of the other BBC Shakespeares.

Howell's first tetralogy garnered some enthusiastic responses: Graham Holderness (1992:224) detected 'the creative intervention of a genuinely radical director' and Dennis Bingham (1988:222) praised Howell for mastering 'the art of transforming theatre into television'.[10] In her overall approach – underlining the cost of maintaining a violent warrior culture, emphasising the entanglement of Margaret in the monstrous war games – Howell inevitably diminished the male heroes of the plays. While questioning militaristic heroes is very much a feature of late twentieth-century Shakespeare production generally and is certainly not only the preserve of women directors, Howell's distinctive contribution here was to accompany this with a rewriting of Shakespeare's first tetralogy as a 'herstory', by her sympathetic treatment of Margaret of Anjou.

Howell's rewriting of Shakespeare's history seems respectful,

however, alongside Joan Littlewood's assaults on *Richard II* and
Henry IV, but Littlewood was only exercising her right to
interrogate history, bringing the past to bear on the present and the
present to bear on the past. In a book like this, which posits an
alternative to mainstream history and a hearing to previously
marginalised voices, such a gesture has to be celebrated; whatever
audiences thought of Littlewood's politics, aesthetics or theatrical
practice, they came out of her productions of Shakespeare's history
plays with their complacent notions of history and Shakespeare
shaken to the core.

Roman History Plays

Shakespeare's other history plays, the Roman plays, are a very incongruous group: they were written at different periods of Shakespeare's working life, they have different preoccupations and politics and they have a very different sense of 'Romanness'. However, like Shakespeare's English history plays, they do share common ground in featuring male characters jostling for position in terms of political power, and in presenting a large amount of stage violence and stage battles. Nonetheless, the three plays considered here – *Titus Andronicus, Antony and Cleopatra* and *Coriolanus* – also accord considerable space to disruptive female characters.

Titus Andronicus is a revenge tragedy full of onstage gore, mutilation, murder and violence against women. Tamora, the Queen of the Goths, who has been vanquished in battle at the beginning of the play, leads a revenge action against the victorious Titus, a revenge which includes her inciting her sons to rape and mutilate Titus' daughter Lavinia. In the course of an action-packed narrative, Tamora also marries an emperor, commits adultery with Aaron the Moor, gives birth to his child and eats a meat pie containing the cooked remains of her sons, before dying violently. The violence against Lavinia, who is not only raped but silenced by having her tongue cut out and her hands cut off, is particularly gruesome, but although she is silenced and has no lines to speak, Lavinia is a haunting stage presence until she dies in the final bloodbath of the play. All this excessive violence – involving stage property heads and chopped off hands – makes *Titus* a complicated and problematic play to stage.[1]

Jane Howell's *Titus Andronicus*, which was filmed in 1985, was the last production in the BBC Shakespeare series. Despite continuities between *Titus* and the plays Howell had already directed for the BBC series – all the plays feature violent, aggressive male characters acting atrociously, and assertive, uppity women who challenge traditional gender boundaries – Howell was not immediately engaged by *Titus*.

Jane Howell: Again I thought it was a load of old rubbish *initially* and then I found a way through. I like the problems of doing Shakespeare on television because there's no guidelines, and with *Titus* I suddenly realised that in that rather ludicrous scene with people with hands cut off and somebody raped, all sitting down for a family tea, that there was a child, young Lucius, Titus' grandchild, watching. Then I had a personal hook into the play. My son used to have very bad nightmares and I thought he could have easily dreamed this play. The idea didn't come off totally but that aspect interested me a lot, the notion of the *watcher*.

Consequently Howell built up the character of young Lucius and plotted his journey from his initial position of watcher, the serious student, wearing glasses and distanced from the world of warfare at the beginning of the play, to the position of participator, assisting in the violence orchestrated by Titus, even in scenes where Shakespeare's text does not have young Lucius onstage. Meanwhile his father, the older Lucius, was presented as becoming completely corrupted by the violent world of Roman power-mongering.

Howell's *Titus* also contained other watchers: masked servants, soldiers and senators, anonymous Romans who, because of their masks, appeared impassive in the face of the violence they were watching.[2] These watchers, of course, reflected on the watchers/audience of the play, and a chilling image of a clinical voyeurism was created alongside a strong sense of the moral culpability of witnessing such events and failing to protest about them. The masks were also suggestive of Greek and Roman theatre, but Mary Maher (1988:147) additionally points out that the lack of mouths in the soldiers' and servants' masks 'tells the audience that the world of the Andronici is not characterized by political freedom and democratic ideas'. The masks pointed to the question of who can speak and who cannot, a question which is particularly loaded in a play concerned with the speaking or telling of history, and one in which a woman, Lavinia, is so brutally and memorably silenced by having her tongue ripped out.

In this production there was also an emphasis on the extent to which both the major women characters, Lavinia and Tamora, participated actively in the violence of their society. Both characters were seen to be driven to this by the damage inflicted on them first: Tamora by seeing her son sacrificed by Titus, Lavinia by her rape and mutilation. The silenced Lavinia was a particularly forceful presence in Titus' revenge action, and finally was seen actively to commit suicide, deliberately handing the knife to Titus for him to kill her. In addition, Lavinia was given the power of deciding when the final bloodbath should begin as it waited on a signal from her, the lifting of her veil. In the gruesome abattoir scene depicting the killing of Chiron and Demetrius – the rapists of Lavinia who were hanging upside down with blood pouring from their slashed throats – Anna Calder-Marshall's Lavinia clearly enjoyed collecting their blood in a bowl. This performance of Lavinia gave the character agency and made her far more than a mere victim; Lavinia wanted revenge and she enjoyed witnessing the suffering of those who had made her suffer.

It was less surprising that Eileen Atkins as Tamora would be a forceful presence, and Atkins was consistently chilling in her representation of Tamora's ruthlessness. Tamora's Gothic otherness was also stressed, particularly through costumes which picked up on modern resonances of the word 'Gothic', which ally it with punk, leather, nose rings and chains.

Howell made sure that at the end of the play, the audience was left with a bleak sense of the cycle of violence and corruption continuing unabated. The older Lucius, now in control of Rome, was an oath-breaking thug, who had killed Aaron's baby son even though he had sworn not to. The impact of the baby's death was made more powerful, as Alan Dessen (1989:105) points out, because Howell chose to use a real baby for the earlier scenes.

Jane Howell: I played a few games with the baby, Aaron's son, who was killed to stress the idea of 'Count the cost of this excessive, macho culture. If you must do this, just know what it costs.'

As with her production of the first tetralogy, Howell used stage violence very deliberately to ask questions of the cultures which applaud the warrior code and also of those cultures which elevate the representation of violence to the level of high art.

Antony and Cleopatra also features a great deal of violence and scrutinises the warrior code in its study of the ageing and increasingly ineffectual Antony. However, the death of Antony in Act 4 means that the final act of the play is dominated by Cleopatra. Cleopatra is a complex figure and in some ways suggestive of subversive female power – she is the living representative of the goddess Isis, she is a queen, she wears Antony's sword and dresses him in her clothes (2.5.22-3), she is sexually assertive and has a history of affairs with powerful men. The potential to build up the power of the feminine in this play is enormous, but when Yvonne Brewster directed *Antony and Cleopatra* for Talawa in 1991, she also found contemporary events, specifically the Gulf War, influencing the way her production evolved. In a programme note she commented:

> When this production was first planned, war had not yet been declared on the Iraqis. By the time we came to work on this glorious text, we, as an all black company, could not escape some of the indelible images of this most recent of wars... appropriation, greed, colonisation, black oil, black foot soldier fighting black foot soldier...

However, theatrically speaking, Brewster took the focus away from violence and battles. This she also justified in the programme note:

> This is an intimate play. The battles are all offstage and the crucial scenes often take place between a small number of characters.

While the *Tribune* (31 May 1991) complained 'Brewster throws away, wilfully it seems, the superheroism', Brewster saw herself as making a virtue of necessity:

Yvonne Brewster: I thought, 'I can't afford all this "The army crosses the stage" business.' Then I thought, 'How can I do this with 15 people without everybody changing hats and boots and all this nonsense?'

Eros fascinated me, Eros is the messenger of love, and all the messengers in *Antony and Cleopatra* bring messages of love or war, or the love of war, or the war of love. So I put all the messengers together and Eros became a big part.

I made 12 major characters out of the play and the doubling was very deliberate, but it was hard; it took me a year to do it. I had to get it right before I even spoke to anybody because it seemed mad.

Brewster was particularly drawn by the prospect of having a black Cleopatra:

Yvonne Brewster: Dona Croll, who I think is a fine Shakespearean actor, played Cleopatra and so there we had a Cleopatra who looked like Cleopatra did. The production got a following; it became a bit of a cult thing with black people.

Brewster also felt drawn to the play by the age of the lovers who are its protagonists:

Yvonne Brewster: I thought, 'Hold on a minute, this bloke Antony, what's he doing? What is the relationship between those two? Is she looking after him in his dotage?' Antony was almost dead by this time and Cleopatra was no spring chicken either and, not being a spring chicken myself, I was looking at love in advanced age, and that's what fascinated me about the play.

She also had a strong directorial line on Cleopatra as a figure of great power:

Yvonne Brewster: I think it's Cleopatra's play, not Antony's, but often it's done as Antony's play. It's a play I could do every five years and it would be completely different, but it does bring out a kind of situation that women find themselves in. I felt that Cleopatra wrapped Antony up in her psyche, but I didn't know how best to do that in the theatre.

I don't like sets, I like suggestions, and working with my designer Helen Turner we had come up with three stainless steel chairs on a wonderful sandy type floorcloth with half a pyramid. You could make a ship or Cleopatra's tomb out of that. But then we made this 20 foot square quilt and that was Cleopatra's 'receiving blanket'; it could become the sea – because it was the colour of the sea on one side – and on the other side there was the most enormous appliqué, in raw silk, of Isis.

When Antony was coming up into Cleopatra's tomb, she was at the head of the half pyramid and she threw down the quilt, he rolled into it and Cleopatra and her women pulled it up. Cleopatra actually wound Antony up into her whole self, into her bosom. People would sit around in the theatre afterwards and talk about it, especially older women.

Brewster expands on the mystical side of her production by reference to the rhythm of *Antony and Cleopatra* and to her treatment of Mardian the eunuch, a character whom she kept onstage for most of the action:

Yvonne Brewster: The female flow in the play is fascinating, and the play repeats itself and tells things twice, but if you try and cut out the repetition, you lose the rhythm of the play. That rhythm is why I had the quilt as a receiving kind of object with, on the back side of it, the sea.

I thought that Mardian, as a eunuch, had a spiritual element to him, and he became whatever was necessary in the play. He became the man with the figs and here he was a priest figure coming from a more Animistic faith – remember, it is Egypt. The man with the figs is also the way out, and that's a priestly function: to take you to the end.

She toughened one aspect of the play:

Yvonne Brewster: At the end when Caesar (Ben Thomas) came in, he was quite clearly *so* homosexual that he didn't give a toss about Cleopatra. He paid her respects but in a very grudging kind of way. One forgets that Augustus Caesar was the one who allowed the massacre of the children in Bethlehem; he's not going to be impressed by Cleopatra.

The *Guardian* (20 May 1991) commented:

> Ms Brewster's most original touch is her interpretation of Octavius Caesar as not just a cold calculator but a murderous pragmatist. At the end of the scene aboard Pompey's galley he has his host quietly strangled and later sees his political partner, Lepidus, taken into custody.

> The former idea runs clean against the text...[b]ut one forgives it since Octavius is marvellously played by Ben Thomas as a ruthless Machiavel.

Thomas' award-winning portrayal of Caesar generated a sense that the 'noble' warrior code that Antony followed was out of date. Generally, however, even while Brewster felt the play gained new meanings because of the military context of her production – the Gulf War – her *Antony and Cleopatra* took the theatrical focus away from men's battles and gave the play to Cleopatra.

The hero of Shakespeare's other late Roman play, *Coriolanus*, is almost the ultimately effective warrior, at times little more than a macho killing machine. However, the warrior is finally defeated and killed because of the interventions of his mother, Volumnia, and wife, Virgilia, who beg him not to destroy Rome. Volumnia is traditionally a particularly forceful stage presence, an overbearing, overwhelming, voluble figure who lives vicariously through her son and through him achieves the status denied her as a woman in early Roman society. By contrast, Coriolanus' wife, Virgilia, who is silent when Volumnia speaks out, is often a somewhat pale stage presence. However, in Gale Edwards' acclaimed production of *Coriolanus* for the Sydney Theatre Company in 1993, Virgilia became extremely forceful, demonstrating that a character doesn't need lines in order to make a significant contribution to the action.[3]

Gale Edwards: That production made a very feminist statement on the world. Virgilia hardly speaks, she has no voice in the play, she's just the loving wife. Meanwhile Coriolanus gives a sword to his son and tells the kid to grow up big and strong like him. But at the end, when Coriolanus is stabbed and the stage is running with blood and Aufidius has clearly become a monster out of control, we went to this image of the child picking up the sword and his mother, Virgilia, coming in slowly behind him and she took away the sword.

It was fantastic. She disempowered him; it was like the feminine, the female saying, 'You don't need to live in a male dominated world of violence.' The world of that play is incredibly male, the political world as well as the violent world of war, and I just felt that the female voice, although it was 'silent', was the only one that could offer hope or peace or harmony or any kind of sense at all – and I loved that.

Heather Mitchell's Virgilia was also a very strong stage presence elsewhere in the production: she consistently and very visibly resisted Volumnia's bullying, and an extremely sharp sense of conflict between the women, their values, and their influence on Coriolanus was generated. Virgilia might have been given very few lines to speak by Shakespeare but this Virgilia, the wife whom

Coriolanus calls his 'gracious silence' (2.1.172) was also capable of shouting angrily at Volumnia in the few lines she *does* have. In addition Virgilia, alone on stage at the end of 1.3., gave an unscripted scream of anguish at the thought of the horrors of war, and this was the signal for the battle scenes at Corioli to commence.

Edwards' critique of the violent world of the men in *Coriolanus* was also expressed in the excessive stage violence of her production.

Gale Edwards: I'm very fascinated by violence, and *Coriolanus* is a play about violence, war and warmongering. It's about men who violate other men as well as women.

I'm very brave in putting violence onstage and it was a *very* violent production; when Aufidius stabbed Coriolanus at the end, he stabbed him fifty times. Aufidius would just keep stabbing and it was horrendous, absolutely horrendous. On the opening night, which was just extraordinary, people in the audience cried out, 'No, stop!' at the bloodbath.

The stabbing of Coriolanus continued until Aufidius' arm was worn out and Aufidius was staggering with exhaustion, panting heavily. The *Sydney Morning Herald* (30 July 1993) thought the climax 'shocking, gory and piteous'. However, the unnerving, excessive violence wasn't confined to the scene of Coriolanus' death or to the battle scenes; in this production the crowd actually bashed one of the tribunes to death.

Although Edwards to a certain extent revelled in the staging of all this violence, her intention was always to shock in order to condemn. While the violence did occasionally become almost mesmerising in its visual excess, Edwards remains very proud of *Coriolanus*:

Gale Edwards: *Coriolanus* was probably one of the best productions I ever did in my life but it was a long time in coming. I had wanted to do the play for years. I had worked with John

Howard on *The Rover* and he was Edmund in my *King Lear*, and he is a great, great actor and an exciting person to be in the room with. We were talking drunkenly around the table one night about vehicles for him and I said, 'One day you must play Coriolanus', and then two or three years later it became possible to do that at the Sydney Theatre Company.

Howard is known for his slightly unpredictable, dominating stage presence: The *Bulletin* (17 August 1993) saw his Coriolanus as Ramboesque, the *Telegraph Mirror* (31 July 1993) saw 'a blood-soaked Terminator' and the *Australian* (30 July 1993) vividly described Howard's first entrance as Coriolanus from the dominating position of upstage left:

> With fire in his belly and flint in his heart, we first see him, helmeted and with metallic shoulder pads, emerging from a fog of dry ice like some ancient Terminator.

Edwards' vision of the play also placed the relationship between Coriolanus and his major adversary, Aufidius, at the centre:

Gale Edwards: Philip Quast (Aufidius) was able to be the kind of lion that would work in the arena with John Howard. Coriolanus and Aufidius were narcissistic in their adoration of each other and there was a homoerotic centre to the play. We took Aufidius' speech 'Let me twine/Mine arms about (Coriolanus') body' (4.5 107–8) very seriously, and so there was this kind of perverse attraction between these two enemies who were trying to kill each other, but killing, fucking, orgasm were all the same thing.

Edwards claimed in the production programme:

> I believe that *Coriolanus* acquires a new relevance when viewed against the backdrop of the late twentieth century. In the recent events of Eastern Europe we have seen the overthrow of dictatorships, the collapse of economies, the emergence of

democracies and the descent into criminal tribalisation. Coriolanus would feel quite at home in our world.

Consequently, although Brian Thomson's set primarily evoked the Roman world, Roger Kirk's costumes mixed Roman and modern having, for example, the tribunes Brutus and Sicinius 'looking like real estate shysters' (*Sydney Morning Herald*) in suits.

Edwards also wrote in the programme of the fight to control *Coriolanus*:

> As a director of this play, one is constantly aware of it bucking and rearing beneath the reins, refusing to be either one thing or another.

However, overall Edwards was very satisfied with the production:

Gale Edwards: We did a *Coriolanus* that was shorter, neater, cleaner and more vital than its original, but it was a really, really good go at the play.

Edwards' assertion that she is 'very brave' in the use of stage violence is borne out by her highly praised but gruesome 1996 production of Webster's *White Devil* for the RSC. Currently convincing, close-up, in-your-face violence on stage, as on film, is very fashionable. However, in some ways Edwards' exploration of the silent and traditionally innocuous Virgilia in *Coriolanus* was as effective in questioning the warrior code of that play as the strenuous and bloody violence onstage. Howell's exploration in *Titus Andronicus* of Lavinia, a woman silenced by means of appalling violence, was similarly revealing. Deprived of words, this Lavinia still moaned and murmured her pain in a way which was, if anything, more disturbing than many of the tub-thumping speeches going on around her. Both Edwards and Howell rendered silent women characters 'speaking' by their direction.

All of Shakespeare's Roman history plays considered here include violent women: Tamora incites violence in *Titus Andronicus*; Cleopatra beats up a messenger and insists on going into battle alongside Antony; in *Coriolanus*, Volumnia revels in the violence inflicted by her son.[4] By addressing a real range of emotions in relation to women, these plays challenge the feminine stereotypes of passivity, compassion and nurturing love, even though the action is still dominated by men fighting battles, men in hand-to-hand combat, male armies charging across the stage, and lives given over to the macho warrior code.

Productions of the Roman history plays today tend to question this warrior code more and more stringently and often use them to comment on the continuing militarism of contemporary society. It is encouraging to see women directors taking on and interrogating these plays, particularly given the still dominant assumption that staging violence, in performance as well as in real life, is the preserve of men. Nevertheless, an idea which was at the heart of Jane Howell's treatment of Margaret of Anjou, in Shakespeare's first tetralogy of English history plays, is also relevant here: doing violence as well as men do it may not always be the healthiest way forward.

Part 3 – Women Directors: A Herstory

None of the directors interviewed for this study felt part of a long history of women directing Shakespeare, something which is unsurprising because the history of women's achievements in this area has been largely suppressed. This section of the book is designed to establish the fact that women *have* been directing Shakespeare for a long time even though their achievements have been marginalised in standard theatre histories. However, it is also important to acknowledge that if a woman director feels as if she is a pioneer, it is almost irrelevant whether or not she really *is* a pioneer. If she feels the pressures of pioneering, then those pressures are real and will affect her work – whether positively or negatively.

This 'herstory' does not pretend to be comprehensive – it is more a preliminary survey of the very rich field of women's achievements in the production of Shakespeare. Although I have attempted to look at a range of directors who have worked in different theatrical spheres, and whose marginalisation has worked in different ways, there is a focus on women who have themselves written about their careers in autobiographies and memoirs. These are not unproblematic sources – Lillie Langtry's autobiography, for example, completely omits to mention her affair with the future Edward VII and the role that affair played in launching her stage career. However, when women directors have chosen to write their autobiographies, when they have elected to speak in their own words about their theatre work, they are clearly making a bid to enter theatre history, and to prevent their work being misinterpreted, belittled or forgotten. While this in some ways makes it all the more troubling that so much of their work *has* been forgotten, these women's self-advocacy means that their achievements are more readily recoverable.

Self-advocacy tends to be a tool of the relatively assertive, empowered and literate woman and so the discussion here inevitably falls somewhat into the trap characterised by Tracy Davis (1989:64) as the 'chronicle-of-stars' approach which creates a focus on 'the very successful, famous, and therefore atypical elite' of women working in theatre (Davis, 1989:63). However, when even women who achieved star status in their time, such as Eliza Vestris, have been given scant attention in most Shakespeare theatre histories, there is an urgent need to construct an initial 'chronicle-of-stars', simply in order to compensate for the way in which women's work has been neglected, to begin reclaiming these women's achievements, and to start formulating a new theatre history.

This herstory of Shakespeare in the Theatre is divided into three historical periods: before Edy Craig; Edy Craig and after; the sixties to the mid seventies. Edy Craig was the first woman in English theatre who consciously identified herself as a theatre producer/director, who wrote about this, who directed productions without also acting in them and who clearly worked in the way we would see a director functioning today, that is, taking overall responsibility for the artistic vision of a production. Craig was also a worker for women's suffrage, and the existence of the suffrage and suffragette movements at the end of the nineteenth and beginning of the twentieth centuries clearly made an important contribution to how contemporary women directors defined themselves.

Craig's career also coincided with a general change in the way theatre directing was perceived, when the modern notion of the theatre director was crystallising as distinct from the producer, the actor-manager, or the manager-interpreter who had 'directed' productions previously. Edward Braun (1982:7–8) in his study of seminal directors (all men, although he mentions Vestris, Littlewood and Mnouchkine) comments: 'Ever since Aeschylus supervised the presentation of his tragedies at the Athenian festivals of the fifth century BC it is safe to assume that someone has had overall responsibility for the rehearsal of any play that has reached the stage'; however, it is only in the last hundred years or so that this person has been identified as a 'director'.[1] Because Edy Craig's career reflects and contributes to contemporary changes in thinking about theatre directing, and about women's position in society, it is a particularly useful marker in this herstory. As the changes wrought by the growth of feminism in the sixties also had a marked impact on women's theatre practice, the sixties and onwards also provides another appropriate punctuation point.

Before Edy Craig

As women were excluded from the English professional theatre until the Restoration, it is reasonable to assume that professional director figures would have been male up until that time.[2] However, outside professional theatre, Katherine of Sutton, the abbess of Barking from 1367 until her death in 1376, staged and presumably directed her own plays, thereby following in the illustrious playmaking footsteps of Hroswitha of Gandersheim (c.935–after 973) and Hildegard of Bingen (1098–1179). In terms of the production of Shakespeare's plays, some have made claims for women functioning in a proto-directorial/managerial capacity as early as the Restoration, the period when women first began working in English theatre in significant numbers. Lady Davenant, Elizabeth Barry and Anne Bracegirdle have all been seen in this light.[3]

The first directorial woman I would like to focus on is Sarah Baker of Kent (1736/7–1816), a successful dancer/actor/manager who was described by Thomas Dibdin as a 'directress of the British Drama' (Dibdin, 1827:I, 94). Baker was not a director of Shakespeare in the modern sense of the word: she produced rather than directed Shakespeare's plays, and Dibdin (1827:I, 96) records that during rehearsals Baker ran a 'sort of levee for those of her establishment who had business with her'. Anne Mathews also describes Baker as 'too much occupied at her usual station, in letting boxes, and selling tickets, &c., to be present at the rehearsal' (Mathews, 1844:40). But while Baker did not take responsibility for the interpretative vision of Shakespeare her company was offering, she *did* have control over which plays were performed. It is also clear she was a good judge of what pleased her audiences – Baker was a phenomenally successful businesswoman and made a fortune running several theatres on her Kent circuit. However, she has generally been written about as a dotty eccentric, a joke, a theatre 'character' (Dibdin, 1827; Mathews, 1844). JS Bratton points out that this has significantly helped to detract from Baker's achievement as 'a successful independent woman in the theatre' (Bratton, 1994:45) who ran a 'matriarchal' company (51) and took on the male establishment (49–50).

Any woman who is unorthodox and successful is very susceptible to being defined as an eccentric, but such caricaturing needs to be recognised as a way of belittling that woman's achievements. It is a strategy of containment which was still being used two centuries after Sarah Baker by some reviewers discussing the Shakespeare productions of Joan Littlewood, constructing Littlewood as a 'loony left' eccentric, a theatre 'character' who shouldn't be taken too seriously. Both the semi-literate (according to Dibdin), generous, but extremely successful businesswoman, Sarah Baker, and the stoutly nonconformist, anti-establishment Joan Littlewood represented threats to the privileged status quo because of their dangerous combination of unorthodoxy and success. One effective way of defusing that threat was to classify them as eccentrics.

Another strategy Bratton identifies in the marginalisation of Sarah Baker is 'the reading of her management style as "domestic"' (Bratton, 1994:52), a tactic which turns up repeatedly in relation to one of the most important directors of the nineteenth-century stage: Eliza Vestris (1797–1856). Vestris had an extraordinary career as a director, manager, actor, singer and dancer. Yet too often writers have discussed Vestris' work as if, instead of managing a theatre, she was doing the housekeeping or as if, instead of revolutionising stage design, she was tastefully ('taste' is a word used ad nauseam in relation to Vestris) rearranging knick-knacks in the drawing room.

Vestris herself sometimes used the discourse of domesticity very strategically: in her opening address at the Olympic Theatre, where she had just taken over control as manager, she identified herself as an heroic pioneer, comparing herself with Joan of Arc, and asked her audience to:

> Cheer on the enterprise, thus dared by me!
> The first that ever led a company!
> What though, until this very hour and age,
> A lessee-lady never owned a stage![4]

She then added more conventionally:

> In this, my purpose, stand I not alone –
> All women sigh for houses of their own.

Positioning herself alongside 'all women' and claiming a 'domestic' basis to her ambitions helped Vestris appear more conventional than was suggested either by her move into theatre management or by her sensational early career as a popular travesty performer, famous for displaying her legs. However, the discourse of domesticity always sat somewhat awkwardly with a woman who didn't have any children, who was extravagant to the point of two bankruptcies, who had an adventurous love life, who inspired pornographic literature and who married a man younger than herself, an event which inspired much scurrilous comment at the time.

Nevertheless, invoking the discourse of domesticity in relation to Vestris is a recurring and limiting motif in commentary on her work. One aspect of Vestris' working practice which laid her open to this was what Clifford Williams (1973:99) describes as her 'considerate management', whereby Vestris (unusually for the time) offered her performers security and dependable salaries instead of the lottery of benefit performances. In Vestris' theatres:

> Authority was delegated and responsibility assumed unless and until it proved either misplaced or diminished. Good manners and efficient work were presumed. Individual cases of distress, professional or personal, were brought to the notice of the management and help given (Williams, 1973:99).

This consideration contrasted starkly with the autocratic regimes of other actor-managers of the time. Vestris also made her various theatres comfortable for her performers:

> The Green-Room was exceedingly comfortable during the Mathews and Vestris management…In fact, the reign of Vestris and her husband might be distinguished as the *drawing-room management* (Vandenhoff, 1860:53).[5]

The phrase 'drawing-room management' suggests Vestris was feminising and domesticating the theatre; however, she could equally be seen to be actively colonising a public space and installing her own personal values and agendas. She was contributing to the push towards a family oriented, middle-class theatre, which may sound like anathema today, but in the 1830s and 1840s helped to reform audience behaviour, which frequently included fights, riots and disturbances, drowning out performers' voices.

Another tactic used to belittle Vestris has been simply to refuse her credit for what she did. Clifford Williams' biography of Vestris, for example, diminishes her achievements even as he claims to celebrate them. Williams disparages Vestris in two obvious ways. First, he constantly refers to her as 'Madame', which makes her sound as if she's running a brothel. (When he is announcing one of Vestris' ground-breaking moments, when she became 'the first of a new species: an actress/manageress in London', Williams (1973:96) then refers to her, patronisingly, as 'the Fair Lessee'.) The second technique is to undermine her achievements by adding a diminishing proviso to his praise. For example, having claimed that Vestris' theatrical innovations were such that she was pre-empting Ibsen's *Doll's House* and 'Potential Norahs and Torvalds were being made at the Olympic in the 1830s' (Williams, 1973:114), he then instantly undercuts this: 'it must be emphasised that no claim is being made for Madame Vestris as a conscious pioneer'.

Jay Halio (1994:23) achieves a similar diminishing effect when, in the context of discussing the theatre history of *A Midsummer Night's Dream*, he introduces Vestris as 'the Italian contralto', thus placing her primarily as a singer rather than as an interpreter of Shakespeare. When he cannot avoid writing approvingly of Vestris' restoration of Shakespeare's text, Halio again manages to disparage her by claiming her collaborator JR Planché deserves 'much of the credit for such integrity as the script retained'. As Gary Jay Williams comments (1997:98): 'had a male actor-manager been in Vestris's place, one doubts that Planché would have been given all the credit', and certainly Planché himself paid tribute to Vestris' impact on contemporary theatre, and the personal care she took over her productions (Planché, 1872:251–2).[6]

One of Vestris' undervalued achievements was that she produced a distinctly feminised version of Shakespeare compared with the rather macho Shakespeare produced by many contemporary actor managers. This feminisation, or emphasis on the female and the traditionally feminine, is something which can be seen in terms of her interpretations of the plays, her repertoire, and her stagecraft.

When Vestris and her husband Charles Mathews took over Covent Garden, the nation's leading theatre, many, including the former lessee Macready, felt they were not fit for the job. At Covent Garden Vestris was expected to produce the national playwright, Shakespeare, but she did not have a tragic, heroic lead actor in her company. So, logically, and in striking contrast to the dominant practice of her male contemporaries, she proceeded to produce Shakespeare with an emphasis away from the grand tragedies with their towering lead roles. Instead, Vestris tended to favour ensemble plays and plays which give more space to women characters. She opened Covent Garden with *Love's Labours Lost*, which was almost unknown on the contemporary London stage; and she often revived another play based around the humiliation of men by women, *The Merry Wives of Windsor* (Vestris played both of the merry wives at different stages in her career). However, her biggest hit was with *A Midsummer Night's Dream*, when she produced a very clearly feminised version of fairyland.[7]

Vestris' *A Midsummer Night's Dream* was popular and it was extravagant: it required 70 extras and included 14 musical numbers, although this was a reduction on the normal practice of the time. In addition, the production presented a very suggestive image of female power which was centred on fairyland.

Vestris herself played Oberon, the centre of power in the play, with 'dignified grace' and 'as she stood there with her glittering armour and fantastic helmet on an eminence, with a blue-tinted wood gliding by her in the back-ground, presenting different aspects of the same sylvan scenery, the effect was little short of supernatural' (*The Times*, 17 November 1840). However, Jay Halio (1994:24) is dismissive:

> A woman playing Oberon seemed in the nineteenth century to convey better than a man the 'ephemeral idea' of fairyland consistent with the taste of the age...Whatever 'impotence' or contradiction the casting of women for both Oberon and Titania might bring to the quarrel between the fairy king and queen was outweighed by this consideration.

Halio's reading of 'impotence' and 'contradiction' is very loaded and ignores the possibility, despite extensive discussion of the homo-eroticism of the original all-male stagings of Shakespeare's plays, that this all-female vision could have been erotic on a lesbian as well as a heterosexual level. It was also appropriate for Vestris to play the powerful director figure Oberon at a time when she was manager of the home of the national theatre. Gary Jay Williams (1997:93, 6) also points out that:

> A woman fairy king would have addressed the patriarchal Victorian culture in complex, fascinating ways. Once again a woman was on the English throne, and in this production of a play resonant with the anxieties of Elizabethan men not in control of their women...an eroticized woman theatre manager stepped into the role of a male ruler.

Vestris recast the obnoxious taming of Titania by rendering all the principals of this action female (Puck was played by a young girl), and so fairyland became a female-dominated space. The subject of traditional notions of femininity and masculinity was also provocatively to the fore: Vestris appeared as Oberon, with her legs on display and with a slender, phallic spear beside her; the girl Puck first arrived onstage sitting on top of a mushroom, which pushed up through a hole in the floor of the stage; the extremely Amazonian Hippolyta wore a costume which quite precisely presaged the rational dress advocated by Amelia Bloomer, a knee-length tunic and bloomers (Fletcher, 1987:28).

By appropriating the role of Oberon so successfully, Vestris helped nurture a tradition which increased the number of roles for women in nineteenth-century Shakespeare; many subsequent Oberons (and Pucks and Ariels) were played by women.[8] However, crucially, as Trevor Griffiths (1979:396) acknowledges, Vestris:

> was the first person to present Shakespeare's text of *A Midsummer Night's Dream* for more than two hundred years, and she did this at a time when unShakespearean adaptations of many of the plays still held the stage... The loss of four hundred words is to be regretted, but we should regard this production primarily as the reclamation of seventeen hundred for the stage.[9]

Griffiths also speculates as to why Vestris' 'massive' (1979:396) achievement has been marginalised; in a later commentary (1996:24) he suggests that:

> Partly this is because Vestris's two successors as *Dream* producers, Samuel Phelps and Charles Kean, had longer managerial careers and more effective partisans and publicists, partly it is because Vestris herself, the object of erotic speculation as 'a woman with a past', was a dubious figure for a theatre that was bent on establishing its own respectability in order to attract a more respectable audience.[10]

In fact simply being a woman and a theatrical pioneer rendered Vestris problematic for conservative theatre historians and they reacted by failing to pay her her due. Alan Fischler (1995) has indicated something of the extent to which this is the case, in his review of the way in which so many of Vestris' innovations in theatre practice, such as the use of realistic, low-key acting, realistic box sets, scrupulous rehearsing and re-rehearsing, have subsequently been attributed to others, especially men.[11]

The American-born actress Mary Anderson (1859–1940) deserves special attention in tracing a history of women directing Shakespeare, because she was the first woman to do battle with Shakespeare in his birthplace, Stratford-upon-Avon. In her memoirs Anderson never identifies herself as a director but she *does* record intervening in a directorial fashion in the productions of Shakespeare's plays in which she starred. For example, she discusses her research on and editing of the text for *The Winter's Tale* (Anderson, 1896:246), with which she had a huge success, at Henry Irving's Lyceum theatre in 1887. Dennis Bartholomeusz (1982:118) talks of the text of Anderson's *Winter's Tale* being 'emasculated' as 'anything that taxed the brain over much was dropped'. Nevertheless, Anderson's high handed treatment of *The Winter's Tale* created an ideal vehicle for her acting (she played Hermione and Perdita, the first recorded instance of this doubling), and her *Winter's Tale* was so popular it played for 166 nights. Earlier in 1884 Anderson also had considerable success playing Juliet in her production of *Romeo and Juliet* at the Lyceum, and William Winter, who saw her play Juliet 35 times (1969:II, 176), records (1969:II, 173) that Anderson travelled to Verona specifically to study the location of the play so that she could ensure a genuine Italian flavour for her production.

My claim that Anderson was the first woman director at Stratford is of course contentious – her stage manager Napier Lothian might equally be labelled the director of the 1885 *As You Like It*; however, the production was popularly seen to be Anderson's and it was Anderson who was the draw card. Stratford was besieged with national and international reviewers who had never visited its theatre before and who had to find accommodation in Leamington Spa because Stratford itself was overwhelmed by theatre-goers. The production was completely sold out, despite the fact that ticket prices were quadrupled, and raised over £100 pounds for the Shakespeare Memorial Theatre where Anderson became a life-governor.

Reviews mostly concentrated on Anderson's reading of Rosalind. Many felt that her masculinity or mannishness as Ganymede was surprising and several disapproved because they felt Rosalind's femininity should be shining through her disguise. Several reviewers also commented on Anderson's determination, when playing Rosalind as Ganymede, to cover her legs as much as possible with her cloak. This must have disappointed those reviewers (for example the *Sporting Times*) who seem to have travelled to Stratford primarily to get a look at her legs. Anderson's famous contralto voice was also much appreciated but she was sometimes felt to be turning the play into a tragedy.

Anderson had very strong, romantic feelings about Shakespeare and Stratford, and records spending time sitting 'alone in the room where the great bard was born' (Anderson, 1896:130-31) as well as arranging to be locked into Holy Trinity Church (where Shakespeare is buried) during the janitor's tea break. Anderson then recited Juliet's death speeches whilst kneeling at Shakespeare's grave and was terrified when a storm immediately broke out (Farrar, 1884:53-4).

Despite her great successes on stage, in 1889 Anderson married and retired from the theatre (except for giving charity performances). In her memoirs she identifies her discomfort with the public gaze, intrusions on her privacy by fans, and the repetitive nature of her life when appearing in one of her long-running hit productions, as crucial factors in her retirement. Of course, in addition, many actresses retired from the stage on marrying because the profession was still not deemed respectable. Even in the most 'virtuous' of women, and Anderson's scrupulous attention to virtue was very much part of her public profile, the exposure of the actress onstage to the public gaze was seen as very problematic.

The intensely 'virtuous' Anderson makes an interesting comparison with her complete opposite in the virtue stakes — the 'scandalous' Eliza Vestris. Although both women are remembered as actresses, their directorial achievements have been obscured, despite the fact that Vestris exerted ultimate artistic control over most of her productions – and indeed was liable to fly into a tantrum if her control was challenged – and despite the fact that Anderson tried in her memoirs to make a record of her directorial-style work.

Anderson's success at the Lyceum invites comparison with Ellen Terry's work in the same theatre. Terry (1847–1928) was the mother of two directors – Edy and Edward Gordon Craig – but she was never primarily a director herself, although she clearly did do directorial work. Something of the politics of identifying a nineteenth-century actress as what we would now call a directorial figure can be discerned from the propaganda war waged between Terry's children, Edy and Edward Gordon Craig, shortly after her death. Edy Craig published Terry's correspondence with George Bernard Shaw and promoted the image of her mother as a serious intellectual. Edward Gordon Craig wrote a book dedicated to refashioning the great actress Ellen Terry as his adoring mother, 'little Nelly' (Craig, 1931:vii), a woman who would have loved to live a domesticated life but tragically had to go out to work. In another book paying tribute to the career of Terry's professional partner, Henry Irving, Gordon Craig also categorically denounced suggestions that 'without Ellen Terry to help him in the production of a play, [Irving's] productions would not have been so beautiful' (Craig, 1930:94) and asserted:

> Ellen Terry was all actress: with a woman's taste for lovely things, responding to music, to painting, to sculpture and architecture, as a highly gifted woman of temperament ever responds to these things – but creative as a stage producer, no (Craig, 1930:94).

Gordon Craig is contradicted by Terry herself (1982:111), who in her memoirs discusses, for example, her contribution to lighting design at the Lyceum. Terry also explains that she was the one performer Henry Irving did not give direction to – so her performances were self-directed – and that in relation to performances by other women in the company, 'Sometimes [Irving] would ask me to suggest things to them, to do for them what he did for the men' (Terry, 1982:108). If Irving was directing the men, then it seems rational that Terry must have been directing the women.

Terry was also very comfortable with the notion of women managing/directing stage productions: she admired Sarah Bernhardt for showing 'herself the equal of any man as a manager. Her productions are always beautiful; she chooses her company with discretion, and sees to every detail of the stage-management' (Terry, 1982:140). Terry herself was directed by several women early in her career although some of these experiences sound traumatic. Terry (23) relates Madame Albina de Rhona would call out directions at her: '"Take down your hands... *Mon Dieu*! It is like an ugly young *poulet* going to roost!" 'and on one occasion de Rhona 'flew at me like a wild-cat and shook me' (24); in another production the director Leonora Wigan shouted at Terry (44) from the stalls '"*Stand still!*... Now you're of value!" "Motionless! Just as you are! *That's* right."' Ellen Kean's directions included (12) '*You must plaster that "but" on the white wall at the back of the gallery*' and, in coaching Terry for the role of Arthur in *King John*, Ellen Kean 'stormed at me, slapped me', although, 'When the rehearsal was over, she gave me a vigorous kiss' (16). Ellen Kean's crucial role in training Terry is acknowledged in the memoirs of Squire and Marie Bancroft (1909:179), who describe Terry as 'Ellen Kean's child-pupil', and even Gordon Craig (1931:80) admits that Ellen Kean was a seminal influence in Terry's career.

Ellen Kean stands usefully, like Marie Wilton (Lady Squire Bancroft), for the many married women whose directorial role is hard to recover because it was subsumed by their husband's.[12] Vivien Gardner (1992:10) comments: 'Whilst the actress-manager was never a significant rival *numerically* to the actor-manager in the nineteenth century, she did constitute a significant challenge to the traditional notions of a woman's place', and this is partly why so many women managers preferred 'to allow male colleagues to be the public face of the management'. To be seen as a managing, directing woman, even in the comparatively unorthodox world of the theatre, was problematic. However, in her memoirs, Ellen Terry (1982:7) remembers Ellen Kean as an equal to her actor-manager husband Charles and 'the leading spirit in the theatre: at the least, a joint-ruler, not a queen-consort' (1982:11).

One nineteenth-century woman director who did operate completely independently of her husband was Lillie Langtry (1852–1929), now mostly remembered as a professional beauty and mistress to royalty. Langtry produced several Shakespeares including *As You Like It, Macbeth* and *Antony and Cleopatra.* Her theatre productions were fussily, but fashionably, decorative – her *Antony and Cleopatra* (1890) included an 'Alexandrian Festival', an 'Egyptian Dance by the Princess's Ballet', a 'Triumphal Reception of Antony by Cleopatra', a 'March of Roman Legions', a 'Bacchante Dance' and, as *The Times* (19 November 1890) reported, the ceremonious introduction of a mummy. Nevertheless Langtry was a shrewd businesswoman and managed to fill theatres by the drawing power of her beauty and her name.[13]

James Brough (1975:275) characterises Langtry's theatre management and direction as decisive, full of attention to detail in 'costumes, scenery, makeup, contracts'. He states:

> A succession of managers had to be taught not to question her taste for extravagance in putting on a play.
>
> 'No doubt you are right,' she would tell them, 'but I want it, and it *is* my money, isn't it?' (Brough, 1975:275)

A different view is taken by Norman Marshall (1962:13), who describes Langtry as an unreliable, careless and irresponsible director. Of a revival of *As You Like It,* he comments:

> Usually Lily [sic] Langtry herself directed the plays in which she appeared, but as she had acted Rosalind before, she saw no

necessity for rehearsing with the company until shortly before the opening. Bored at the idea of having to attend rehearsals merely to direct other actors, she engaged [Lewis] Wingfield to produce and went off on holiday to Paris.

However, in her autobiography *The Days I Knew*, Langtry (1925:216) tells the story very differently: she claims she engaged Wingfield to 'lessen my work' but she returned from Paris to find that:

> Wingfield had not only arranged the scenery, but he had re-arranged the play in a manner so audacious that the Company, headed by Arthur B. [Bourchier], had struck work, and, the first night being advertised, I had to put in a tremendous lot of time to replace the scenes in the sequence familiar to Shakespeare and myself.

Langtry's autobiography is not an unimpeachable source but it does reveal her as intelligent, well read, and 'a serious student' of Shakespeare (Langtry, 1925:173). The notable gaps in *The Days I Knew* – such as the lack of references to Langtry's royal love affairs - suggest a woman very carefully and strategically constructing an image of herself for posterity. Langtry here makes a clear bid to be taken seriously as a theatre artist – as an actress, manager, director and producer – but Marshall's portrait of her as the spoilt beauty, bored with directing, attempts to undermine this.

While it is Langtry's fame for activities other than theatre direction which make it easy to forget her as a director of Shakespeare, the example of Sarah Thorne (1837–1899) is the all too familiar one of a woman working in areas particularly susceptible to being marginalised: the provinces, teaching and actor training. Thorne was a successful actress, who was praised for the naturalness of her acting (Morley, 1966:81) and was offered work in theatres all round the country. As a manager and director, Thorne worked mainly in Margate, Kent, a town where, as Malcolm Morley's history of

Margate and its theatres reveals, women often managed and directed theatre: Sarah Baker in the eighteenth century; Ellen Ternan, Charles Dickens' friend, directing her husband's school students in productions of Shakespeare in the nineteenth century (Morley, 1966:97); Sally Miles in the 1960s. Sarah Thorne's career, however, is particularly striking. Thorne managed the Theatre Royal Margate for most of the period from 1867 up until her death in 1899. Under Thorne's management the theatre frequently produced Shakespeare and Thorne usually performed in these productions.[14] In addition, from 1885, she ran a school of acting for Ladies and Gentlemen who were taught 'voice production, gesture and mime, dialects and accent, make-up, the portrayal of characters, the value of pace and the value of pauses' (Morley, 1966:110) at a rate of £20 for three months or £30 for six (109).

Thorne frequently directed her pupils in productions of Shakespeare. Violet Vanbrugh trained at Thorne's school, pronounced her to be 'a good producer and stage-manager' (Vanbrugh, 1925:31), and greatly valued the extensive grounding in Shakespeare that she and her sister Irene gained whilst working with Thorne (39). Many of Thorne's pupils went on to successful careers in the theatre – one of the most notable of these being the groundbreaking director Harley Granville-Barker.

The women directors considered so far in this herstory were not *primarily* directors – but then this is also true of their male counterparts of the period who were also acting and managing as well as directing, even if what could be identified as directing only consisted of dominating and stamping their individual preferences on their productions. With the exception of Sarah Baker, all of these women also acted in their productions, and this has distracted attention away from their directorial functions. This is particularly true of the star actresses who achieved huge box office success: Mary Anderson, Ellen Terry and Lillie Langtry. While individual aspects of some of these women's careers have rendered their directorial activities particularly vulnerable to marginalisation – Terry's acting, Langtry's love life, Thorne's location in the provinces – it is important to acknowledge that there has also been a basic drive not to recognise these women as directors at all; and that is a fallacy which must be contested.

Edy Craig and After

Edy Craig (1869–1947) is a crucial figure in this herstory, not only because she saw herself primarily as a director but also because she was a feminist and brought her politics into her theatre productions. Craig was multi-talented: she had experience of acting (often alongside her mother, Ellen Terry, and Henry Irving); she ran an acclaimed, if financially unviable, costume workshop in London; she produced and directed theatre, especially pageants, all over the UK for the Actresses' Franchise League, which was working to publicise the fight for suffrage; and her first company, the Pioneer Players (1911–25), a woman-centred company, put on a large number of plays for Sunday matinee performances. These plays focused on women's issues, were often written by women, and offered good acting opportunities for women (Dymkowski, 1992: 222). Later in her life, working alongside her partners Christopher St John (the pseudonym of Christabel Marshall) and Clare (Tony) Atwood at Smallhythe in Kent, Craig established a memorial to Ellen Terry and produced theatre there for many years, especially with her Barn Theatre Society (1931-9). Great actors of the day appeared in Craig's productions, yet Bernard Shaw commented of Craig and her brother: 'Gordon Craig has made himself the most famous producer in Europe by dint of never producing anything, while Edith Craig remains the most obscure by dint of producing everything' (St. John, 1949, letter XLV:85).

Craig directed Shakespeare in several different contexts ranging from full-scale productions to 'scenes from Shakespeare' vehicles for Terry, from Shakespeare birthday celebrations at the Old Vic to Terry memorial performances. Although some scenes performed at Smallhythe 'were lifted complete from current West End productions' a proportion would also 'be specially prepared, often rehearsed in Edy's London flat' (Thomas, 1989:10). Certainly Adlard (1949:147) attributes the *Macbeth* at Smallhythe that she remembers to Craig's vision:

> It was a grand performance, Gielgud a tired, worn, haunted Macbeth and Martita Hunt as his Lady, looking like a lovely but wicked fairy, with a brushed-up aureole of red curls framing her white face. Edy's magic turned a tiny stage into the dim, cold halls of a Scottish castle and the whole production was a triumph.

Craig also directed several full-scale Shakespeare plays for the British Empire Shakespeare Society in the 1920s – *Henry VI*, *Richard III*, *Henry VIII* – as well as a *Merry Wives of Windsor* for Ashford Conservative Association in Kent in 1936.[15]

In an article on 'Producing a Play' published in 1907, Craig explicitly discusses her metamorphosis into a director.[16] Craig states that her actions caused 'quite a flutter in the dove-cots of the London newspapers' because 'I was the first woman stage-manager on record; I was the pioneer of a new departure in theatrical enterprise!' and she was asked by the press how she felt about 'the grave responsibilities of a revolutionary!' (311). Craig explains that she learnt directing from watching Henry Irving (311). Later, on Ellen Terry's provincial tours, 'I was not called either stage-manager or stage-director, but I did the work.' In this article Craig (311–12) also argues against her brother Edward Gordon Craig's views on theatre directing; by contrast with Gordon Craig's controlling vision, Edy Craig wants all theatre workers, including those playing the smallest of roles, to think, be responsive and not allow themselves to become machines. She also comments (314) that, for a woman, directing in America is much more comfortable than in England where men resent 'a woman "bossing" them in a professional capacity'.[17] Craig here may have been playing down the directorial work of women in the past, but her conscious perception of herself as a director makes her career a turning point in any history of women directors.

Nearly thirty years after this interview Edy Craig is quoted in the *Hastings and St Leonards Observer* (20 May 1933) as saying that directing was a 'branch of [theatre] work which was specially suited to women' and that women directors were better than men where actresses were concerned: she implies that actresses spend time flirting with male directors but with a woman director an actress is keen to get on with the job. She also somewhat optimistically claims, 'If you know your job there is no actor who will resent you because you are a woman'; however, of directors in general she comments: 'There are a lot of men who do not know their jobs and get away with it' – something Craig doesn't think a woman director would 'get away with'.

Craig did not achieve much commercial success as a director. In Eleanor Adlard's collection of reminiscences about Craig she emerges as a perfectionist who could create theatre (especially costumes) from the most unpromising materials but who didn't suffer fools gladly and was formidable when angry. John Gielgud, who is Craig's second cousin, adds to this impression of a difficult woman: Craig was 'an original stage director, but in her best years she was evidently too managing to be tactful or popular' (1972:23). Nancy Hewins, who did the lighting for a Craig *Macbeth*, takes a different view: Craig 'was nothing if not frank and the things she said to me were rather stimulating, and launched at me as a rule when I was at the top of a ladder. I enjoyed it' (Hewins, 64). Although Craig clearly inspired devotion in some, and leading performers of the time would work for her in her Smallhythe productions, Gielgud echoes many when he comments that Craig failed 'to gain the recognition she deserved' (1972:21) and that she was 'unlucky to have lived at a time when women were not greatly trusted with leading positions in the world of the theatre (except as actresses) and in consequence she always had a good deal of suspicious resentment to contend with' (1972:24). An article in *Time and Tide* (29 December 1922) also attributes Craig's failure to get commercial work 'in part to the determination of the male to keep the work of the theatre to himself'.

Certainly in terms of her Shakespeare productions, Craig is vulnerable to being forgotten as a director because of her lack of commercial success: when stars worked for her they usually worked for free; she often worked with one of the groups most marginalised in traditional theatre histories – amateur theatre; she did one-off productions which only played for a single performance and didn't get reviewed. The fact she was a feminist and lived in a lesbian ménage à trois probably didn't endear her to traditional theatre historians either.

Craig's career was largely contemporaneous with a period when, partly because of the women's suffrage campaigns, more and more women were moving into real positions of power in the theatre. Annie Horniman used her money to help establish the Abbey Theatre, Dublin and the Gaiety Theatre, Manchester; Florence Farr, suffrage activist Elizabeth Robins, and Marion Lea all managed theatres in their own right. Meanwhile at the Old Vic, the producer Lilian Baylis, known for her relentless economies and her dedication to God and opera, began to produce Shakespeare. Baylis, following the example of her aunt, Emma Cons, ran the Old Vic as a matriarchy (Roberts, 1976: 64–5), surrounding herself with women workers. Indeed the Old Vic was rumoured to be a 'lesbian stronghold' (Findlater, 1975:240) and both Baylis and Cons certainly operated within the lesbian networks of North Lambeth (Auchmuty, 1993: 83–6, 92–7). Because of its reputation, the Old Vic might seem to be the theatre most likely to employ the lesbian and feminist Edy Craig, but Christopher St John records Baylis as saying 'We don't want another woman here. And anyhow we don't want Edy. She would upset the staff' (Adlard, 1949:25). However, the first person to direct a season of Shakespeare at the Old Vic, in April 1914, *was* a woman, Rosina Filippi.

Filippi (1866–1930) was an experienced actress, a playwright and teacher, who claimed to be the half sister of Eleonora Duse. Once Filippi arrived at the Old Vic, she and Baylis were almost constantly at war. For example, Baylis placed slips in the theatre programmes telling the opera patrons:

> that although they might want to come and see the plays, they must clearly understand that they must not spend their Opera

pennies upon them. If they couldn't afford to pay for the two shows, they must come only to one, and that one Miss Baylis insisted must be the Opera (Thorndike, 1938:113–14).

Filippi complained about this and about having to stage plays 'with art muslin, two changes of scenery and two hired orange trees' (Findlater, 1975:105) and she demanded that electric lights be put in (Rowell, 1993:100) which the cost-conscious Baylis had been putting off.

Filippi's inaugural season of *The Merchant of Venice* (Hermione Gingold played Jessica), *Romeo and Juliet* (Filippi's daughter Rosemary played Juliet) and *The School for Scandal*, was not a box office success and the experiment in producing Shakespeare was temporarily abandoned. However, during the First World War, four other women followed Filippi's lead and directed productions at the Old Vic: Hutin Britton and her husband Matheson Lang directed *The Taming of the Shrew*, *Hamlet* and *The Merchant of Venice*; Estelle Stead co-directed *The Merry Wives of Windsor* and *As You Like It* with Andrew Leigh; Constance Featherstonehaugh (Mrs Frank Benson) directed *She Stoops to Conquer* and Mrs Edward Compton directed *The School for Scandal* (Findlater, 1975:119). The reason for the women's sudden access to the Old Vic stage was, of course, the scarcity of men, who had all gone off to fight. While there is no evidence that these productions were especially changed or marked by the fact that they were directed by women, the resulting large number of women who were suddenly directing at a major London theatre was a radical departure from normal theatre practice.

Despite the fact that she led the way for women directors at the Old Vic, Rosina Filippi is scarcely remembered now. This might partly be accounted for by her move into the lower status areas of teaching and actor training. John Gielgud, who played Mercutio in one of Filippi's 'Scenes from Shakespeare' productions at her school in Whitehead's Grove, recalls Filippi in 1920–21 conducting 'rehearsals with much authority and humour' although she put him out by playing 'twiddly bits' through his delivery of Mercutio's 'Queen Mab' speech (Gielgud, 1987:29). Gielgud also remembers that Filippi had 'a broad, motherly face, grey hair and a rich, jolly laugh' (Gielgud 1987:29). The motherly aspect was very important to Filippi, whose pupils knew her as 'Rosina Mother' (Thorndike, 1938:112).[18] However, playing up the mothering, nurturing, domesticated side of her work probably didn't help Filippi when it came to getting her directing work taken seriously.

The First World War also provided an opportunity for suffrage activist Lena Ashwell (1872–1957) to direct Shakespeare.[19] As an actress Ashwell's forte was realism and modern plays, but she had acted in Shakespeare alongside Henry Irving. Ashwell also ran the Kingsway Theatre for several years where she promoted plays written by women (Cicely Hamilton's *Diana of Dobsons* was a big hit) and dealing with women's rights.

During the war Ashwell began organising concerts to entertain the troops in France and she received 'a great number of requests for Shakespeare' (Ashwell, 1922:47). In response to this patriotic desire for the national bard, Ashwell arranged a scaled-down *Macbeth* (4 scenes) with Ashwell herself playing Lady Macbeth and, along with her team of women administrators, fund-raisers and performers, she then went on to organise hundreds of concerts and play productions. Women directing under the auspices of the Lena Ashwell Players included Penelope Wheeler, Cicely Hamilton, and New Zealander Rosemary Rees. Towards the end of the war Ashwell negotiated for her Paris company to play Shakespeare matinées at the Comédie Française (Ashwell, 1922:191), but the opportunity was lost when Lord Beaverbrook changed his mind and withdrew his support.

After the experience of running several acting and concert companies comprising over 600 artistes that toured battlefields in France, Malta, and Egypt and performed in sometimes appalling and dangerous conditions, Ashwell decided to carry on running a theatre company in peacetime. One of Ashwell's main aims was to bring theatre to as wide a community as possible. As a consequence, from 1919 to 1929, the Lena Ashwell Players toured outer London; most years they also played Bath, Rugby and occasionally York.

The Lena Ashwell Players gave Laurence Olivier one of his first professional engagements (minor roles in *The Tempest* and *Julius Caesar*) but Alan Webb, who introduced Olivier to the company, describes the experience of working for Ashwell in dismissive terms:

> our principal work was to travel about...giving performances of the classics in schools and church halls. The pay was miserable and the conditions worse, but what was one to do?...None of us took what we were doing very seriously, since we were all aiming for the West End and this was as far from the West End as we could be without being in South Africa or Australia. However, most of us tried to be diligent during actual performances (Kiernan, 1981:34-5).

Olivier, however, was not diligent and Ashwell sacked him for unprofessional conduct onstage. Olivier – who called the Lena Ashwell Players 'the Lavatory Players' because the changing rooms were usually lavatories (1982:32 and 1986:165) – is witty at the expense of Ashwell's company and describes them as consisting of 'would-be West End actors desirous of a change from constant disappointment, a few really·scruffy old derelicts, and a handful of desperate hopefuls like myself' (Olivier, 1982:31). But he does put Ashwell in exalted company when he is discussing successful women directors and managers: 'look at Helli Weigel with Bertolt Brecht, Maxine Elliott, Katharine Cornell in New York, our own Lena Ashwell, and for heaven's sake what about a dainty blossom called Lilian Baylis?' (1982:203).

At one stage Ashwell was running three companies simultaneously and trying to present a different play every week. With this pressured schedule, clearly, she could not direct all the companies' productions herself. However, Ashwell did direct several Shakespeares for her company and, what is more, she gave several other women performers opportunities to direct: Esme Church, Beatrice Wilson and Nancy Price all directed Shakespeare for her.[20] Ashwell's theatre ventures were finally brought to an end by financial losses, after years of subsidy by her second husband, Henry Simson, who lost £17,000 on the Players (Ashwell, 1936:250).

Ashwell also lectured and wrote about Shakespeare; her book *Reflections From Shakespeare* offers itself as 'perhaps, the first book' on Shakespeare 'by a woman of the (theatre) profession' (Ashwell, 1927:17). This book is unlikely to find many modern disciples offering, as it does, a heady cocktail of ecstatic devotion to Shakespeare 'the Seer' and teacher, enthusiastic Christianity, rapt visions of Merry England in the time of Shakespeare, reincarnation theory, seances, ghosts, ectoplasm and numerology. Ashwell's framework for understanding Shakespeare's women characters is that they reflect his life experiences: his bad marriage, his love for the Dark Lady of the Sonnets, his desertion by the Dark Lady, and his retirement to peace at Stratford. Ashwell is also very impatient of sentimental performances which she thinks render Shakespeare's strong women characters weak.

In her autobiography, *Myself A Player*, Ashwell is also forthright on the subject of directing: she insists that directors (and first-night critics) ought to do their jobs from the seats at the back of the gallery (1936: 263); she doesn't like modern dress Shakespeare; she detests directors who have 'every movement mapped out before a rehearsal began, even to the placing of one's hand in a certain place at a certain word, so that the actor was imprisoned from the start. Here began the most vicious of all the changes which have affected the theatre' (1936:256). She stresses the creativity of the actor, something a non-acting director cannot understand, and rather sweepingly equates the non-acting, tyrannical directors with Stalin, Mussolini and Hitler (1936:260).

Ashwell was also very aware of the gender politics of theatre:[21] 'The power is largely in the hands of men' (1936:261) who are mostly on the lookout for actresses who fit the current type of beauty. However, Ashwell was not above exploiting a sexual dynamic in her wartime concert parties and plays, when her predominantly female performers were playing for all-male audiences of soldiers (Holledge, 1981:99). Ashwell argued that her companies brought beauty, physical and spiritual, into the ugly world of the war and that the success of her war effort demonstrated beyond all doubt that theatre was not a luxury but an essential; 'my whole object from the beginning had been the demonstrating that the arts were essentially and vitally necessary to human beings, as necessary as the Red Cross' (Ashwell, 1922:132).

Ashwell not only wrote an autobiography – *Myself a Player* – which despite the title's emphasis, witnessed to her career as a director, she also wrote a book chronicling her wartime theatre companies' exploits, and another specifically on Shakespeare. Despite this strenuous self-advocacy, her work is little known today.

One of the most significant aspects of Ashwell's work was her promotion of other women as directors. One of her actor/directors, Esme Church (1893–1972), later acted at the Old Vic, became Head of the Old Vic School of Acting and in 1943 inaugurated a children's theatre on tour project entitled the 'Young Vic'. Church became Director of the Bradford Civic Playhouse in 1944 and taught at the Northern Theatre School. For the Old Vic, Church directed *The Merry Wives of Windsor* in 1942 and *The Merchant of Venice* in 1943 (at the New Theatre) but her most famous Old Vic Shakespeare was her 1936 *As You Like It*, starring Edith Evans and Michael Redgrave, a production so successful that it was revived the following February at the New Theatre.

At 48 Edith Evans was returning to Rosalind, a role she had already played ten years earlier. The production was Watteau inspired, and Muriel St Clare Byrne (1949:16) considered Church 'gave a pictorial and emotional unity to the whole play: never had it appeared so enchantingly fresh and lively'. However, Church's Orlando, Michael Redgrave, ridicules her direction in his autobiography:

> Esme Church, our producer, was of the 'Yes, dear that'll be lovely, let's do it again' school. I cannot for the life of me recall a single note she gave me during our four weeks' rehearsal, or whether she gave me a note at all. (Redgrave, 1983:104–5)

Redgrave's own view on *As You Like It* (105) is that he 'can think of one prescription only for any young actor who is to play Orlando: fall in love with your Rosalind', but he doesn't credit Church with realising that he and Evans, who were lovers, might not have needed heavy directorial notes.

A more generous assessment of Esme Church is given by fellow director Margaret Webster (1969:329), who thought Church 'a fine artist and much-underrated director'. The example of Esme Church, however, demonstrates yet again how easily a director (male or female) is forgotten. Not only did Church's *As You Like It* achieve West End success but photographs of her production – particularly of Evans and Redgrave (see plate 11) – are well known. But the production is remembered as the Edith Evans and Michael Redgrave *As You Like It*, not as Esme Church's.

Fifty years after Mary Anderson's visit to Stratford with her *As You Like It*, Irene Hentschel (1891–1979) became the first woman to direct Shakespeare at the Stratford festival. Hentschel, another protégée of Ashwell, specialised in modern plays so it was perhaps surprising that she was asked to guest direct *Twelfth Night* in 1939, but the build-up to Britain's participation in the Second World War was already beginning to provide more opportunities than usual for women.

For *Twelfth Night* Hentschel brought in the team of women designers, 'Motley', who 'were to work constantly at Stratford in the 1950s' (Beauman, 1982:159). The production design was controversial (see plate 12), as were the casting and interpretation of the play. Most reviews mentioned the fact that Hentschel was the first woman to direct at the Shakespeare festival and many agreed with the *Birmingham Mail* (13 April 1939) that the production 'shrieks at the conventions, flouts all the traditions'. The *News Chronicle* (14 April 1939) commented that Hentschel 'pays no attention to the masculine tradition that the new boy should show modesty and respect' and the *Stratford Upon Avon Herald* (21 April 1939) sleazily remarked that the production was 'a demonstration in which (as always when ladies kick up their heels) there was much to fix and fascinate the gaze'.[22] The decision to locate the action amongst eclectic Victoriana was much criticised – but Ivor Brown, who carefully skated round directly assessing Hentschel's direction (she was his wife) thought that the 'affected, over-worked mourning of Olivia' naturally suggests 'a Victorian mood' (*Observer*, 16 April 1939).

Critics were particularly shocked by Hentschel directing some scenes very farcically, by the production's inconsistency in period (Malvolio was Dickensian, Sir Toby Edwardian, Orsino Byronic Regency), and Hentschel's direction of Olivia not as 'the stately and mature lady we are used to but a charming little wilful heiress scarcely out of the school-room' (*Daily Telegraph and Morning Post*, 14 April 1939). Hentschel's reinterpretation of Olivia is particularly interesting given comments she made two years earlier on the distinctive contribution made by a woman director/producer. In an interview in the *Daily Express* (23 August 1937) Hentschel was reported as claiming the value 'of women producers is psychological. How can a man, demands Miss Hentschel, understand the feeling of a young girl in love?').[23]

Like the First World War, the Second World War was important in providing new opportunities for women directors, and it is depressing to consider that women directors were only given more access when men were away fighting and dying for their country, and theatre had a lower profile than usual.

Dorothy Green (1886–1961), who was a very popular actress at Stratford and had played a very large number of Shakespearean roles there, directed *The Winter's Tale* in the middle of the war years in 1943. *The Winter's Tale* was a play Green knew well, having, on various occasions in the past, played the roles of Emilia, Hermione and Paulina. Green had also directed the play previously: in his autobiography Anthony Quayle, a great admirer of Green's acting, remembers being directed by her as Autolycus in *The Winter's Tale* at RADA. Green 'gave out nothing but encouragement' although 'The worse we acted, the more she smoked' (Quayle, 1992:175).[24] Green's wartime *Winter's Tale* at Stratford was scarcely reviewed at all (the *Birmingham Mail* (10 May 1943) was complimentary while the *Stratford Upon Avon Herald* (7 May 1943) was not) and this was in line with the reduced scale of operations at Stratford during the war years and the focus in the newspapers on the war, which often left little room for anything else. However, the result is that one of the very few examples of a woman directing Shakespeare at Stratford has been almost completely forgotten.

1946 was a season of new beginnings at Stratford. Barry Jackson was hoping to turn it 'into another Salzburg' (Beauman, 1982:167) and he set about improving production standards by bringing in new talent. He brought in Paul Scofield as a lead actor, the youthful Peter Brook to direct *Love's Labour's Lost*, and he gave Dorothy Green the chance to do, as the *Birmingham Gazette* (11 May 1946) put it, 'a man's job' and direct *Henry V.*

Green directed Paul Scofield as Henry in absolute contrast to Olivier's portrayal of the role in his then very recent, immensely popular, film of *Henry V.* Green's production:

> deliberately tried to play down the militaristic elements. As Henry, Paul Scofield seemed to be searching for an interpreta-tion antithetical to Olivier's, a Henry less heroic, more humanized, more subdued and reflective, perhaps even more broadly comic.[25]

The majority of the reviews were positive, with local papers being the most enthusiastic. However, those reviewers who disliked the production disliked it intensely, and for them Green did not make *Henry V* enough of a hero. For *The Times* (13 May 1946) Scofield's performance lacked 'fire' and:

> the warrior King suffers more than anyone else from Miss Green's unwillingness to let her actors suit the action to the word. He is always tethered to a throne or to a council table when he should be on his legs.

Trewin (1964:38) also complained that 'we wanted the Muse of Fire'. A more sympathetic review suggested that as Henry, Scofield:

humanises Henry for modern sympathies…playing a convincing fighting man rather than a legendary monarch. If this tends to nullify the glory of a dubious war it also gives Henry more appeal for a war-scorched generation than he could otherwise command. (*Stage*, 16 May 1946)

The end of the Second World War also provided Fabia Drake (1904–90) with an opportunity to direct *Henry V*. In the space between VE and VJ day, Drake, who had been teaching and directing at RADA during the war, directed Henry V with a cast of actors drawn from the American army stationed in London.[26] Drake persuaded Renee Asherson, who had just appeared in the Olivier film of *Henry V* as Katherine, to reprise the role and Asherson's fiancé Robert Donat was so impressed with the results that he then asked Drake to direct Asherson and himself in *Much Ado About Nothing* at the Aldwych Theatre. Drake has very positive memories of this *Much Ado*: Asherson was a 'delicate, charming Beatrice' and Donat's 'humour gave such colour to Benedick's soliloquies that I have never, before or since, heard them win so much delighted amusement from an audience' (Drake, 1978:133). Drake also took a strong line on Claudio, too often 'cast as a "soft boy"', but who 'needs to have a jealous fire in his veins that will erupt, like Etna, when his honour is at stake' (Drake, 1978:134). In 1946 Drake's star actress Renee Asherson also appeared as Juliet in a *Romeo and Juliet* directed by Clare Harris at the King's Theatre, Hammersmith.

Ngaio Marsh (1895–1982) also directed Shakespeare during the Second World War. Although she had a professional theatre career – for example, she had success with *Six Characters in Search of an Author* at the Embassy Theatre, London in 1950 – Marsh also directed student productions of Shakespeare for Canterbury University, Christchurch, New Zealand for a period of over 20 years. Some of these student productions were major box office successes, went on tours of New Zealand and Australia, and included many rising stars (best known today would be Sam Neill and John Schlesinger). Outside of New Zealand, Marsh is primarily known for writing crime novels, but her theatrical career would come as no surprise to her readers, given that nearly all her novels have some theatrical content. Her detective, Roderick Alleyn, was named after Edward Alleyn, the Elizabethan actor who founded Dulwich College (the school Marsh's father attended); favoured characters often quote Shakespeare; and the novels open with a list of characters as if for a play. Marsh's final novel *Light Thickens* includes extensive details of a production of *Macbeth* (a play Marsh directed several times) and mostly reads as her ideal production.

Marsh's first Shakespeare, her wartime *Hamlet* (1943), was in modern dress. Marsh argued she 'wanted, first of all, to get rid of Eng. Lit. and say to the players themselves and then to whatever audiences we might win: "This is an immediate affair, it happens now and all the time. The predicament is ours"' (Marsh, 1982:239). Rachel Rogan (1994:16) points out that wartime shortages may also have influenced this decision, but Allen Curnow (1943) testifies to the fact that Marsh achieved the effect she intended with his comment on the opening of the production: 'As on some New Zealand coast defence post, so at Elsinore.' The final tableau – a silhouette of two soldiers carrying Hamlet shoulder-high – would have been particularly poignant for those in the audience with family and friends on active service.

Marsh's success with *Hamlet* launched her career in theatre and for Marsh directing students in Shakespeare was a 20-year 'love affair' (Marsh, 1982:243) which brought her 'greater satisfaction ...than anything else that has come my way' (Marsh, 1982:236). Her productions were notable for their pictorial composition – not surprising in someone who trained as a painter – their meticulous planning, their attention to detail, and their hostility towards the New Zealand accents of her students. Marsh would have to be seen today as an agent of British cultural imperialism in her massive promotion of received pronunciation Shakespeare, but at the time she was seen as an important pioneer who was laying the foundations for New Zealand theatre.

Marsh's student productions can be studied in detail, as Paul Bushnell has demonstrated, because so many of the prompt books and production photographs are still in existence. In addition Marsh wrote about her craft as a director, and as a famous crime novelist she still has an international profile which has resulted in her life and works receiving attention in a way that other directors' careers have not. Marsh is particularly interesting for this herstory, however, because she made a real bid to get into the Shakespeare theatre history books by writing an essay for the academic journal *Shakespeare Survey* about one of her productions – her Watteau-style *Twelfth Night* (1951) for the short-lived but fully professional British Commonwealth Theatre Company. In this article she describes her production in detail, warns prospective directors of the dangers of interfering with Shakespeare's text and spells out her own interpretation of the play. Marsh believed that every Shakespeare play had a core idea, and for *Twelfth Night* this was 'Illyria' and the revelation of 'several aspects of love' (Marsh, 1955:70).

The issue of self-advocacy is again crucial here. Marsh was confident enough to stake a claim for her *Twelfth Night* to be remembered and taken seriously by the academic readership of *Shakespeare Survey*, and although her production doesn't feature in stage histories of the play, that article ensures that something of her production – and perhaps even more significantly Marsh's own views, in her own voice – can be retrieved.

Marsh was also enabled in her theatre work by her personal wealth. She didn't *have* to make a huge profit every time with her Shakespeare productions (although she did direct several that were extremely successful financially), because her main source of income was her detective fiction. Nancy Hewins (1902–78) was also enabled by her background circumstances to have the confidence to do things differently – although here education was more significant than wealth. Hewins' father was a founder of the London School of Economics and Hewins read Modern Greats at Oxford. She became addicted to Shakespeare via the Old Vic, took theatre classes from Edy Craig and went on to light professional mainstream theatre, ballet and huge pageants at Greenwich and Hyde Park. With her professional all-female company, Osiris, Hewins toured for 36 years, up until 1963, and in that time produced 22 plays from the Shakespeare canon plus Marlowe's *Dr Faustus.*

When Hewins wrote her autobiography, she couldn't find a publisher, so she deposited the manuscript in the London Theatre Museum. In this manuscript Hewins comments on the lack of attention accorded Osiris: 'I dare say if the company had had a Russian name it would have been regarded as a remarkable experiment' (262). Osiris was remarkable not only for being an all-female company which existed largely in isolation from the legitimate theatre world, but also for providing extensive professional training for women in all aspects of theatre. It was also a collective which fed, clothed and looked after its members but didn't pay them enough to pay tax – during the war the company had to make gas mask cases to sell as well as averaging 260 performances a year (Hewins, 306). The company toured in two Rolls-Royces, while company members usually camped in tents. Osiris notched up some extraordinary achievements: *Hamlet* with only 6 performers; performing 5 plays in one day for the company's twenty-first birthday; playing Stratford in the Old Rectory gardens in 1955 and presenting 11 different plays in a fortnight.

Hewins started by founding the all-female Isis Players to tour Shakespeare to elementary schools in London and, when she found that the school children were receptive, without preconceived prejudices about theatre, and that they 'accepted an all woman cast for Shakespeare plays', Hewins then founded Osiris, which had its first professional performance in 1930.[27] Paul Barker (1995), one of the very few writers to have taken an interest in Hewins, cites references to Dorothy L Sayers and Margaret Rutherford as indicative of the Hewins style and quotes Jane Freeman, an ex-Osiris Player, who partly bases her characterisation of Ivy, in the BBC television series *The Last of the Summer Wine*, on Hewins.

Hewins was 'too busy' to marry (Hewins, 17) and is slightly mocking of the parents of her young performers, who 'were apt to think that any theatre company must be a hotbed of Vice' or 'a seething maelstrom of elemental passion' (Hewins, 203). The company recruited 'well-built girls' of 'average height, because a very tall or short girl would stand out and not fit so easily into a variety of parts' (Hewins, 208). Hewins stresses 'I never engaged a tough, square, hearty, masculine type of woman' (Hewins, 207) and seems to be skirting around accusations of lesbianism here, something which Paul Barker (1995) points out 'would have been death' publicly although there was one 'definite pair' within Osiris.

All Hewins' performers had to do stage management and operate lights as well as performing, and sometimes wore several layers of clothes to make doubling easier. Performers were so used to swapping roles that Hewins (285) records a *Macbeth* where there was confusion in the final duel because the performers playing Macbeth and Macduff were used to playing both parts and had forgotten who was who, and whose turn it was to die that afternoon.

Hewins' directing was constrained by the logistics of touring and performing in school halls, but although school audiences posed a tough challenge, Hewins (142) pragmatically targeted them because they 'could provide guaranteed audiences without which the company could not have been run'. The focus on schools meant that the reviews the Osiris productions garnered were usually school essays, and although the productions were seen by very large numbers of people, there are few records left apart from Hewins' autobiography.

Hewins' marginality in theatre history, is, of course, bound up with the perceived eccentricity of her all-female company. Playing Shakespeare with an all-female cast might actually seem like an important gesture of appropriation in relation to plays which premiered with all-male casts and which, when cast according to the designated sex of the characters, will always provide far more employment opportunities for male performers than female. However, while modern all-male productions of Shakespeare's plays have a certain kudos – because they have historical credibility even though they resurrect the sexism of the early modern playhouse – professional all-female productions like Hewins' are primarily seen as curiosity pieces.[28]

Margaret Webster (1905–72) provides a classic example of a woman director who achieved critical and box office success in her lifetime and yet today is undervalued and almost forgotten.[29] Webster directed *The Merchant of Venice* at Stratford in 1956 and *Measure for Measure* at the Old Vic in 1957; both productions were critically well received at the time and now are hardly ever discussed.

Webster (1969:280) learnt a great deal about directing from Edy Craig, whom she admired immensely and who lived in the flat below Webster's parents in Bedford Street, London. As the daughter of the actress, suffrage worker and chair of the Women's Franchise League, May Whitty, Webster was surrounded, from a very early age, by women who were feminists and activists. The fact that Webster's father, Ben, came from a theatre dynasty whose successes spanned several generations was also important; Webster's family were achievers. They were also politicised: Webster and her parents were involved in the early unionisation of theatre in England as well as the fight for women's suffrage.

Webster began her theatrical career as an actress and she worked for some time for Ben Greet's Company, performing a wide array of Shakespearean roles in unpredictable, outdoor, makeshift theatre spaces. Later Webster played several roles at the Old Vic including Lady Macbeth in 1932, and the Duchess of York (alongside John Gielgud) in *Richard II*.

Webster's first major directorial project involving Shakespeare took place in Kent, where she directed a Women's Institute outdoor pageant production of *Henry VIII* which had an all-female cast of 800 women. She had been directing for some time, mainly for tryout theatres or Sunday societies, when, at the time of the Edward VIII abdication crisis, Maurice Evans phoned her from New York asking her to come to America and direct him in *Richard II*. She worked flat out for five weeks with a cast largely inexperienced in Shakespeare, and created a smash Broadway hit which no one had expected. *Richard II* ran for 132 performances on Broadway and was revived several times before George Schaefer adapted the production for television in 1954.[30]

In his autobiography Evans (1987:120) claims much of the credit for *Richard II* but Amanda Rudisill (1972:51) sees things differently: Evans blocked the production before Webster arrived but she 'drafted a different and improved version. Mr Evans then left the arrangement of the play to her.' Evans' autobiography often tries to construct Webster as his artistic handmaid and stakes a claim on the credit for their *Hamlet* (1938) and *Macbeth* (1941), but even Evans has to concede that Webster was indisputably the artistic force behind their *1 Henry IV* (1939) and *Twelfth Night* (1940). Independently of Evans, Webster also scored some notable Shakespearean triumphs. Her *Othello* (1942/3) played to packed houses for 296 performances on Broadway, although it initially couldn't get any backers because it cast the African American actor, Paul Robeson, as *Othello*.[31] Webster also controversially cast African American Canada Lee as Caliban in her *Tempest* of 1945. She directed *Henry VIII* (1946), *Richard III* (1953) and, for Marweb – her financially draining bus and truck company which toured America in the late forties – *Hamlet, Macbeth, The Taming of the Shrew* and *Julius Caesar*. Because her company included two African American actors, some performances in southern states got cancelled. Other achievements included directing four 40-minute Shakespeare comedies on a small-scale replica of the Globe, for the Merrie England concession at the New York World's Fair of 1939.

Webster wrote extensively about her work, but her philosophy as a director is mainly articulated in the book she wrote late in life, *Don't Put Your Daughter on the Stage*. Here Webster reveals herself to be wary of the interventionist director who 'stars himself [sic]' and she claims of her own Shakespeare productions 'I never set out to impose myself on a play, but always to reveal it' whilst making 'the plays march' and making them 'exciting' (1972:89). She would take 'immense trouble' over small parts, directing all her crowd scene actors very precisely, giving them lines as well as business; indeed she was sometimes 'criticized for domesticating the plays and cluttering them with visual "business"' (1972:90). She worked in great detail on meaning and historical context although she was always ready to cut or transpose in order to make a play accessible to her audience (Spector, 1986:103). Writing in 1971, Webster felt her productions probably had 'too much scenery' but she adds defiantly that that was 'the age of scenery, and a lot of ours was good' (1972:91). Eva Le Gallienne (1953:247), herself an experienced director, paid tribute to Webster's 'clean, precise theatrecraft, her honesty, her rare understanding of the actor's problems, and her unfailing kindness and good nature'.

Webster is frank about prejudice against her as a woman director: one actor refused to audition for *Richard II* 'because he would not, he said, be subjected to the whims of a woman' (1969:379–80); she overheard gossip about her direction of *Richard II* – 'One woman and all those men – she must be fierce' (1969:381); Alec Guinness was reported to be apprehensive about working with her as 'women directors are customarily expected to be strong-minded and rather head-mistressy' (1972:131). When advised by friends to play the 'little woman' to make life easier when working alongside Terry Helburn, 'one of the very few people in my theatre life who made me conscious that I was a woman doing what is more often a man's job', Webster refused (1972:68). And when Glen Byam Shaw offered Webster *The Merchant of Venice* at Stratford, Webster had reservations: 'The British do not like women directors and they do not like people who have made reputations in America' (1972: 301).

Webster's major problem with *The Merchant of Venice* was that her Portia, Margaret Johnston, wouldn't play the trial scene in the way Webster wanted: as if in 4.1., when Portia enters the court of Venice, she does *not* know how to save Antonio and so has to think on her feet. Webster had hoped this reading would add a sense of uncertainty and tension to a well-known scene. Johnston first agreed, and then refused to enact this reading and Webster records how she diplomatically chose to avoid confrontation but she adds that, despite her and Johnston's 'excellent notices', 'I still haven't seen the Trial done "my way"' (1972:302). She was 'despondent' about Johnston's U-turn and reflects: 'Probably if I had been a few years younger, vainer and a fraction more dictatorial, I would have refused to go on with the job' (1972:302).

Webster's other memories of her *Merchant of Venice* focus around Antonio:

Anthony Nichols was a strong and authoritative Antonio. This was important to me. One should not ignore the title of *The*

Merchant of Venice. I began the play with the lonely figure of Antonio watching, apart, the chatter and bustle of the Venetian scene, and ended it with him, still alone, as the happy lovers dance away in the early dawn at Belmont (1972:302–3).

At a time when it was not as usual as it is now to play Antonio's homosexuality overtly, Webster wanted a sympathetic recognition of his apartness. This was presumably something she understood. Webster herself was someone 'apart': more American than English in Stratford; 'un-American' according to the McCarthy investigation she had been subjected to recently; and apart as a lesbian, travelling round the Cotswolds with her partner Pamela Frankau during breaks in rehearsals (1972:302).

Webster directed a very pretty, musical, decorative *Merchant* with contrasting moments of real nastiness: Emlyn Williams was an unsympathetic, villainous Shylock. Some reviewers detected anti-Semitism, but Webster contextualised this Shylock by providing a repellent and noisy Jew-baiting rabble, who made the most of Shylock's defeat in the court scene and whose appalling behaviour made sense of Shylock's attempt to strike back when he could. Shylock physically collapsed at the end of this scene and it was hinted that the knife he had brought to use against Antonio was now going to be used against himself. Johnston's Portia was generally applauded and the first two casket scenes were full of business which made them a lot less tedious than reviewers had anticipated; in particular the Prince of Aragon was vigorously sent up and became a comic hit with the audience.

The height of prettiness was perhaps reached early on (many reviewers felt the opening moments were the weakest) when, as Bassanio spoke of Portia, a vision of her appeared onstage through a 'diaphanous curtain' (*Evesham Journal,* 21 April 1956). However, the majority of reviews were enthusiastic and several felt they were seeing what the *Birmingham Mail* (18 April 1956) called 'A Woman's *Merchant of Venice*'. Many also felt Webster's American identity brought in freshness of vision. Webster's autobiography politely records that she enjoyed Stratford although (1972:302) 'It is not always easy for a visiting director to work in an existing repertory company. You have to accept prearranged casting and pre-established methods, and sometimes the company are a little "set in their ways".'

The following year, immediately after directing Verdi's *Macbetto* at the New York City Centre, Webster directed *Measure for Measure* at the Old Vic, hampered by a broken ankle, a feeling that the Old Vic was 'a club, closed to non-members, to which I had been graciously accorded a temporary visitor's card', and what she saw as unhelpful actors (1972:304). Webster's reading of *Measure for Measure* included a 'Heaven-Earth-Hell pattern', which was reflected in a multi-levelled set, and a concern with 'triple identity: every man is three people – the man he would like to appear, his public image; the man he himself likes to think he is; and the man he *really* is, the basic stripped essence' (Webster, 1972:303).[32]

Webster was dissatisfied with this *Measure for Measure*; years later when she directed the play at Boston University she *did* 'have an Isabella who was, as I am convinced she must be, truly young, innocent, passionately dedicated to becoming "the bride of Christ"' (1972:347). It is interesting that in both the Stratford *Merchant of Venice* and the Old Vic *Measure for Measure*, in Webster's own perception, her main difficulties were with her leading lady. However, Judi Dench, who, in her second professional role, was Juliet in Webster's Old Vic *Measure for Measure* remembers things differently:

Judi Dench: Peggy Webster was hard on John Neville, who was playing Angelo. She made herself very unpopular as a result. After watching John she said: 'What was it that made Gielgud so good in this role?' She was also very unpleasant to the designer in front of everybody. I remember she had a broken leg at the time, which may explain some of it.

The costume designs 'were of an abstract, modern nature and the actors disliked them intensely' (Jacobs, 1985:26) but after Webster 'verbally lambasted her designer in front of the entire company' they all united in the designer's defence, even though some felt that the designs 'made people look absolute idiots' (Barbara Leigh-Hunt, quoted in Jacobs, 1985:26).

Despite all this, most reviewers liked the production: 'Miss Webster conjures better acting and speaking from the company than we have seen or heard for some time there. She keeps the play moving unfalteringly even over the shoals of its second half, and fits its parts beautifully together' (*New Statesman*, 30 November 1957); 'Margaret Webster has directed the play with an unusual coherence' (*Illustrated London News*, 30 November 1957).

Webster tried very hard to make sure her work was not forgotten – she did lecture tours and recitals drawing on her experiences, she wrote books on Shakespeare, on her family history, on her own life and on her productions. While her work in the States is remembered – Amanda Rudisill (1972:230–31), for example, claims Webster's influence was far-reaching, particularly in terms of Shakespeare and student campus theatre, the growth of Shakespeare festivals and bus and truck companies – Webster's work has a comparatively low profile in the UK. The fact that Webster was directing Shakespeare in the UK in the mid to late fifties, the same time that Joan Littlewood was directing much of her Shakespeare and Renaissance drama, is also suggestive. Webster and Littlewood trod *very* different paths as directors – one worked in the traditional mainstream, the other in alternative politicised theatre – but while both succeeded in a man's world, and both wrote books about their work, both also had a major struggle to get their achievements in directing Shakespeare recognised in the country of Shakespeare's birth. Littlewood comments:

Joan Littlewood: I saw Margaret Webster act. She was at the Old Vic but she'd be all right because she was sensitive and very intelligent. It doesn't matter if you disappear. Nowadays they don't know what we did.

The Sixties and Seventies

The sixties are known as the decade which heralded new freedoms, particularly in terms of sexual liberation, and a loss of reverence for tradition. In terms of Shakespeare production, directors felt increasingly free to open up radical new outlooks on the bard and a generation of university educated, leftish male directors quickly set about relocating Shakespeare's plays in terms of settings, character sympathies and politics. Although the sixties also saw a new wave of enthusiasm for feminism, this had less impact on the Shakespeare establishment and there was no sudden increase in opportunities for women directors. Joan Littlewood carried on as usual without funding. Dancer, choreographer and theatre director Wendy Toye directed *As You like It* (1959) for the Old Vic and *A Midsummer Night's Dream* (1964) starring Ralph Richardson, a production Toye 'still remembers with great affection' (Cook, 1993:153).[33] Judi Dench was Phoebe in Toye's *As You Like It* and pays tribute to her skill as a director:

Judi Dench: Wendy Toye made me want to run to rehearsal. What was wonderful about her was her enthusiasm. She knew what she wanted and went for it. I don't particularly like the play *As You Like It* but I had a wonderful time being directed by Wendy.

Another notable achievement was that of Joan Kemp-Welch, who directed *A Midsummer Night's Dream* for television in 1964. Much later, in 1976, Kemp-Welch also directed *Romeo and Juliet* for television in an eight-part production for schools.[34] Kemp-Welch's *Dream* used Mendelssohn's music, ballet, and performers known for their comedy skills as the mechanicals: Benny Hill was Bottom, Alfie Bass Flute, Bernard Bresslaw Snout.

One Shakespeare arena where women were particularly conspicuous by their absence during the sixties was the newly formed RSC at Stratford-upon-Avon. It is only since the fifties that Stratford-upon-Avon has become such a major focus for the production and reproduction of Shakespeare. Sally Beauman's history of the RSC reveals how difficult it was to get London reviewers to travel to productions at Stratford before the fifties and Alan Sinfield (1985:158) describes the theatre at Stratford at the end of the Second World War as being generally seen to be 'artistically, culturally and politically insignificant'. This may be why Irene Hentschel and Dorothy Green were able to break the male monopoly on directing there around that time.

During the fifties, with the high-profile success of Anthony Quayle's artistic directorship and appearances there by stars such as Laurence Olivier and Vivien Leigh, Stratford's reputation improved. In the early sixties, with the formation of the RSC under Peter Hall, the prestige of the theatre at Stratford rose still further and now RSC productions are routinely reviewed by every major national newspaper. But it is precisely the crucial period of the early to mid sixties, when Stratford and the RSC were becoming more and more established as the prestigious centre of the Shakespeare theatre industry, that – despite the increasing general awareness of issues like gender inequality – women directors were completely absent.

Women directors have been particularly scarce on the often maligned mainstage at Stratford; a total of six women have directed there, something which seems ironic given that the space was designed by a woman, Elizabeth Scott, whose success over her male competitors in securing the contract to design the memorial theatre was much commented on at the time.[35] Women directors who have worked for the RSC in the last 30 years have tended to direct in the smaller theatre spaces and have worked more often with new plays than with Shakespeare.

In *Joan's Book*, Joan Littlewood regales her readers with the story of how close she came to directing at the RSC: Peter Hall had offered her a production of *1 Henry IV* so she went to the RSC's London base, the Aldwych Theatre, to look around, only to be thrown out by the 'odd-job man' (Littlewood, 1994:633–4). Littlewood abandoned the project very soon afterwards, irritated because Peter Hall wouldn't let her cast Zero Mostel (then being blacklisted for standing godfather to Paul Robeson's son) as Falstaff (Littlewood, 1994:635).

After Margaret Webster's *Merchant of Venice*, it actually took 15 years before another woman directed a Shakespeare at Stratford and that woman was Buzz Goodbody (1946–75).[36] In 1967 Goodbody joined the RSC as John Barton's personal assistant. Barton had been impressed by one of Goodbody's student productions and wanted a '"Girl Friday" slave and companion, but university-trained, who was keen on the theatre' (Chambers, 1980:26). Goodbody, a feminist and a communist, began directing on the fringes of the RSC, graduating to assistant director and eventually taking on Theatregoround, the section of the company which was aimed at what Dympna Callaghan calls one of theatre's 'most despised constituencies: schoolchildren' (Callaghan, 1991:166).

Goodbody was overtly political and this was much in evidence both in her productions and her public statements to the press. On the news of her appointment as first woman director at the RSC several newspapers (for example, the *Western Press*, 28 January 1970) carried the following statement by Goodbody:

> I'm engaged in some political work at home and I'm a Marxist-Socialist revolutionary.
>
> I find that Shakespeare does not contradict modern revolutionary thinking.

Goodbody was also repeatedly asked to make statements about being a woman director. She admitted she had encountered prejudice at the RSC but said she tried to ignore it and:

> I don't think there is any essential difference between a woman and a bloke when it comes to directing. I certainly don't approach people differently just because I'm a bird.
>
> If you can communicate something to somebody, it doesn't really matter what you look like or whether you're a bird or not (*Sun*, 9 June 1970).

However, it's hard to imagine Goodbody's male colleagues at the RSC being subjected to the sort of commentary this interviewer (like many others) offers. Readers are informed that Goodbody's surname is apt and 'She's leggy, curvy, well-endowed in the right places.' Even the obituary in the *Sun* (15 April 1975) described Goodbody as 'the shapely brunette stage director'.[37]

Goodbody also commented on how the rehearsal room dynamic could be affected by her sex:

> Actresses are in a paradoxical position because they are more independent than most women, but they are used to, if not sleeping with the director, at least flirting with him because he is a man and they are used to having him boss them around. I have to convince them that I have a different kind of strength. (*Daily Telegraph*, 13 July 1973)[38]

In the same interview Goodbody looked forward to a future beyond the RSC 'running one of the new provincial theatre companies' but she warned 'By 35 or 40 you can't take the strain any longer in a company like this' because 'you haven't got the physical stamina any more'.

Goodbody directed a cut-down *King John* for the RSC Theatre-goround, an educational outreach programme which toured extensively and played in a wide variety of venues, not all of them theatrically congenial. *King John*, with its emphasis on political shenanigans, seemed appropriate for an election year (1970), and the background conflict in South-East Asia. The production was satirical, broadly comic and featured Patrick Stewart as a childish and ludicrous *King John* who died farcically. Costumes were inspired by playing cards; AA Milne's poem on King John was quoted in a programme which also contained an anthology of derogatory remarks about politicians. John Russell Brown (1974: 3–7) identified a severe case of misdirection. Goodbody had:

> directed that the characters should enter marching like toy soldiers, that they should smirk, giggle and repeat phrases in

parrot-like chorus. They prayed in unison with mechanical gestures and toneless voices. Blanche's wedding was proposed with humorous over-emphasis and, at the end, a comic 'phew' was introduced to the text. For his death-scene, the king was carried on stage lumped unceremoniously over a lord's back. The director wished to stress the repetitions, self-satisfaction and self-interest of politics, and she did so with wearying completeness. The suffering, uncertainty, passion and moral considerations, so often suggested by the text, were crowded out, submerged in what director was telling us.

By contrast Colin Chambers (1980:28) suggested: 'Here at Stratford was the flavour of Littlewood, the living newspaper, a fast-moving, fluent, cartoon-strip production for all its faults, sardonic, grotesque – rolling Punch and Judy and a Plantagenet Ubu into one with the fun and excitement of sport.' The *New Statesman* (19 June 1970) also invoked Littlewood: 'Miss Goodbody has clearly been influenced by the fashion, derived from Joan Littlewood…for documenting history in stylised, simplified and often comic form.' Chambers (1980:29) adds appositely:

> Brook, who was an inspiration for Buzz Goodbody, was 'taken by the vigour' of *John*, which he found 'full of life, energetic, disrespectful'. What would the critics have said if his name had been on the programme instead of an unknown woman's?

King John was given a run on the RSC mainstage after the Theatregoround tour, but Goodbody's next Shakespeare was her major RSC mainstage production: *As You Like It* with Eileen Atkins as Rosalind, a production the *Morning Star* (14 June 1973) called the 'Women's Lib' *As You Like It.* Colin Chambers (1980:33) suggests that this *As You Like It* was an 'attempt, after the all-male National Theatre production of 1967, to win the play back for women', but Penny Gay's discussion (1994:64) of this 'so-called "Hair" production' (it included rock songs and paper hearts raining onto the audience) argues that the emphasis on sex and gender issues proclaimed in the programme and poster, created expectations of a feminist critique that were not borne out by the production (Gay, 1994:65). However, Goodbody was including so many references to contemporary culture – pop, the swinging sixties, androgynous youth fashions – that that other contemporary issue, 'women's lib', was likely also to be in circulation for many in the audience.

Goodbody wanted to place her characters in 'a convincing social context' and yet saw the world of Arden as unreal: 'Hardly anyone seems to do any work: the shepherds and shepherdesses – Phoebe, Sylvius and so on – are not really country people. I see them as art college students – drop-outs who live in the country and have mummies and daddies in town with large incomes' (*Birmingham Post*, 9 June 1973). This sense of unreality bred a forest of Arden made of thin metal scaffolding tubes. It also made the last scene – which Goodbody didn't believe in (Gay, 1994:65) – difficult. An additional problem was the relationship between Goodbody and Eileen Atkins who was playing Rosalind (Chambers, 1980:30); at the time the *Sunday Telegraph* (17 June 1973) commented: 'It did not require inside knowledge to sense a lack of rapport between the director and her leading lady.'

Being feminist in conception, it's not surprising that the production was disliked by many reviewers who were generally only willing to praise Richard Pasco's Chekhovian Jaques, although several reviewers did mention, condescendingly, that the audience around them, inexplicably, seemed to be enjoying themselves. The reviewers' praise of Pasco often suggested that he had succeeded in spite of the rest of the production he was in, but in an interview Barbara Leigh-Hunt (Pasco's wife) claims Pasco 'firmly believes that [Goodbody] got out of him one of the best performances he's ever given' (Hay, 1984:16). Sheila Hancock (1987:172) comments:

The male critics wax sentimental nowadays over Buzz Goodbody, but when she was alive they were far less perceptive about her work. They viciously attacked her one main-house production of *As You Like It*, which destroyed her confidence for large-scale work, and ironically she died before her best reviews – *Hamlet* – were published.

In 1974 Goodbody became Artistic Director of The Other Place at Stratford where she directed two Shakespeares: *King Lear* in 1974 and *Hamlet* in 1975. *King Lear* was heavily cut to accommodate school visits which included post-performance discussion. Here again Goodbody directed as a feminist; the sisters were strong women in conflict with an infuriating father and their husbands – France, Cornwall and Albany – were all cut. Goodbody also directed as a Marxist; the production opened with a politicised prologue, spoken by Tony Church (Lear) and Mike Gwilym (Edgar) which juxtaposed contemporary and seventeenth-century attitudes towards poverty, old age and law enforcement. This prologue was only used for 15 performances (Chambers, 1980:61) and was a digest of a more substantial anthology assembled to offer provocative and educational material to schools. The prologue certainly provoked the *Sunday Times* (21 July 1974), which described an 'unpromising' opening which turned Shakespeare into a charity for the homeless, 'a sort of theatrical Shelter' and characterised the production as 'short on cosmic grandeur', combining 'harrowing force' with occasional 'lapses of bizarre vulgarity'.

The production featured a great deal of direct address and interaction with the audience. The focus on the women in the play was enhanced by the production's additional emphasis on domesticity, families and sexuality, some of it incestuous:

> [Goodbody] took solo sessions with the daughters and Tony Church, who had to shut his eyes and explore their bodies with his hands, describing what he felt as their father Lear: they went as far as forcing Goneril's legs apart when Lear curses her womb, to drive the point home (Chambers, 1980: 63).

The national critics – who were not invited to the production (Chambers, 1980: 39) – complained about the lack of tragic dignity, but the production was popular. It toured in the US, and the adapted text was subsequently used in a production in Brisbane, which starred Warren Mitchell and a young Geoffrey Rush.[39] However, once Goodbody was dead, the reviewers did an about-turn: *The Times* forgot the 'vulgarity' of her *Lear* and called the production 'the most dispassionate re-examination of the play since Peter Brook's 1962 version', and particularly praised the great spectacle Goodbody had achieved with 'a few banners on a bare floor'. The *Lear* adaptation became one of 'economy' (*Guardian*, 15 April 1975), whereas the previous year reviewers had complained of unduly savage cutting.

Goodbody's final Shakespeare was *Hamlet*, the first *Hamlet* I ever saw. I can still remember the excitement and the intensity generated in the sweltering heat of The Other Place in summer. Ben Kingsley was a dark, slightly balding Hamlet, full of unpoetic anger and rage. Denmark was peopled by businessmen in suits. The inner play seemed particularly bizarre to me: now, reading the *Guardian*'s description of 'figures in white paper masks lasciviously pawing each other whilst a copulatory rhythm is beaten out on a tabor', I can understand why.[40]

The production was played realistically, and was low key and very fast paced, with scenes overlapping each other. Flashlights were used in the opening sequence, and were shone straight into the faces of the audience as the soldiers searched for the ghost. The production was low on introspection, the metaphysical and the heroic, but high on dynamic action; even the final fencing match degenerated into an ugly, very violent brawl. Charles Dance's Fortinbras was a thug whose arrival was accompanied by the ominous offstage sound of jackboots marching. Kingsley's Hamlet slapped Gertrude frantically, over-reacted to the words 'father' and 'mother' and threw himself hard against a wall in frustration after he failed to kill the praying Claudius. Horatio was a Mancunian proletarian who didn't really seem likely to drink poison and join the dead aristocrats surrounding him at the end of the play. Ophelia covered her face with lipstick and wore Polonius' dressing gown when she mourned him. Laertes was fond of Polonius and overly fond of Ophelia. Claudius, a 'pin-striped, administrative mogul of the modern commercial state' (*Morning Star*, 27 May 1975), often seemed a reasonable man, who was upset at Ophelia's collapse. The reviews were all extremely appreciative.

Goodbody didn't read the reviews as she committed suicide before the production opened. Colin Chambers points to some of the pressures Goodbody may have felt and suggests that she feared 'that after almost seven years she would not "make it"' with the RSC, something which would prove 'to those who wanted to see it, that a woman could not be as good a director as a man' (Chambers, 1980:11). He also comments:

> As a director with the RSC, Buzz Goodbody felt the disadvantage of being a woman in an overwhelmingly male Company, run, however sympathetically, by men…The RSC was used to women in front of audiences or typewriters, taking voice or dancing classes, casting or planning, making wigs, hats and costumes, but on the rehearsal floor it was a different matter. Buzz Goodbody blamed herself when things went wrong, and felt that if she were successful they would say, 'what a good director', but if a failure, 'the woman can't do it' (Chambers, 1980:12).

In public, however, Goodbody expressed optimism:

> Actors simply aren't used to women directors. But all this will change as more women come into the theatre from the universities. Meanwhile one just has to learn to be tactful.

> Directing is as much handling people as having significant ideas about the theatre. You should have a talent for both. You have to be an all-round type – part psychiatrist, part favourite friend, part stool pigeon (*Observer*, 26 January 1970).

In the same interview Goodbody commented that she had 'encountered prejudice against both her youth and her sex in her brief two-year-old career…with the Royal Shakespeare company' but had learnt 'to handle this without too much trouble'.

Margaret Sheehy (1984:12) claims that the RSC developed 'a pervasive, guilt-ridden, tribal memory of the suicide of Buzz Goodbody' which created a notion that 'women crack under the pressure' and that this contributed to the subsequent under employment of women directors at Stratford. It was actually 1983 before the RSC let another woman director loose on Shakespeare when Sheila Hancock directed *A Midsummer Night's Dream* for the RSC tour. In her autobiography, Hancock (1987:16–17) has some trenchant comments to make on the subject of women workers servicing the work of male directors at the RSC.[41] Despite enthusiastic audiences during the months on tour, Hancock's *Midsummer Night's Dream* received unenthusiastic reviews when it played in Stratford. Hancock feels that her production 'had one or two new things to say about the women in the play' and this was ignored by reviewers, most of whom 'are from the same middle-class, middle-aged, academic, white, male mafia as the directors' (Hancock, 1987:172). Elsewhere Hancock has spoken of the RSC 'academic male mafia – the boys from Oxbridge who have got a stranglehold' (Martin, 1984:19). Although Hancock also talked provocatively about how she would like to direct Shakespeare and put 'female sensuality, gentleness, compassion and friendship into the plays' (Martin, 1984:20), Hancock hasn't directed at the RSC since *A Midsummer Night's Dream*.

Although women directors started getting more work at the RSC in the eighties, this has tended to be outside the Shakespeare/Renaissance area.[42] Experiences have varied widely: Brigid Larmour, who had extensive experience of directing Shakespeare outside of the RSC, found the company a 'deeply sexist organisation' (Manfull, 1997:16); Jude Kelly had a 'privileged time' rehearsing there with her newborn baby by her side (*Sunday Times*, 7 April 1996); Di Trevis found that family upheavals and directing at the RSC were an unsustainable combination. Deborah Warner perhaps has had most success with the RSC, directing a brilliant *Titus Andronicus* at the Swan Theatre in 1987, followed in 1988 by *King John* at the refurbished Other Place. Warner 'desperately' wanted to work for the RSC (Cook, 1993:102) and had a long history of directing Shakespeare for her own theatre company, Kick, founded in 1980, before she joined the RSC. Warner has become one of the most high-profile women directors of Shakespeare in the UK, going on to direct *King Lear* and *Richard II* for the RNT. Despite, for example, provocatively casting Fiona Shaw as Richard II, Warner maintains that 'as a classical director, her gender is less significant than the fact that she doesn't have a university background'.[43]

Since then the roll call of Shakespeare productions directed by women at the RSC is very small: in 1989, Cicely Berry directed *King Lear* at The Other Place, which was also where Katie Mitchell directed *3 Henry VI* in 1994; Gale Edwards directed *The Taming of the Shrew* on the mainstage in 1995. Given the large number of Shakespeare productions churned out by the RSC each year, the percentage of women directors seems woefully small. The artistic director of The Other Place at Stratford is currently a woman, Katie Mitchell; however, it's slightly depressing to reflect that artistic director at The Other Place was precisely the hierarchical position Buzz Goodbody occupied over 20 years ago. In addition, while The Other Place is generally perceived to be an exciting, alternative space within the RSC, it can only accommodate tiny audiences compared with the mainstage, and when women directors work there they are perpetuating the cliché that women only direct in small, fringe venues.

What is most noticeable about women directing Shakespeare in the period of post-sixties feminism is that realistically speaking, if a woman wants to direct Shakespeare, she still stands a far better chance if she founds her own company, works in the provinces, works in fringe, works in a summer company, works in education – indeed if she works almost anywhere except the RSC.

Feminist consciousness-raising has made people more aware of the fact that few women get to direct Shakespeare in the most prestigious theatre spaces in the UK but it hasn't done much to alter that fact, and it's sobering to reflect that even the most conspicuously successful women directors today don't compete (in terms of range of plays and numbers of performances) with some of their predecessors. However, it is worth celebrating the fact that there *is* a history of distinguished, diverse and challenging direction of Shakespeare by women even though this history's very existence has been ignored for so long.

It is also important to acknowledge that with the recent revival of popular interest in Shakespeare – because his plays have proven pulling power at the film box office as well as in the theatre – directing Shakespeare is as prestigious as it has ever been. This probably means that women directors will have to carry on fighting very hard if they want to direct Shakespeare's plays in upmarket venues.

However, despite enormous odds the history of MsDirecting Shakespeare from Sarah Baker and Eliza Vestris, through to Edy Craig, Margaret Webster and Buzz Goodbody, shows that women have been succeeding in this area for over two centuries.

Reflections

My interest in investigating the work of women directors of Shakespeare was very much encouraged by an early interview with Melbourne-based Kim Durban about her all-female production of *The Two Gentlemen of Verona* in 1988 at St Martin's Youth Theatre, Melbourne. This production of *The Two Gentlemen of Verona* seemed to offer one of the most intelligent approaches to the play I had ever encountered, and yet as an all-female, youth theatre production, it received very little critical attention. Durban's production highlights many of the issues which have emerged as crucial during the course of my research and so it seems fitting to finish with a brief consideration of this *Two Gentlemen of Verona*.

At the end of *The Two Gentlemen of Verona*, Proteus, the unfaithful lover of Julia, attempts to rape Silvia, the beloved of Proteus' best friend Valentine. In an astonishing fit of magnanimity, Valentine forgives Proteus as soon as he asks for forgiveness, and offers to hand Silvia over to him. Silvia, of course, is not asked what she thinks of this and Julia, who is present disguised as a boy, faints with the shock. Julia's faint allows her identity to be discovered and Proteus then reverts to his role of Julia's lover. Silvia's silence is deafening. Durban describes how she staged this moment:

Kim Durban: At the end of the production the two 'boys' walked off hand in hand, leaving the girls behind in wistful silence. Then they joined up, not so happily, and walked off together. Basically the girls had been forgotten; the boys were so much into each other that they'd forgotten their lovers. It's very teenage. Those boys get into an uncomfortable collusion because they're not able to face their own feelings.

Silvia's silence was particularly important to Durban:

Kim Durban: I'm very interested in female silence. I see it as my responsibility as a director to construct very carefully and deeply, the society in which these silences take place.

Silvia was blonde with little ringlets and she looked completely untouchable and inviolable, which meant that the attempted rape scene caused great concern. I wanted it to be as uncomfortable as possible. My performers, who were all girls aged between 10 and 16, were shocked at the way Valentine forgives Proteus and we had furious arguments about it. They all said, 'Shakespeare is a sexist pig.' I tried to suggest that Shakespeare was writing his play within a very closed system and that, even if *they* thought it was an appalling act and no forgiveness should be given, it was actually a very deliberate and conscious choice for the men in the play to forgive one another. But because I was furious too, I staged the ending so that it *was* uncomfortable.

Although Durban has a passion for Shakespeare and is a very successful director who has won accolades for major professional productions, she has very rarely been offered the chance to direct Shakespeare professionally:

Kim Durban: The perception is that Shakespeare is risky and expensive with very large casts, even if you do a cut-down version. It's seen as very sticky to give a woman a large production, particularly in a mainstage theatre; the resource risk is considered too great. However, I've had lots of employment opportunities where there are a lot of actors at my disposal because they're kids or students, and so when they say, 'What play would you like to do?' I've picked a Shakespeare. That's how I've managed to do so much.

Durban is also very politically aware. She identifies herself as a feminist, is a founding member of the Australian Women Directors' Association and, when I interviewed her, was passionate about reinstating the women directors of the past – such as Irene Mitchell in Melbourne – who have been forgotten.[1] It is hardly surprising, under the circumstances, that Durban is also conscious of the risk of her own work 'disappearing' from theatre history.[2] She is also very aware of her cultural location in Australia and her distance from the generally perceived centre of Shakespeare production, the RSC:

Kim Durban: I admired what I'd read about the RSC, the intelligence, the application to discipline, the precision, the history. This turned out to be romantic fog. I travelled to Stratford, I saw six productions and they were of six different colours from brilliant to the most awful schlock. Some of the actors I'd seen one night being brilliant were appalling the next day in something else, and I understood all over again how important directors are in the deal.

I don't any longer look to the RSC or England as the pinnacle of Shakespeare production. My visit gave me a very healthy respect for the work we do in Australia, because a lot of it is without bunk, it's direct, it's an attempt to communicate, it has energy. I found when I talked to artists in England, the ones who had no sympathy would say, 'Oh, so you want to do that? Someone did that here in 1953.' There's a kind of boredom with the whole notion of trying to do something different, there's a climate of scorn.

Durban's attitude is a determined one – if she can't do Shakespeare in the prestigious arenas where she directs contemporary drama then she will go into the less prestigious ones and direct Shakespeare there. She is determined to convert the 'disadvantages' of working in those arenas into advantages:

Kim Durban: Many people who came along to *Two Gentlemen of Verona* were threatened by the thought of watching young girls acting Shakespeare for hours, but it gave me a wonderful opportunity because those girls were the right age to be the subject of the kinds of discussions the play asks for.[3] *Two Gents* is about

youthful people who are capricious, who are learning to understand their own energies, trying to understand what it means to fall in love. The young girls playing the fathers did brilliantly because they well understood the situation of youngsters yearning for love but being under the thumb of a father figure. The girls were also pretty good at performing the loving boys who turn into liars, because they knew all about that.

They were also quite mocking of the gushy love stuff in the play and kept saying, 'Why are these lovers going on and on and on?' So we discussed why people *do* go on and on in love and I decided to make it a full-blown romantic production. I picked out a few slushy songs by Frank Sinatra and Nat King Cole that seemed to be very much about the content of *Two Gents* and threaded them through the action as a kind of a score. We used them for linking moments and to comment on how fake it all was; to say, 'It's fun but it's fake.'

In its clever use of romantic music, this production anticipated a successful RSC production of the play in 1991. In addition, Durban's *Two Gentlemen of Verona* was feminist, enlightened and enlightening. It was also entertaining, took risks and, as usually happens with theatre on the margins, was hardly reviewed at all.

Durban's *Two Gentlemen of Verona* raises many of the recurring themes of this study – the fight to find a space in which to direct Shakespeare; the usefulness of the margins when the mainstream denies you access; the confrontation with the sexism of Shakespeare's text; the focus on women characters and a determination to make their silences speak eloquently; the lack of critical response or appreciation. These questions don't apply *exclusively* to women directors of Shakespeare but, as this book has shown, they do apply far *more* to women directors than to men.

Perhaps the most crucial question of all, however, is, as Joan Littlewood pointed out, 'What about the future?' It is important, and encouraging, to acknowledge the extent to which things are improving. Little by little women directors *are* getting more credit and a higher profile in theatre, and in theatre history. Two very recent publications on *A Midsummer Night's Dream* (Griffiths, 1996; Williams,1997), for example, both give Eliza Vestris the serious consideration that is her due. Despite the persistence of the old boy network in the theatre and media, women *are* also directing more Shakespeare – at least, away from the RSC. Buzz Goodbody's hope that things would improve 'as more women come into the theatre from the universities' (*Observer*, 26 January 1970) has, to a certain extent, come true and it seems reasonable to predict that there will increasingly be more MsDirected Shakespeare around.

Something of the distance travelled in the last 30 years can be gauged by reference to the advice to women directors/producers published in 1960 by Alison Graham-Campbell, who devoted her life to amateur theatre, and Frank Lambe. Having stated that:

> We ourselves tend to regard women play producers in the same light as women car drivers: the really good ones can be brilliant, but they constitute a small minority; the rest seldom merit even half marks for proficiency (Graham-Campbell and Lambe, 1960:43).

the authors describe the woman director in very revealing terms:

> The woman producer has instinctively more understanding of the woman player's viewpoint; she knows the responsibilities of the woman who is wife and mother and has to run a home; she knows that meals have to be prepared, shops visited, children attended to, husbands pacified, and illnesses coped with; she is more able and willing to organise rehearsal schedules which take the vital time factor into account (Graham-Campbell and Lambe, 1960:44).

It is interesting to ponder what Joan Littlewood and Margaret Webster, two of the leading women directors at the time of this book's publication, would have made of this 'advice'.

Nevertheless, while it is important to acknowledge how much things have improved since Eliza Vestris started taking artistic and directorial responsibility for her productions of Shakespeare, there is still a long way to go. Women still have to fight harder than men for the opportunity to direct high-profile Shakespeare productions. And yet the future may offer new possibilities for women who want to overcome the existing male bias in the Shakespeare industry. Debates about the future of theatre in the face of competition from multi-media point to the fact that any woman who can operate a video can create a MsDirected Shakespeare of her own.

Finally, the determination and dedication to their art shown by *all* the women directors examined in this book suggest that if, like Kim Durban, women directors continue to be denied access to the most prestigious arenas of Shakespeare production, they will, nevertheless, carry on MsDirecting Shakespeare in the spaces that *are* available to them. So the answer to Joan Littlewood's question, 'What about the future?', seems to be that women directors will continue to provide startling new insights into Shakespeare's plays and their treatment of gender. And it is to be hoped that they, and the women who have been MsDirecting Shakespeare for centuries, will finally gain the acknowledgement they deserve.

Notes

Introduction

1. *As You Like It* also contains the transgressive figure of the woman priest, Celia.
2. For example, Ralph Berry (1977), Michael Billington (1990). This stricture is not true so far of Cambridge's *Shakespeare in Production* series.
3. For recent discussions of women directors see, for example, Michelene Wandor (1986:108–13), Clare Venables (1980), Rebecca Daniels (1996), Helen Manfull (1997), Ellen Donkin and Susan Clement (1991), Claire Armistead (1994).
4. In Britain in 1984 women comprised 12% of artistic directors (this being the real power position in a theatre); 41% of assistant directors; 24% of freelance directors; 17% of resident associate directors (Dunderdale, 1984). More up to date figures (Kenneth Rea, 1989:24) tell a similar story with the additional rider that 'while the percentage of young women directors has risen…more women tend to leave the profession by the time they are 50' (26). While the record of productions carried by *Shakespeare Survey* reveals increasing numbers of women directing Shakespeare, as a proportion of the whole, women directors still account for a small percentage of Shakespeare production in Britain.
5. Quoted in Carole Woddis (1991:7). Many of the actresses interviewed by Woddis comment on the lack of opportunities for women directors although several of them – Janet Suzman, Prunella Scales, Judi Dench, Carmen Munroe, Julia McKenzie – have directed productions themselves.
6. Pessimism about directing the classics is also expressed by Ellen Donkin and Susan Clement (1991:1). Linda Walsh

Jenkins and Susan Ogden-Malouf (1985:66) also warn of the dangers of Method acting in relation to 'an unhealthy gender role', a phrase which could apply to many of Shakespeare's female characters. More positively, Gay Gibson Cima (1991) helpfully lists 22 suggested directorial strategies for subverting canonical plays, which could be useful for feminist directors. In practice, stressing the grim sexist realities of the societies in which the women characters are operating is a commonly adopted strategy. Critiquing the male gaze in the theatre, and avoiding sexist blocking and casting is advocated by Sue-Ellen Case (1988:119).

Part 1 – MsDirectors

1. All bold print material is quoted from interviews with the author. All interviews took place in May and June, 1996 with the exception of interviews with Gale Edwards (January, 1997) and Helena Kaut-Howson (September, 1997).

2. Kenneth Rea's study (1989) reveals it is the norm in the UK for directors to have some acting experience (76% had; others had acted as part of their training and only 14% had no acting experience at all). Rebecca Daniels (1996:17) found a similar pattern in American women directors although Helen Manfull (1997) interviewed women directors who mostly had no acting experience. Over sixty years ago, director Auriol Lee (*Daily Express*, 23 August 1937) cynically commented that directing is 'the only thing for an actress to do when "they're fat and getting on".'

3. See Rebecca Daniels (1996) for a complementary study of several of these issues in relation to American women directors.

4. Private letter, 21 June 1996.

5. Samuel Leiter (1991) is exceptional in discussing Littlewood's Shakespeare productions in some depth. Littlewood also directed several other Renaissance plays including: *Volpone, The Alchemist, Every Man in His Humour, The Dutch Courtesan,*

Arden of Faversham, Edward II, Fuente Ovejuna (The Sheepwell) and an adaptation of *La Celestina.* For Littlewood's Jonson productions see Cave (1999).

6. *Othello* (October 1997) was produced after the interview with Brewster took place and so is not discussed in detail.

7. In 1984 Margaret Sheehy (12) complained that the vast majority of British theatre directors were Oxbridge educated men, while Pam Brighton (1984:50–51) stressed the power of the 'Oxbridge mafia, whether male or female'. However, by 1989 Kenneth Rea (24) was suggesting a move away from this pattern as students who want to become directors increasingly choose universities which, unlike Oxford and Cambridge, have drama courses.

8. See Lizbeth Goodman (1996:110) for Wright's thoughts on Harriet Walters' performance as Lady Percy. Here Wright also talks about 'the language of feminism' being 'appropriated' (111).

Part 2 – The Plays

The Taming of the Shrew

1. See Penny Gay (1994); Carol Rutter (1988); Graham Holderness (1989).

2. *Taming of A Shrew* quotation from additional passages (C.1).

3. Another Australian inflection was added to the play's theatre history when Sue Rider directed Aboriginal actress Deborah Mailman as Katherine in a production of *The Shrew* at La Boite, Brisbane (1994). Baptista and Biondello were played by Aboriginal actress Lesley Mariller; Bianca was a blonde white woman Kathryn Lister. This production was set immediately after World War 2, with Petruchio as a returned Digger, and was revived the following year, again with an Aboriginal Kate, Roxanne McDonald.

Much Ado About Nothing

1. *Plays International,* May 1988:28 commented disparagingly on the level of the farce business but had to add: 'The first night audience seemed to love it all.'
2. See Susan Bennett (1996) for an extended discussion of the phenomenon of nostalgia in theatre reviewing.
3. Interview with Judi Dench conducted courtesy of her secretary Sue Jennings. Besides *Much Ado About Nothing,* Dench has directed *Romeo and Juliet, Macbeth* and the musical derived from *The Comedy of Errors, The Boys from Syracuse.*
4. Dench is comparatively unusual in this view (see Introduction p.3); for example, performer Harriet Walter (Rutter, 1988:xx–xxi) feels 'It's easier to defy a male director' because 'If a woman's production fails...in a sense she has failed for all women directors.'
5. For Webster and Toye see pp.223–9, 230.
6. Penny Gay (1994:171) also suggests a mismatch between the evidence of Trevis' reviews and the production video.

A Midsummer Night's Dream

1. For other women-directed *Midsummer Night's Dreams* see Part 3 – Eliza Vestris, Wendy Toye and Joan Kemp-Welch. Although American productions are outside the remit of this book, there is a readily available discussion of Jill Dolan's exciting, gender bending, cabaret version of this play which turned the forest into a gay disco, Athens into an 'upscale Yuppie fern bar' (Dolan, 1993:154), Titania (played by a man) into a 'punk drag queen' (155) with a whip and Oberon into a 'fashionable, sexy, butch lesbian' (155).

The Tempest

1. The productions in question were: Belvoir Street, Sydney, directed by Neil Armfield; and La Boite, Brisbane, directed by Patrick Mitchell. All three of these 1990 *Tempests* had female Ariels.

The Winter's Tale

1. Howell also directed the play at the Irving Theatre, Leicester Square in 1956, at Hornchurch in 1966 and at the Bristol Old Vic in 1970. For Annabel Arden and Annie Castledine's acclaimed production of the play for Théâtre de Complicité, see Helen Manfull (1997:65–9).
2. Moore talks of an Indian and Balinese influence paradoxically evoking an Elizabethan image (*Adelaide Advertiser*, 11 July 1987).

All's Well That Ends Well

1. A programme note by Catherine Bates described Helena thus: 'Baffling doctors with her mysterious healing powers and her cryptic, often incantatory speeches, Helena represents a female world of received wisdom and proverb lore that lies beyond the ken of the pragmatic and scientific men of the French court.'

The Merchant of Venice

1. For another 'gay mafia' production see Penny Gay's discussion of Carol Woodrow's controversial *Merchant of Venice* for the Bell Shakespeare Company in Australia, a production which set the opening scene in a gay sauna, (Gay, 1995).

King Lear

1. In discussing Deborah Warner's production of *King Lear* at the Royal National Theatre (1990), Bennett (1996:41) points out that this was Warner's second *King Lear* and that Warner's 'apparently radical' Kick production of *King Lear* in 1985 was 'the decisive contribution towards [Warner] getting a major offer from a major theatre company'. It is also significant that Warner's first *King Lear* was for the company she had formed herself, Kick, where she was able to direct any play she wanted.

    NB all line references to *King Lear* in this chapter are to the Folio text.

2. *Guardian*, 21 March 1994. Robin Thornber reviewing the production in the same newspaper on 4 March 1994 was far more favourable. Bennett's discussion (1996:54–6) of reviews of Barrie Keeffe's *King of England* (a version of *King Lear* where Lear becomes a Trinidadian living in London who wants to return to the land of his birth) reveals that the race dynamics of this play worried several reviewers.

3. Mitchell played Lear for the Queensland Theatre Company, in Brisbane, May 1978, using a text based on Buzz Goodbody's adaptation of the play (p.236–7).

4. Women Lears include: Ruth Maleczech (directed by Lee Breuer – see, for example, Solomon (1997:130–44); and Marianne Hoppe (directed by Robert Wilson – see, for example, Blair (1991:305). Maria Casarès played the role in Paris.

    A recent survey of women playing male roles in Shakespeare is to be found in Taranow (1996); a discussion of young girls playing Shakespeare's male roles in the American goldfields appears in Ferris (1992).

5. Deborah Paige's *King Lear* (Sheffield 1997) took place long after I interviewed her and so is not discussed in detail here. However, Paige's *King Lear* was notable for the casting of deaf actor, Tim Barlow, as a militaristic, old soldier Lear. Paige was quoted as saying she felt Barlow 'as a deaf person...would have experienced isolation, something which is very much

part of the king's ordeal' (Sheffield *Telegraph*, 24 October 1997). Two contemporary contexts which were evoked in the programme were the Scottish and Welsh devolution votes and the Royal family's troubles: as the *Big Issue* commented: 'A royal household expels its most favoured daughter, bringing disaster on itself.' Reviews mentioned Beckett and Tarantino. Playing alongside *King Lear* was *Gorbelly*, an adaptation of *King Lear* for 8–13 year olds by Richard Hurford and directed by Catriona Murray.

Macbeth

1. See Manfull (1997) for a discussion of Julia Bardsley's *Macbeth*, at the Haymarket Theatre, Leicester, where Bardsley not only directed but also played the witches. Previously, Nancy Meckler directed *Macbeth* at Leicester in 1985, with Bernard Hill as Macbeth and Julie Walters as Lady Macbeth.
2. References to reviews of Wright's *Macbeth* in national papers are to Scottish editions where appropriate.

English History Plays

1. For example, there have been important *Richard II*s directed by Margaret Webster (see p.224–5), Deborah Warner and Ariane Mnouchkine. Deborah Warner directed a *King John* (1988) and Katie Mitchell directed *Henry VI Part 3* (1994) at The Other Place for the RSC.
2. A picture spread also appears in *Theatre World*, March 1955. There is an illustration of the set design in the hardback edition of Howard Goorney's *The Theatre Workshop Story*.
3. Callaghan (1993:121) points out that 'the portrayal of male homosexuality in [Littlewood's] productions (*Richard II*, *Edward II*, and *A Taste of Honey*) seem to indicate a more enlightened attitude towards sexuality than that of most of her

contemporaries'. Littlewood herself offers a typically unapologetic view on homosexuality offstage, rather than on, in an interview in 1994: 'I invented heterosexuals in the English theatre. They only had homosexuals until I came along' (Bramwell, 1997:108).

4. Littlewood had also directed the play in 1951–2. See p.232 for the aborted proposal that she should direct *Henry IV* for the RSC.

5. The Quatercentenary celebrations included an exhibition celebrating Shakespeare's life and a demonstration of Baconian vandalism – which turned an advertisement for the Shakespeare festival into an advertisement for a *Bacon* festival. Anti-Baconians responded by ceremonially burning a copy of Bacon's essays.

6. A sketch of this setting appears in the *London Illustrated News*, 29 August 1964.

7. Thanks to Peter Rankin for his memories of the refugee sequence.

8. See also Howell's discussion of the death of chivalry in *Part 1* (Fenwick, 1983a:22–3, 30–31).

9. Susan Willis' account of the filming of *Titus* also stresses the trust fostered by Howell in her production team (1991:294).

10. Less enthusiastically, Lorraine Helms (1994:126) concedes slightly grudgingly that Howell's *1 Henry VI* 'did evade the sexism that has often been gratuitously introduced into other interpretations of the play'.

Roman History Plays

1. Deborah Warner's much discussed and much praised production of this play for the RSC (1987) became famous for the impact of its stage violence. Warner also directed *Coriolanus* for Kick in 1986.

2. See Henry Fenwick (1986:19) for Howell's discussion of how the use of the masks came about.

3. The year after Edwards' very successful production Brenda McRobbie directed *Coriolanus* for the Fractal Theatre Company in Brisbane.
4. Even the Roman play not considered here, *Julius Caesar*, includes a violent woman. However, Portia directs violence against herself, firstly by wounding herself, very suggestively, in the thigh and then by committing suicide.

Part 3 – Women Directors: A Herstory

1. The vexed question of terminology needs to be mentioned here: what is now in Britain called a 'director' was in Craig's time called a 'producer'. The terms are used interchangeably here because theatre production in the sense of fund-raising, promotion, etc. is *not* under discussion in this book; play directing *is*.
2. Sue-Ellen Case (1988:29) encourages us to acknowledge the unrecorded women theatre makers through the ages, such as mimes and *commedia* actors, whose work is particularly difficult to excavate because so few written texts remain. This *caveat* also applies to early women directors.
3. See Gilder (1960:259); Howe (1992:26). Langhans (1991:5) also lists Teresa Cornelys, Mary Ann Yates, Charlotte Charke, Madame Violante, Anne Oldfield and Hannah Lee as possibly acting in a managerial capacity. See also Davis (1989:69). The anonymous and anti-women play *The Female Wits* (c. 1697) shows a woman playwright, Marisilia, a character caricaturing Mary Delarivier Manley, acting in a directorial capacity.
4. Text reproduced from Planché (1872:180–81). Fletcher (1987:19) comments on the way the address moves from 'male-related images' to 'those more acceptably feminine'.

    An anonymous 1866 collection of theatrical memoirs attributed to Mathew Mackintosh, *An Old Stager* (1866:55), records that in 1820 Vestris played Lady Teazle under the management of Mrs Henry Siddons in Edinburgh, so this address is knowingly economical with the truth. Gilder (1960:259) mentions Harriet Waylett as managing a theatre before Vestris. In 1835 Louisa Nisbett managed the Queens theatre.

5. Vandenhoff (1860:3) also comments 'at Covent Garden it was Charles Mathews, *lessee*, Madame Vestris, *manager*; for, in management, Charley was a cipher by the side of "Her humorous ladyship".'

6. *An Old Stager* also bears witness to Vestris' clearly directorial contributions to productions.

7. Vestris also produced *Hamlet, Much Ado About Nothing, As You Like It* and *Twelfth Night*. With *Twelfth Night* she transposed the opening scenes, disrupting Shakespeare's intentions but setting a precedent many subsequent directors have followed. Vestris also was the first to restore the tragic ending to *Romeo and Juliet*, but she gave up on this as it was unpopular with audiences (Gilder, 1960:283)

8. Williams (1997:93) points out that 'after Vestris, the role of Oberon was played by a woman in every major English and American production of the play until 1914, with one exception'.

9. Odell (1963: volume 2:203–4) also stresses Vestris' achievement here.

10. Samuel Phelps' partner at Sadlers Wells, Mary Warner, also has some claim to be seen as a woman producer/director of Shakespeare not only for her work alongside Phelps but also in her own right as manager of the Marylebone theatre, where she produced several Shakespeares. For Charles Kean's debt to Ellen Kean see p.203–4.

11. Someone who did give Vestris her due was Laura Keene, who became the first actress also to manage a Shakespeare producing theatre company in the States. Keene claimed she had worked with and was following the example of Vestris (Turner, 1990: 75, 77)

12. The Bancrofts' major Shakespeare production, the *Merchant of Venice* which marked Ellen Terry's return to the stage, did not involve Marie Bancroft, who was ill that summer (Bancrofts, 1909:201); however, both Bancrofts researched for the play in Venice in 1874.

13. Langtry's début in the theatre was coached by Henrietta Hodson (Mrs Labouchere), a former actress, who acted initially as Langtry's manager. The two women parted company when Langtry started missing rehearsals in the States and Labouchere 'took the slating that (Langtry's) Rosalind received as a reflection on her own prowess as drama coach' (Brough, 1975:272).

14. Thorne also managed the unusual feat of extracting theatrical performances from Edward Gordon Craig – as Hamlet, Macbeth, and Romeo (Craig, 1968:76–7; Terry, 1982:209).

15. See Gandolfi (1995) and Cockin (1998). Craig also directed non-Shakespearean Renaissance plays including Fletcher's *Faithful Shepherdess* (a play also produced by her father Edward Godwin) at the West End Phoenix theatre, working in collaboration with Sir Thomas Beecham, and Webster's *White Devil* at the Renaissance Theatre in 1925.

16. Craig uses 'stage-manager' where modern British usage would have 'director'.

17. Cockin (1998:79), however, cites a misogynist report on Craig in the Brooklyn press.

18. In her acting manual *Hints to Speakers and Players*, Filippi's 'Letters to My Students' are signed 'Rosina Mother'.

19. For a discussion of Ashwell's productions of Ben Jonson see Cave (1999).

20. Nancy Price later directed extensively for the People's National Theatre. Cox's (1997) list of productions of *Much Ado About Nothing* includes Beatrice Wilson's at the Strand Theatre in 1924, starring Athene Seyler and Nicholas Hannen.

    Irene Hentschel (see pp.216–7 and Helen Ferrers also directed modern plays for Ashwell.

21. Ironically, Ashwell's worst experience in theatre management came when she was suddenly let down by two women, referred to by the pseudonyms Jane Emerson and Lady Caroline in *Myself A Player* (140–56).

22. This review also speculated about the possibility that Olivia and her attendants might be wearing 'black lingerie' under their mourning clothes.

23. This article features the work of four women directors – Auriol Lee, Leontine Sagan, Margaret Webster and Hentschel – who all had shows about to open in the West End. The rest of the newspaper bears vivid witness to the preparations for war, which contextualises these women's access to the heart of London theatre.

24. Unfortunately Green died of lung cancer.

25. Leiter (1986:214). The commentary on p217 wrongly identifies Green as 'the first woman to direct a play' at Stratford.

26. Drake had herself played Henry at the age of fifteen, directed by Edy Craig in 1919 in an entertainment for Anzacs waiting to be repatriated.

27. Quotation from the insert in Hewins' manuscript autobiography.

28. Examples of all-female Shakespeares include Ariane Mnouchkine's planned all-female *Twelfth Night* – in the end only Aguecheek and Curio were crosscast (Bradby and Williams, 1988:104). Ellen Terry (1982:191) saw an 'extraordinarily well done' all-female *As You Like It*; Louie Dunn ran an all-female Shakespeare company in Melbourne in the 1930s; Alisa Solomon (1997:185) records a less successful all-female *As You Like It* in 1995.

29. This is far less true in the States than in the UK. See Leiter (1991) and Spector (1986).

30. Margaret Shewring discusses this broadcast as 'an attempt to capture Evans's performance for future generations' (1996:140) and acknowledges the production's origins in Webster's 1937 production without ever mentioning Webster by name. Shewring also discusses Mnouchkine's and Warner's productions of *Richard II* but completely omits Joan Littlewood's production.

31. Robeson had played Othello previously in London (in a panned production directed by Ellen Van Volkenburg) but race tensions at the time were far higher in the States than in England and the Webster/Robeson production was a big risk.

32. Richard Proudfoot has recently written about this production in detail.

33. Judith Cook records that Wendy Toye was justifiably upset 'that in a recent biography of Sir Ralph Richardson, another director was credited with directing' the production.

34. Schools television is an area where several women directors have recently had some success The BBC *Shakespeare Shorts* series (which introduces a play by looking at one character and one scene in detail) included *Romeo and Juliet* directed by Yvonne Brewster; *Twelfth Night* directed by Jane Howell; and *Julius Caesar* directed by Deborah Paige.

35. Beauman (1982:100). The six are: Hentschel, Green, Webster, Goodbody, Trevis, Edwards. In 1994 Claire Armistead (186) pointed out that no woman had then directed on the RSC's London Barbican but since then Gale Edwards' *Taming of The Shrew* has appeared there.

36. Tina Packer, who was to direct so much Shakespeare later in the States, managed to direct a modern dress *Taming of the Shrew* at Stratford, a production which had 'hints of the Wild Western knockabout and more than a touch of the Grouchos' as well as having Katherine's husband and father 'interestingly ...appear to have a good deal in common' (*Stratford-upon-Avon Herald*, 20 April 1973); however, this production was not RSC sponsored.

37. Chambers (1980:29) and Callaghan (1995:279) also discuss interviewers' tendencies to focus on Goodbody's appearance.

38. Pam Brighton (1984:58) also considers the sexual dynamics of the rehearsal room, and how these may change when the director is a woman.

39. Chambers (1980:62). *King Lear* ran 17 May to 10 June 1978, at the Queensland Theatre Company, Brisbane. See Alan Edwards, director's programme note.

40. Review of the Roundhouse, London, revival, *Guardian*, 5 February 1976.

41. On this question of women occupying lower profile positions at the RSC, Barbara Leigh-Hunt comments: 'A lot of the stage management teams at the RSC are women – and very good at it' and: there was a time even 20 years ago when the best stage

directors in the business were women; Sir Laurence Olivier always had a woman stage director – Diana Boddington – and there was a remarkable stage director at the Aldwych named Ruth Atkinson, whom we called the Captain' (Hay, 1984:16).

Stage direction/management is still an area where comparatively large numbers of women get work in the theatre, but it is one of the most low profile areas of theatre work.

42. Eg Penny Cherns, Jane Howell, Jude Kelly. Manfull's interviews include several with women who have worked for the RSC as directors and assistant directors: Annie Castledine; Deborah Warner; Sue Sutton Mayo; Katie Mitchell; Di Trevis; Garry Hynes; Phyllida Lloyd; Sarah Pia Anderson and Brigid Larmour.

43. Armistead (1994:190). Fiona Shaw's career as a director and in particular her direction of *Hamlet* is discussed in Goodman (1996:144–5).

Reflections

1. The Association was founded in 1992 and has published the papers from their in-house forums 1995–6. For Irene Mitchell see Susan Pilbeam, 'Three Australian Women Theatre Directors' in the AWDA collection.

2. Private letter.

3. The actors were also close in age to the boy actors who originally played Julia and Sylvia. It is worth noting that Durban deliberately asked for an all-female cast.

Bibliography of Works Cited

Adlard, Eleanor (ed) (1949) *Edy: Recollections of Edith Craig*, London: Frederick Muller

Anderson, Mary (1896) *A Few Memories*, London: Osgood, McIlvaine and Co.

Anon (1922) 'Personalities and Powers: Edith Craig', *Time and Tide*, December 29: 1262–4

Anon (1981), *The Female Wits* in Fidelis Morgan (ed), *The Female Wits: Women Playwrights on the London Stage 1660–1720*, London: Virago

Ansorge, Peter (1972) 'Lots of Lovely Human Contact', *Plays and Players*, July: 18–21

Appleton, William W (1974) *Madame Vestris and the London Stage*, Columbia University Press

Armistead, Claire (1994) 'Women Directors', *Women: A Cultural Review* 5 (2): 185–91

Ashwell, Lena (1922) *Modern Troubadours: A Record of the Concerts at the Front*, London, Copenhagen and Christiana: Gyldendal

—(1927) *Reflections From Shakespeare: A series of lectures*, London: Hutchinson and Co.

—(1936) *Myself a Player*, London: Michael Joseph Ltd

Auchmuty, Rosemary (1993) 'By Their Friends We Shall Know Them: The lives and networks of some women in North Lambeth, 1880-1940' in Lesbian History Group (eds) *Not A Passing Phase: Reclaiming Lesbians in History 1840–1985*, London: Women's Press: 77–98

Bancroft, Marie and Squire (1909) *Recollections of Sixty Years*, London: John Murray

Barker, Paul (1995) 'A Woman of Some Importance', *Independent on Sunday*, 4 June: 16-18

Bartholomeusz, Dennis (1982) *The Winter's Tale in Performance in*

England and America 1611–1976, Cambridge: University Press

Beauman, Sally (1982) *The Royal Shakespeare Company: A History of Ten Decades*, Oxford: University Press

Bennett, Susan (1996) *Performing Nostalgia: Shifting Shakespeare and the Contemporary Past*, London: Routledge

Berry, Ralph (1989) *On Directing Shakespeare: Interviews with Contemporary Directors*, London: Hamish Hamilton

Billington, Michael (1990) *Directors' Shakespeare: Approaches to 'Twelfth Night'*, London: Nick Hern

Bingham, Dennis (1988) 'Jane Howell's First Tetralogy: Brechtian Break-Out or Just Good Television?' in JC Bulman and HR Coursen (eds) *Shakespeare on Television: an anthology of essays and reviews*, London: University Press of New England: 221–32

Blair, Rhonda (1991) '"Not…but"/"Not-Not-Me": Musings on Cross-Gender Performance' in Donkin and Clement: 291–308

Bradby, David and Williams, David (1988) *Directors' Theatre*, London: Macmillan

Bramwell, Murray (1997) 'A Cup of Tea with Joan Littlewood' in Joanne Tompkins and Julie Holledge (eds) *Performing Women/Performing Feminisms: Interviews with International Women Playwrights*, Australasian Drama Studies Association Academic Publications 2

Bratton, JS (1994) 'Sarah Baker: The Making of a "Character"' in Richard Foulkes (ed) *Scenes from Provincial Stages: Essays in Honour of Kathleen Barker*, London: The Society for Theatre Research

Braun, Edward (1982) *The Director and the Stage: From Naturalism to Grotowski*, London: Methuen

Brighton, Pam (1984) 'Directions', in Susan Todd (ed) *Women and Theatre: Calling the shots*, London: Faber: 47–61

Brough, James (1975) *The Prince and the Lily*, London: Hodder and Stoughton

Brown, John Russell (1965) 'Three Kinds of Shakespeare', *Shakespeare Survey* 18: 147–55

—(1974) *Free Shakespeare*, London: Heinemann

Bushnell, Paul R (1993) 'Ngaio Marsh, Shakespearean Director' in Robin Eaden, Heather Kerr and Madge Mitton (eds) *Shakespeare and the World Elsewhere*, Adelaide: University Press

—(1996) 'The Most Ephemeral of the Arts' in Carole Acheson and Carolyn Lidgard (eds) *Return to Black Beech: Papers from a Centenary Symposium on Ngaio Marsh 1895–1995*, Christchurch: 83–93

Callaghan, Dympna (1991) 'Buzz Goodbody: Directing For Change' in Jean I Marsden (ed) *The Appropriation of Shakespeare: Post-Renaissance Reconstructions of the Works and the Myth*, Hemel Hempstead: Harvester Wheatsheaf: 163–181

—(1993) 'Shakespeare at the Fun Palace: Joan Littlewood' in Marianne Novy (ed) *Cross-Cultural Performances: Differences in Women's Re-Visions of Shakespeare*, Urbana and Chicago: University of Illinois Press

—(1995) 'The Aesthetics of Marginality: The Theatre of Joan Littlewood and Buzz Goodbody' in Karen Laughlin and Catherine Schuler (eds) *Theatre and Feminist Aesthetics*, London: Associated University Presses: 258–85

Carter, Joyce (1994) '*The Tempest* at Salisbury Playhouse: A Case Study', MA Dissertation, Royal Holloway College, University of London

Case, Sue-Ellen (1988) *Feminism and Theatre*, London: Macmillan

—(1990) *Performing Feminisms: Feminist Critical Theory and Theatre*, Baltimore: John Hopkins University Press

Cave, Richard, Schafer, Elizabeth and Woodland Brian (1999, forthcoming) *Ben Johnson and Theatre*, London: Routledge

Chambers, Colin (1980) *Other Spaces: New Theatre and the RSC*, London: Methuen

Cima, Gay Gibson (1991) 'Strategies for Subverting the Canon', in Donkin and Clement

Cockin, Katharine (1998) *Edith Craig (1869–1947): Dramatic Lives*, London: Cassell

Cole, Susan Letzler (1992) *Directors in Rehearsal: a Hidden World*, London: Routledge, Chapman and Hall

Cook, Judith (1993) *Directors' Theatre: Sixteen Leading Directors on the State of Theatre in Britain Today*, London: Hodder and Stoughton

Coren, Michael (1984) *Theatre Royal: 100 years of Stratford East*, London: Quartet Books

Cousin, Geraldine (1986) 'The Touring of the Shrew', *New Theatre Quarterly* 2 (7): 275–281

Cox, John F. (1997) *Much Ado About Nothing: Shakespeare in Production*, Cambridge: University Press

Craig, Edith (1907) 'Producing a Play', *The Munsey Magazine*, June: 311–14

Craig, Edward (1968) *Gordon Craig: The Story of His Life*, London: Victor Gollancz

Craig Edward Gordon (1930) *Henry Irving*, London: J M Dent

—(1931) *Ellen Terry and Her Secret Self*, London: Sampson Low, Marston & Co.

Curnow, Allen (1943) 'Hamlet in Modern Dress', *New Zealand Listener*, 20 August

Daniels, Rebecca (1996) *Women Stage Directors Speak*, London: McFarland

Davis, Tracy C (1989) 'Questions for a Feminist Methodology in Theatre History' in Thomas Postlewait and Bruce A McConachie (eds) *Interpreting the Theatrical Past: Essays in the Historiography of Performance*, Iowa City: University of Iowa Press: 59–81

—(1991) *Actresses as Working Women: Their Social Identity in Victorian Culture*, London: Routledge

Dessen, Alan C (1989) *Titus Andronicus*, Shakespeare in Performance, Manchester: University Press

Dibdin, Thomas (1827) *The Reminiscences of Thomas Dibdin*, 2 vols, London: Henry Coulburn: Volume 1

Dickens, Charles (ed) (1879) *The Life of Charles James Mathews*, London: Macmillan, 2 vols

Dolan, Jill (1988) *The Feminist Spectator as Critic*, Ann Arbor: University of Michigan Press

—(1993) *Presence and Desire*, Ann Arbor: University of Michigan Press

Donkin, Ellen and Clement, Susan (eds) (1991) *Upstaging Big Daddy: Directing Theater as if Gender and Race Matter*, Michigan: University Press

Drake, Fabia (1978) *Blind Fortune*, London: William Kimber

Dunderdale, Sue (1984) 'The Status of Women in the British Theatre', *Drama* (2):9–11

Dymkowski, Christine (1992) 'Entertaining Ideas: Edy Craig and the Pioneer Players' in Gardner and Rutherford: 221–33

Edmonds, Jill (1992) 'Princess Hamlet' in Gardner and Rutherford: 59–76

Evans, Maurice (1987) *All This…and Evans Too! A Memoir*, University of South Carolina Press

Farrar, JM (1884) *Mary Anderson: The story of her life and professional career*, London: David Bogue

Fenwick, Henry (1981) 'The Production', *The Winter's Tale*, BBC publications: 17–27

—(1983a) 'The Production', *Henry VI Part 1*, BBC publications: 21–31

—(1983b) 'The Production', *Henry VI Part 2*, BBC publications: 18–29

—(1983c) 'The Production', *Henry VI Part 3*, BBC publications: 20–31

—(1983d) 'The Production', *Richard III*, BBC publications: 20–30

—(1986) 'The Production', *Titus Andronicus*, BBC publications: 17–27

Ferris, Lesley (1992) 'The Golden Girl', in Gardner and Rutherford: 37–55

Filippi, Rosina (1911) *Hints to Speakers and Players*, London: Edward Arnold

Findlater, Richard (1975) *Lilian Baylis: The Lady of the Old Vic*, London: Allen Lane

Fischler, Alan (1995) 'Purloined Posterity: The Reforms and Reputation of Madame Vestris', *Women's Studies* 24 (4): 307–22

Fletcher, Kathy (1987) 'Planché, Vestris, and the Transvestite Role: Sexuality and Gender in Victorian Popular Theatre', *Nineteenth Century Theatre* 15 (1): 9–33

Gale, Maggie B (1996) *West End Women: Women and the London Stage*, 1918–1962, London: Routledge

Gandolfi, Roberta (1995) '*La Prima Regista: Le sfide di Edith Craig nel temp del suffragismo e della nuova arte scenica*', unpublished PhD thesis, University of Bologna

Gardner, Vivien and Rutherford, Susan (1992) *The New Woman and Her Sisters: Feminism and Theatre*, 1850–1914, Hemel Hempstead: Harvester Wheatsheaf

Gay, Penny (1994) *As She Likes It: Shakespeare's Unruly Women*, London: Routledge

—(ed) (1995) *The Merchant of Venice*, The Bell Shakespeare, Sydney: Science Press

—(1998) 'Recent Australian *Shrews*: the "Larrikin Element"' in J Levenson and J Bate (eds) Proceedings of the 1996 ISA conference, University of Delaware/Associated University Presses

Gielgud, John (1972) *Distinguished Company*, London: Heinemann

—(1987) *Early Stages*, London: Hodder and Stoughton (revised edition)

Gilbert, Miriam (1993) *Love's Labour's Lost*, Shakespeare in Performance, Manchester: University Press

Gilder, Rosamond (1931) *Enter the Actress: The First Women in the Theatre*, London: George G Harrap and Co. Ltd.

Goodman, Lizbeth (1993) *Contemporary Feminist Theatres: To Each Her Own*, London: Routledge

—(1996) *Feminist Stages: Interviews with Women in Contemporary British Theatre*, London; Harwood

Goodwin, Clive and Milne, Tom (1964) 'Working with Joan' in Toby Cole and Helen Krich Chinoy (eds) *Directors on Directing: a Source Book of the Modern Theatre* (revised edition): 390–401

Goorney, Howard (1981) *The Theatre Workshop Story*, London: Eyre Methuen

Graham-Campbell, Alison and Lambe, Frank (1960) *Drama for Women*, London: G Bell and Sons Ltd.

Griffiths, Trevor (1979) 'A Neglected Pioneer Production: Madame Vestris' *A Midsummer Night's Dream* at Covent Garden, 1840', *Shakespeare Quarterly* (30): 386–96

—(1996) *A Midsummer Night's Dream: Shakespeare in Production*, Cambridge: University Press

Halio, Jay L (1994) *A Midsummer Night's Dream*, Shakespeare in Performance, Manchester: University Press

Hall, Kim F (1995) 'Shakespeare as Feminist weapon' *New Theatre Quarterly* 41: 55–65

Hancock, Sheila (1987) *Ramblings of an Actress*, London: Hutchinson

Hay, Malcolm (1984) 'Questioning Roles: Questioning Myths', *Drama* (2): 15–17

Helms, Lorraine (1990) 'Playing the Woman's Part: Feminist Criticism And Shakespearean Performance' in Sue-Ellen Case (ed) *Performing Feminisms: Feminist Critical Theory and Theatre*, Baltimore and London: Johns Hopkins University Press

—(1994) 'Acts of Resistance: The Feminist Player' in Dympna Callaghan, Lorraine Helms and Jyotsna Singh, *The Weyward Sisters: Shakespeare and Feminist Politics*, Oxford: Blackwell

Hewins, Nancy *Well, Why Not: the Story of the Osiris Players* Manuscript, The Theatre Museum, London

Holderness, Graham (1989) *The Taming of the Shrew*, Shakespeare in Performance, Manchester: University Press

—(1992) *Shakespeare Recycled: The Making of Historical Drama*, Hemel Hempstead: Harvester Wheatsheaf

Holledge, Julie (1981) *Innocent Flowers: Women in the Edwardian Theatre*, London: Virago

Howe, Elizabeth (1992) *The First English Actresses: Women and Drama, 1660–1700*, Cambridge: University Press

Jacobs, Gerald (1985) *Judi Dench: A Great Deal of Laughter*, London: Weidenfeld and Nicolson

Jenkins, Linda Walsh and Susan Ogden-Malouf (1985) 'The (Female) Actor Prepares', *Theater* 17 (1):66–69

Kiernan, Thomas (1981) *Olivier: the Life of Laurence Olivier*, London: Sidgwick and Jackson

Langhans, Edward A (1991) 'Tough Actresses to Follow' in Mary Anne Schofield and Cecilia Macheski (eds) *Curtain Calls: British and American Women and the Theater, 1660–1820*, Athens, Ohio: University Press: 3–17

Langtry, Lillie (Lady De Bathe) (1925) *The Days I Knew*, New York:

George H Doran and Co.

Le Gallienne, Eva (1953) *With a Quiet Heart*, New York: The Viking Press

Leiter, Samuel L (1986) *Shakespeare Around the Globe: A Guide to Notable Postwar Revivals*, New York and London: Greenwood Press

—(1991) *From Belasco to Brook: Representative Directors of the English-Speaking Stage*, London: Greenwood Press

Lewis, Margaret (1991) *Ngaio Marsh: a Life*, Wellington: Bridget Williams Books

Lipkin, Joan (1991) 'Aftemath: Surviving the Reviews', in Donkin and Clement: 317–24

Littlewood, Joan (1965) 'Goodbye Note from Joan' in Charles Marowitz, Tom Milne, Owen Hale (eds) *The Encore Reader: A Chronicle of the New Drama*, London: Methuen: 132–4

—(1994), *Joan's Book: Joan Littlewood's Peculiar History as She Tells It*, London: Methuen

Mackintosh, Mathew (attrib.) (1866) *An Old Stager*, Glasgow: James Hedderwick

Maher, Mary Z (1988) 'Production Design in the BBC's *Titus Andronicus*' in JC Bulman and HR Coursen (eds) *Shakespeare on Television: an Anthology of Essays and Reviews*, London: University Press of New England: 144–50

Manfull, Helen (1997) *In Other Words: Women Directors Speak*, Lyme, New Hampshire: Smith and Kraus

Manheim, Michael (1994) 'The English history play on screen' in Anthony Davies and Stanley Wells (eds) *Shakespeare and the Moving Image: the Plays on Film and Television*, Cambridge: University Press

Marsh, Ngaio (1955) 'A Note on the production of *Twelfth Night*', *Shakespeare Survey* 8: 69–73

— (1982) *Black Beech and Honeydew: An autobiography*, revised edition, London: Collins

Marshall, Norman (1962) *The Producer and the Play*, revised edition, London: Macdonald

Martin, John (1984) 'Directing Women: A Difference of

Perception', *Drama* 152 (2): 18-20

Mathews, Anne (1844) *Anecdotes of Actors*, London: TC Newby

Milne, Tom (1965) 'Art in Angel Lane' in Charles Marowitz, Tom Milne, Owen Hale (eds) *The Encore Reader: A Chronicle of the New Drama*, London: Methuen: 80–86

Morley, Malcolm (1966) *Margate and its Theatres 1730–1965*, London: Museum Press

Moore, Mary (1994) 'Sexing the Space' in Peta Tait, *Converging Realities: Feminism in Australian Theatre*, Sydney: Currency Press: 227–33

Odell, George CD (1963) *Shakespeare – from Betterton to Irving*, New York and London: Benjamin Blom, 2 vols

Oliver, Laurence (1982) *Confessions of an Actor*, London: Weidenfeld and Nicolson

—(1986) *On Acting*, London:Weidenfeld and Nicolson

Pearce, Charles (1923) *Madame Vestris and Her Times*, London: Stanley Paul

Pilbeam, Susan (1995–6) 'Three Australian Women Theatre Directors: From the Past, the mainstream and the margins' in Australian Women Directors' Association In-house forums, Melbourne: AWDA Publication

Planché, JR (1872) *The Recollections and Reflections of JR Planché*, London: Tinsley Brothers, vol. 1

Potter, Robert (1988) 'The Rediscovery of Queen Margaret: "The Wars of the Roses", 1963', *New Theatre Quarterly* (14:4): 105–119

Quayle, Anthony (1992) *A Time to Speak*, London: Sphere Books

Rea, Kenneth (1989) *A Better Direction*, London: Calouste Gulbenkian Foundation

Redgrave, Michael (1983) *In My Mind's Eye: An Autobiography*, London: Weidenfeld and Nicolson

Reinhardt, Nancy S (1981) 'New Directions for Feminist Criticism in Theatre and the Related Arts' in Elizabeth Langland and Walter Grove (eds) *A Feminist Perspective in the Academy: the difference it makes*, Chicago: University Press

Roberts, Peter (1976) *The Old Vic Story: A Nation's Theatre*,

London: WH Allen

Rogan, Rachel (1994) 'Shakespeare in Performance in New Zealand: Ngaio Marsh's *Hamlet*', unpublished MA dissertation, University of Auckland

Rosenberg, Marvin (1978) *The Masks of 'Macbeth'*, Berkeley and London: University of California Press

Rothwell, Kenneth S (1981) 'The Shakespeare Plays: *Hamlet* and the Five Plays of Season Three', *Shakespeare Quarterly* (32): 395–401

Rowell, George (1993) *The Old Vic: A History*, Cambridge: University Press

Rudisill, Amanda Sue (1972) 'The Contributions of Eva Le Gallienne, Margaret Webster, Margo Jones, and Joan Littlewood to the Establishment of Repertory Theatre in the United States and Great Britain', unpublished PhD thesis, Northwestern University

Rutter, Carol (1988) *Clamorous Voices: Shakespeare's Women Today*, London: The Women's Press

St Clare Byrne, Muriel (1949) 'Fifty Years of Shakespeare Production: 1898–1948', *Shakespeare Survey* 2: 1–20

St John, Christopher (1949) *Ellen Terry and Bernard Shaw: A Correspondence*, London: Reinhardt and Evans

Sheehy, Margaret (1984) 'Why Aren't There More Women Directors?' *Drama* 152 (2): 12

Shewring, Margaret (1996) *King Richard II*, Shakespeare in Performance, Manchester: University Press

Sinfield, Alan (1985) 'Royal Shakespeare: theatre and the making of ideology' in Alan Sinfield and Jonathan Dollimore (eds) *Political Shakespeare: New Essays in Cultural Materialism*, Manchester: University Press: 158–81

Solomon, Alisa (1997), *Re-Dressing the Canon: Essays on Theater and Gender*, London: Routledge

Spector, Susan (1986) 'Margaret Webster's *Othello*: the principal players versus the director', *Theatre History Studies* 6: 93–108

Sprague, AC and Trewin, JC (1970) *Shakespeare's Plays Today: Some Customs and Conventions of the Stage*, London: Sidgwick and Jackson

Steed, Maggie (1993) '*Much Ado About Nothing*' in Russell Jackson and Robert Smallwood (eds) *Players of Shakespeare 3*, Cambridge: University Press: 42–51

Sullivan, Esther Beth (1991) 'Women, Woman, and the Subject of Feminism: Feminist Directions', in Donkin and Clement

Taranow, Gerda (1996) *The Bernhardt Hamlet: Culture and Context*, New York: Peter Lang

Terry, Ellen (1982) *The Story of My Life*, London: The Boydell Press

Thomas, Anthony (1989) *The Story of the Barn Theatre 1929–1989*, Stone-in-Oxney, Kent: published by the author

Thomson, Peter (1974) 'Review of the 1975 Season at Stratford', *Shakespeare Survey* 27: 143–54

Thorndike, Sybil and Russell (1938) *Lilian Baylis*, London: Chapman and Hall Ltd

Trewin, JC (1956) *Paul Scofield*, Theatre World Monograph no. 6, London: Rockliff

—(1964) *Shakespeare on the English Stage 1900–1964: A Survey of Productions Illustrated from the Raymond Mander and Joe Mitchenson Theatre Collection*, London: Barrie and Rockliff

Trevis, Di (1984/5) 'Acts of Life', *Drama* 158 (4):15

Turner, Mary M (1990) *Forgotten Leading Ladies of the American Theatre: Lives of Eight Female Playwrights, Directors, Managers and Activists of the Eighteenth, Nineteenth and Early Twentieth Centuries*, Jefferson, North Carolina and London: McFarland and Co. Inc.

Vanbrugh, Violet (1925) *Dare to be Wise*, London: Hodder and Stoughton

Vandenhoff, George (1860), *Leaves from an Actor's Notebook with Reminiscences and Chit-chat of the Green-room and the Stage in England and America*, London: D. Appleton and Co.

Venables, Clare (1980) 'The Woman Director in the Theatre', *Theatre Quarterly* 10 no. 38: 3–7

Wandor, Michelene (1986) *Carry On, Understudies: Theatre and Sexual Politics*, London: Methuen (revised edition)

Webster, Margaret (1969) *The Same Only Different: Five Generations of a Great Theatre Family*, London: Victor Gollancz

—(1972) *Don't Put Your Daughter on the Stage*, New York: Alfred A. Knopf

Wells, John (1994) 'Joan Littlewood' in *Heroes and Villains: An anthology of animosity and admiration*, London: Victor Gollancz in association with the *Independent Magazine*: 209–12

Williams, Clifford John (1973) *Madame Vestris: a Theatrical Biography*, London: Sidgwick and Jackson

Williams, Gary Jay (1997) *Our Moonlight Revels: 'A Midsummer Night's Dream' in the Theatre*, Iowa City: University of Iowa Press

Willis, Susan (1991) *The BBC Shakespeare Plays: Making the Televised Canon*, London and Chapel Hill: University of North Carolina Press

Winter, William (1913) *The Wallet of Time*, New York: Moffat, Yard and Co.

—(1969) *Shakespeare on the Stage*, New York: Benjamin Blom, reissue of 1911 edition

Woddis, Carol (1991) '*Sheer Bloody Magic*', London: Virago

Index of Plays and Women Directors